IN SEARCH OF
JEFFERSON'S MOOSE

LAW AND CURRENT EVENTS MASTERS
David Kairys, Series Editor

Also in this series:
Icarus in the Boardroom by David Skeel

IN SEARCH OF
JEFFERSON'S MOOSE

NOTES ON THE STATE OF CYBERSPACE

DAVID G. POST

OXFORD
UNIVERSITY PRESS

2009

OXFORD
UNIVERSITY PRESS

Oxford University Press, Inc., publishes works that further
Oxford University's objective of excellence
in research, scholarship, and education.

Oxford New York
Auckland Cape Town Dar es Salaam Hong Kong Karachi
Kuala Lumpur Madrid Melbourne Mexico City Nairobi
New Delhi Shanghai Taipei Toronto

With offices in
Argentina Austria Brazil Chile Czech Republic France Greece
Guatemala Hungary Italy Japan Poland Portugal Singapore
South Korea Switzerland Thailand Turkey Ukraine Vietnam

Published by Oxford University Press, Inc.
198 Madison Avenue, New York, NY 10016

www.oup.com

Oxford is a registered trademark of Oxford University Press

Library of Congress Cataloging-in-Publication Data
Post, David G.
In search of Jefferson's moose : notes on the state of cyberspace / David G. Post.
p. cm. — (Law and current events masters)
Includes bibliographical references and index.
ISBN 978-0-19-534289-5 (alk. paper)
1. Internet—Law and legislation.   2. Computer networks—Law and legislation.
3. Information superhighway—Law and legislation.   I. Title.
K564.C6P67 2009
343.09'99—dc22   2008023699

9 8 7 6 5 4 3 2 1
Printed in the United States of America
on acid-free paper

TO ANNIE AND BEN

"JEFFERSON SURVIVES!"

JOHN ADAMS'S LAST WORDS, JULY 4, 1826[1]

---

1 It's not known whether Adams uttered those words accompanied by a smile or the gnash-
   ing of teeth. In any event, he was wrong; Jefferson had in fact died earlier that same day, the
   fiftieth anniversary of the signing of the Declaration of Independence.

CONTENTS

ACKNOWLEDGMENTS

All writers are vain, selfish and lazy, and at the very bottom of their motives there lies a mystery. Writing a book is a horrible, exhausting struggle, like a long bout of some painful illness. One would never undertake such a thing if one were not driven on by some demon whom one can neither resist nor understand. For all one knows that demon is simply the same instinct that makes a baby squall for attention. And yet it is also true that one can write nothing readable unless one constantly struggles to efface one's own personality. Good prose is like a window pane.

GEORGE ORWELL, *POLITICS AND THE ENGLISH LANGUAGE*

I want to thank . . . everyone I've ever known in my life.

MAUREEN STAPLETON, ACADEMY AWARD ACCEPTANCE SPEECH, 1982

I know what she meant. I have been working on the book you hold in your hands for over a decade, a period virtually co-extensive with my entire professional career as a law professor, and it touches on pretty much everything I've worked on during that period. I was already five or six years into the project before I even realized that it **was** a project, that there might be a book in all of this, and that I needed, among many other things, to start keeping track of all of the people who were helping, just so that I'd be in a position to write these "Acknowledgments" some day. It was already too late, and in any event I had received and was continuing to receive far too much help, from too many directions, to keep track of where it was all coming from—from students chasing down odd bits of Jeffersoniana for me, colleagues pointing me to useful references or explaining some fine points of law to me, scholars in other disciplines—engineers, historians, computer scientists, statisticians, evolutionary biologists—who graciously responded to my often naive and ill-informed requests for information and explanation about their work, and complete strangers, who would on occasion contact me after having read something of mine online and direct me to some useful line of thinking or angle of attack on the problems I was grappling with. I could no sooner list all of these people to thank them personally than I could reconstruct my every move on, say, March 11, 1995, and, were

I to attempt to do so, I would surely omit the names of dozens of people who had helped in some important way and who would feel, justifiably, slighted by the omission. Better, I think—I hope—to say, to all of you: You (and I) know who you are; I am profoundly, and sincerely, grateful for your help. Please accept my apologies for failing to list you personally; you were generous with your time, and I hope you will not think it ungenerous of me not to thank you by name.

I do need to give special thanks to a few people who were truly indispensable, people without whose help and support this book would almost certainly not exist. I had the very good fortune to become part of a small community of "cyberlaw" scholars that was held together by uncommonly strong bonds of affection, mutual respect, and generosity, and I sincerely thank the members of that community—and in particular the operators of and participants in the cyberia and cyberprof mailing lists—whose ideas and arguments helped to shape this book in countless ways. Thanks also to the faculty, administration, staff, and students at Temple Law School, who gave me the space and the support; to David Johnson, the NY Conspiracy, Larry Lessig, Pam Schacherer, and the Dwights, each of whom, in different ways, helped keep me going on what seemed, at times, like a hopeless and improbable project; and to my family, to whom I am indebted for far more than just the contents of this book.

A NOTE TO THE READER

A large work is difficult because it is large, even though all its parts might singly be performed with facility; where there are many things to be done, each must be allowed its share of time and labour, in the proportion only which it bears to the whole; nor can it be expected, that the stones which form the dome of a temple, should be squared and polished like the diamond of a ring.

SAMUEL JOHNSON, PREFACE TO HIS *DICTIONARY OF THE ENGLISH LANGUAGE*

Although this book is a work of "scholarship" (and a good one, I hope), it's not a "scholarly" work, by which I mean two things. First, I have tried to stay focused on the issues and ideas, rather than, in a more scholarly fashion, on the debate **about** the issues, more on whether X is right or wrong than on what various scholars have said previously about whether X is right or wrong, more on trying to make sense of things and less on trying to explain how others have done so. I don't mean to slight the scholarly debates—quite the opposite: I couldn't have written anything remotely resembling this book without drawing upon, as best I could, the vigorous (to put it mildly) scholarly debates that swirl around both of the twinned subject matters of this book—Jefferson's system of thought, and the law of the Net. A book describing and explaining the scholarly debates in those two fields would be a very interesting book, but it's not this book. I find the ideas difficult enough to make sense of and to convey to a reader, without also trying simultaneously to situate each one, to try to explain where it came from, and who held it first, and what the opposing position might be, and who has articulated that opposing position, and why I've chosen one over another, and so on.

I'm assuming, in short, that you, my reader, care less (or not at all) about what Professors X and Y have said about things than you do about the things themselves. I **have** tried to give credit and attribution wherever they're due for the facts, and ideas, and arguments presented in what follows; in the "References and Suggested Readings" section for each chapter, I have tried to bring together enough information to permit the interested reader to uncover the provenance of all of the facts, ideas, and arguments I present. But I have not attempted to provide what every good scholarly work should provide, namely the full panoply of scholarly citation and cross-citation and authoritative support for all of it. A colleague once remarked (only half-jokingly) that the perfect work of legal scholarship would have a footnote at the end of every sentence except the final one, the whole point of the scholarly enterprise being, as it were, to place every idea and every argument in its full context, to show the provenance of every fact asserted, and to give credit for the prior appearance of every idea and argument save the last, the one constituting the author's own original contribution. This is not that kind of work.

A word about Jefferson's words. I use them a lot (and I print them all *in italic type*), and in a somewhat unusual way: I'm trying to bring them inside the narrative, to get you to engage with them not as historical artifacts (though they are indeed historical artifacts) but as expressions of living ideas that are always interesting and sometimes, even, profound. (If I were **really** good at this, I would have written the whole book using **only** Jefferson's words, rearranged to tell the story I want to tell). Jefferson was one of history's greatest prose stylists, and one tinkers with his prose at one's peril. It is, though, eighteenth-century prose, and eighteenth-century prose has any number of peculiarities that can sometimes obscure its meaning to twenty-first-century readers. I have taken some (small) liberties with his words from time to time, in an effort to give it greater fluency for twenty-first-century eyes—altering punctuation (often), paragraph structure (occasionally), and even sentence order (rarely). I have done my best to keep its meaning intact—but even taking out the odd comma (and Jefferson's prose has some **very** odd commas in it) can have subtle and sometimes profound effects on meaning, and I cannot state with absolute certainty that I have always succeeded in doing so.[1] The original sources for all quotations are presented in the supplementary references; if you are unwilling to take my word for it, by all means have at it—nothing would delight me more than to have you checking back with the Jeffersonian originals to point out some nuance I have perhaps missed, or misstated. And if you come up with something interesting, I'd love to hear what it is—www.jeffersonsmoose.org.[2]

---

1 My favorite example: When Robert Frost's now-classic poem "Stopping by Woods on a Snowy Evening" appeared in the first edition of his *Collected Poems*, it read:

> The woods are lovely, dark, and deep
> But I have promises to keep

In fact, what Frost had written was:

> The woods are lovely, dark and deep
> But I have promises to keep

2 I also apologize, in advance, for my use of the term "American" throughout to refer to the United States. It's unpleasantly chauvinistic, and I know that it drives Mexicans and Canadians and Brazilians and Peruvians and other "Americans" to distraction—but there is really no other adjective that works as well to describe United Statesian law, or United Statesesque history, or United Statesish patent procedures, or the like.

And finally, a word to those of you who are tempted to dismiss Jefferson and all things Jeffersonian out of hand—either on general "dead white guy" grounds, or because of his inability to solve, in his own life let alone for the nation as a whole, the terrible problem of slavery, or because of his (many) failures and compromises and defects of character. Jefferson has been the subject of much criticism of late—"viciously maligned," historian Sean Wilentz has written, "in ways normally reserved only for modern American presidents and liberals." Much of it, in my opinion (and Wilentz's), is wrongheaded—but my point here is not to persuade you of that. It's not his character, or even his reputation, that I'm trying to get my hands around, but his ideas, and I ask only that you keep your mind open to the possibility that he still has much to teach us about the world.

IN SEARCH OF

JEFFERSON'S MOOSE

PROLOGUE

THE FOX, THE HEDGEHOG, AND THE MOOSE

If the explorer of the past is wise, he will…attack his subject in unexpected places; he will fall upon the flank and the rear; he will shoot a sudden revealing searchlight into obscure recesses, hitherto undivined. He will row out over the great ocean of material, and lower down into it, here and there, a little bucket, which will bring up to the light of day some characteristic specimen, from those far depths, to be examined with a careful curiosity.

LYTTON STRACHEY

Life must be lived forwards, but it can only be understood backwards.

SØREN KIERKEGAARD

There's something funny going on, I can just feel it in the air.

BOB DYLAN

It's a strange new place, this "cyberspace." It's not really a place at all, of course, more like a bunch of connections between places; as Gertrude Stein famously said of Oakland, California, there's no "there" there. But we talk about it as if it were, and we experience it as if it were; we "visit" websites and then we "leave" them and "go to" others; we meet people "on the Internet," we talk of "entry" and "access," "portals" and "trapdoors," logging in and logging on, home pages and site maps.[1] Whatever it is, place or no-place, it is not quite like anything, or any place, or even any bunch of connections between places, that we have encountered before. It has a strange new geography; the familiar lines on the map around which we organize so much of our lives—the lines around our cities, states, provinces, countries—are harder to discern and seem to matter less "there." There are strange new things there, too—bots, crawlers, avatars, virtual agents, cookies, spiders, viruses. It is no-place, but it somehow seems to span the entire globe, and it keeps growing; as I write this, there are millions of people, from every corner of the planet, interacting with one another "there," with room, it appears, for many more. We go "there" and "back," in an instant, sometimes without even noticing that we are doing so, and we

---

1 David Weinberger, in his wonderful book *Small Pieces Loosely Joined*, contrasts research in a realspace library with the same research on the Web:

> In both cases, you're reading documents, [following] links, and then reading the documents the links point to. The only difference is that in one case the documents are printed on paper and in the other they're sprayed across glass. Despite the similarities, our experience of these two situations will be quite different. Consider the language we'll use. In the first case, we'll take a book from the shelf, find a link, get another book and put the first one back. In the physical carrel, I'm the still center of the universe. I cause things to be brought to me and to be taken away when I have finished with them. Now consider the language we use to talk about the Web experience: we go to a site, we browse, we surf, we find a link and we go to it. When we're done, we leave the site. The library carrel is a place where we sit; the Web is a space through which we travel.
>
> And it's not just a few casual words that happen to use spatial imagery. The economy of the Web is being built around the idea that it's a space. We're building "stores," worrying about the impact of Web "malls," running ads to bring users "in," making our sites "sticky" to keep users from "leaving," providing aids so that users can "navigate." Space isn't a mere metaphor...our experience of the Web is fundamentally spatial....With normal paper documents, we read them, file them, throw them out, or send them to someone else. We do not go to them. We don't visit them. Web documents are different. They're places on the Web. We go to them as we might go to the Washington Monument or the old Endicott Building. They're there, we're here, and if we want to see them, we've got to travel.

"move about" there seemingly unencumbered by geography, gravity, or the other inconveniences of the real, tangible world. Every part of it seems equally close to every other part. And whatever it is, place or no-place, it has become, in an astonishingly short period of time, a global asset of incalculable value—worth, if we were to try to put a monetary value on it, literally countless trillions of dollars. We all spend increasing amounts of our lives "there," yet I doubt that one person in ten thousand could even say what it is or how it works.

Who makes the rules "there," if there's really no there there, and what should they be? What does law look like there? How does it get made, and by whom? Who governs? By what means, and by what right? Online file-sharing, Internet pornography, virtual worlds, spam, online gambling, cyber-terrorism, anonymous remailers, encrypted communication, tele-medicine...? What should the rules be, and who decides what the rules should be?

These are difficult questions—at least, I find them difficult, having spent the better part of the last fifteen years or so thinking about them. Difficult but also important; we have choices before us about the kind of place/thing we want this to be, and about the kind of law we want it to have, and the answers we come up with will affect everyone who uses this remarkable global communications medium—a category that will soon comprise, if current trends continue, almost everybody on the planet. We have a lot of hard thinking ahead of us if we are to resolve them, and if we don't resolve them, we may squander a precious global resource as a consequence.

I need a guide to help me make my way through this strange new landscape with its thicket of hard questions, and I think that Thomas Jefferson will be a good one.

Why Jefferson? That one's pretty easy. Thomas Jefferson has much to teach us about new worlds, and how to think about them; nobody in history, I think it is safe to say, thought more interesting thoughts or asked more interesting questions about the New World than he. He was—as even his most fervent detractors (of whom he has many) readily admit—an awfully smart and interesting guy. If, as Isaiah Berlin had it, the world of great thinkers can be divided into Foxes and Hedgehogs—between those who know Many Things and those who know One Big Thing—Jefferson was both one of history's great Foxes **and** one of history's great Hedgehogs; with the sole exception of Charles Darwin, I can't think of anyone else who merits inclusion in both of those categories.

Jefferson-the-Fox knew an extraordinary amount about an extraordinary range of things—an entire library could easily be stocked with books about Jefferson-the-Architect, Jefferson-the-Botanist, Jefferson-the-Demographer, Jefferson-the-Philosopher, Jefferson-the-Inventor, Jefferson-the-Paleontologist, and so forth. *There is not a sprig of grass that shoots uninteresting to me, nor anything that moves,* he wrote to his daughter—and he meant it. Jefferson seemed to want to know (just about) everything about (just about) everything, and he came astonishingly close to doing so. Jefferson-the-Fox, in the words of a nineteenth-century biographer, could

BOX P.1 HEDGEHOGS AND FOXES

The distinction comes originally from the Greek poet Archilochus—"The fox knows many things, but the hedgehog knows one big thing"—and it marks, Berlin wrote, "one of the deepest differences which divide writers and thinkers, and, it may be, human beings in general."

The metaphor loses much of its force with non-European readers because so many of us haven't the faintest idea what a "hedgehog" is. The European hedgehog (*Erinaceus europaeus*) is an insect-eating mammal belonging to the same Order (Insectivora) as the more familiar voles and shrews. It is the most common small mammal in England. Weighing in at around four pounds, and growing to about twelve inches in length, it hunts at night, eating beetles, worms, caterpillars, slugs, and pretty much anything else that it can catch, and sleeping in underground nests during the day. Its hunting method is straightforward, basically consisting of rooting around for anything that moves and eating it when found. Although the hedgehog is not closely related to the porcupine, it is covered with flexible porcupine-like quills; when startled, it rolls itself into a ball, protecting its head and body from attack. The hedgehog gets its name from a combination of its tendency to be found near hedges and its piglike snout. While its odd shape and short legs give it a clumsy walk, the hedgehog can move with surprising speed. Folklore, at least, has it that when encountering a steep downward slope, a hedgehog can form itself into a ball and roll down the hill (a quality that inspired the video game "Sonic the Hedgehog").

Hedgehogs, Berlin wrote, see everything in terms of "a single central vision, one system less or more coherent or articulate, in terms of which they think and feel—a single, universal, organizing principle." They pursue a Big Goal; their ideas and their thoughts move centripetally, always pointing inward towards the one central vision, the "single, universal, organizing principle." Think Dante, or Plato, or Martin Luther King, men or women who burn with a single-mindedness of understanding and purpose.

Foxes, on the other hand, "pursue many ends, often unrelated and even contradictory, connected, if at all, only in some de facto way." Their world is all complexity and diversity, even chaos, and their thoughts move centrifugally, outwards towards the margins, to contemplate the world's dazzling variety. For the fox, God is always in the details; the essence of the human condition is that there is no essence of the human condition, no single overarching vision or principle or system that can comprehend the world or our place in it. Think Shakespeare; to ask "what is Shakespeare's vision?" is to have already missed Shakespeare's vision, which is that there is no single vision that can ever make sense of it all.

"calculate an eclipse, survey an estate, tie an artery, plan an edifice, try a case, break a horse, dance a minuet, and play the violin," and it was Jefferson-the-Fox to whom President John F. Kennedy was referring when he remarked that a White House dinner with forty-nine Nobel Prize–winners in attendance was the "most extraordinary collection of talent, of human knowledge, that has ever been gathered at the White House—with the possible exception of when Thomas Jefferson dined alone." It was Jefferson-the-Fox who, among his many preoccupations:

- kept a detailed record, while serving as president of the United States, of the first (and last) appearance, each year, of thirty-seven different fruits and vegetables in the Washington food markets
- compiled grammars and vocabularies for more than fifty Native American languages
- took three months off, while serving as America's first secretary of state under George Washington, to go "botanizing" in New England with his friend James Madison (with whom he had earlier engaged in lengthy and anatomically precise correspondence about the genitalia of the mole), the result of which was a lengthy and detailed report on the natural history of the Hessian fly, a major agricultural pest
- not only read (and understood) Isaac Newton's *Principia Mathematica* but designed a new kind of plow in accordance with the principles of Newtonian mechanics
- kept up an extraordinary correspondence with a far-flung network of friends and fellow-scientists regarding agricultural matters as diverse as the advantages of agricultural societies, the construction of mills, the value of agricultural journals, soil erosion, the use of gypsum as soil treatment, the quality of manure (and the use of an "essence of dung" for the purpose), crop rotation, contour plowing versus deep plowing, the possibilities for native silk production, the study and control of insect pests, veterinary medicine, the common and the more scientific use of the word "peccan" (pecan), and the question whether the turkey and honey bee are native to America
- filled the East Room of the White House with the fossil collection from Big Bone Lick in the Northwest Territory
- kept several grizzly bears on the White House lawn while serving as president
- took time out from the deliberations of the Continental Congress in June 1776 to go see a monkey on display in downtown Philadelphia
- smuggled several bags of rice out of northern Italy (at a time when doing so was actually punishable by death) to send back to the United States for cultivation, and introduced dozens of other plant species, including the olive tree, several varieties of grape, vetch, Siberian barley, peaches, Jerusalem wheat (to resist the Hessian fly), yellow-flowered locust, cork oaks, Jamaican lima beans, Spanish broom, and Jerusalem artichokes, to the New World
- delivered, upon his arrival in Philadelphia in 1797 to begin his service as vice president of the United States, the bones of what he believed to be a new species,

Megalonyx, to the American Philosophical Society (of which he had recently been elected president), along with a scientific paper describing the new species (written, incredibly enough, the preceding fall, when he was running for president of the United States)

- wrote, at a time when the mere act of putting pen to paper occasioned excruciating pain in his hand as a result of a broken wrist, a nine-page letter to the president of the French Academy of Sciences devoted entirely to the subject of wind

And it was surely Jefferson-the-Fox who, on July 4, 1776, recorded the purchase of a new thermometer in his diary.

Jefferson-the-Fox had interesting things to say about pretty much everything. Law and governance, surely, but also (as we'll see) networks, and system design, and computer code, and distributed routing, and some of the other things we will need to understand in order to understand law and governance on the global network.

At the same time, Jefferson-the-Hedgehog had, to put it mildly, some very Big Ideas, ideas that helped transform a world in which the conventional mechanisms of lawmaking and governance did **not** work into a world in which, by and large, they did—a few simple but powerful "self-evident truths" that he articulated in prose of great power: that governments "derive their just powers from the consent of the governed," that "all men are created equal," and that they all have "inalienable rights" to "life, liberty, and the pursuit of happiness."

So it's not too far-fetched to think that Jefferson will make a good guide, and that the Jeffersonian perspective on things might help illuminate the strange goings-on in cyberspace in a fruitful way.

The problem, though, is that there are so many different Jeffersons that it is difficult to find "the Jeffersonian perspective" on things. Jefferson-the-Thinker-About-New-Worlds is hidden somewhere among all those other Jeffersons, and uncovering that Jefferson requires entering what Joseph Ellis has called "the labyrinthine corridors of Jefferson's famously elusive mind." No small task. Where do we start, and how do we follow, the Jeffersonian conversation?

Fortunately, he left us both a blueprint and a clue. The blueprint is his book, *Notes on the State of Virginia*; the clue is the moose that he brought to Paris.

VIRGINIA, 1781: *NOTES ON THE NEW WORLD*

I am presently busily employed for Monsieur Marbois without his knowing it, and have to acknowledge to him the mysterious obligation for making me ~~infinitely~~ much better acquainted with my own country than I ever was before.

JEFFERSON TO D'ANMOURS, NOVEMBER 30, 1781 (STRIKEOUT IN ORIGINAL)

In the spring of 1781, Jefferson was finishing up his second term as governor of Virginia, the office to which he had been appointed following his service with the Continental Congress and his justly celebrated work drafting the Declaration of Independence. It was a very difficult and unhappy time in his life. His infant daughter Lucy Elizabeth died in April; his wife, Martha, who had never quite recovered from the pregnancy (her fifth in seven years), was slowly dying.[2]

His tenure as governor, though not quite the miserable failure his political enemies called it, was hardly a resounding success, either. Virginia was at war, and the war was not going well. English forces, led by General Cornwallis and the American turncoat Benedict Arnold, had invaded Virginia the preceding fall, and the government of the new state seemed too disorganized to mount any serious resistance. British troops stormed into Richmond in January 1781, and the entire state government, Jefferson included, abandoned the city rather ignominiously and fled west to Charlottesville. The British continued their advance and in early June entered Charlottesville. They had specific orders from General Cornwallis himself to capture Governor Jefferson, who was then living at nearby Monticello; as British troops

---

2 Martha Jefferson died the following year (September 1782). Just before she died, she scrawled an excerpt from Laurence Sterne's *Tristram Shandy* on a piece of paper:

Time wastes too fast: every letter
I trace tells me with what rapidity
life follows my pen. The days and hours
of it are flying over our heads like
clouds of a windy day never to return more—
every thing presses on

In the almost unimaginably vast trove of Jeffersoniana out there, it is, other than a few inventory lists and the like, the only surviving item written in Martha Jefferson's own hand.

Jefferson himself—whether before or after her death is not known—then wrote out the remaining lines at the bottom of the page:

—and every
time I kiss thy hand to bid adieu, every absence which
follows it, are preludes to that eternal separation
which we are shortly to make!

Martha's death threw Jefferson into a depression from which friends feared he would never recover. "He kept his room for three weeks," his daughter Patsy wrote, and "walked almost incessantly night and day, only lying down occasionally, when nature was completely exhausted, on a pallet that had been brought in during his long fainting fit." When he at last he left his room, "he rode out and from that time he was incessantly on horseback rambling about the mountain on the least frequented roads and just as often through the woods." A miserable kind of existence . . . too burthensome to be borne, Jefferson wrote, all my plans of comfort and happiness reversed by one single event and nothing answering in prospect before me but a gloom unbrightened with one cheerful expectation.

were climbing one side of the hill on which Monticello sits, Jefferson escaped on horseback down the other, and he hightailed it to his estate (little more than a cabin in the woods, really) at Poplar Forest sixty miles to the southwest.

It was not his finest hour. Within two weeks, the Virginia House of Delegates began a formal inquiry into his conduct as governor. Although Jefferson was absolved of all charges that he had been derelict in the conduct of his duties, and the House of Delegates ultimately passed a resolution thanking him for his "impartial, upright, and attentive administration whilst in office," the entire affair left a very, very bitter taste in his mouth. He was, he thought, through with public service forever. *I think public service and private misery inseparably linked together*, he wrote to his friend James Madison; *I have taken my final leave . . . I have returned to my farm, my family and books, from which I think nothing will ever more separate me*. While at Poplar Forest, he turned his attention—with considerable relief, one imagines—to more engaging matters. *Nature intended me for the tranquil pursuits of science, by rendering them my supreme delight*. He had in hand a letter, forwarded to him by Joseph Jones, a member of the Virginia delegation to the Continental Congress, from François Marbois, recently appointed First Secretary of the French legation to the United States—in modern terms, assistant to the French ambassador. Marbois had been *instructed by his government to obtain such statistical accounts of the different states of our Union as might be useful*, and as he was preparing to leave France for the United States he drew up a series of twenty-two questions about life in the New World that he sent to officials in each of the newly independent states.

Marbois's questions read a bit like something an ambitious junior high school student might send to the governor's office in each state as part of a class project (especially if that junior high school student had only a rough command of the English language): What are the "limits and boundaries" of your state? What are its "counties, cities, townships, and villages?" What are its laws? What are its "rivers [and] rivulets, and how far are they navigable?" and the like.[3]

---

3   Marbois's original queries, in full, were as follows:

    Articles of which you are requested to give some details:

1. The Charters of your State.
2. The present Constitution.
3. An exact description of its limits and boundaries.
4. The Memoirs published in its name, in the time of its being a Colony and the pamphlets relating to its interior or exterior affairs present or ancient.
5. The History of the State.
6. A notice of the Counties Cities Townships Villages Rivers Rivulets and how far they are navigable. Cascades Caverns Mountains Productions Trees Plants Fruits and other natural Riches.

Marbois received nothing of value from his correspondents in twelve of the former colonies. Only governors John Sullivan of New Hampshire and John Witherspoon of New Jersey even bothered to respond at all, and then only with perfunctory replies—a "nice to hear from you, welcome to America, sorry I can't be of much help" sort of thing.

No surprise there; after all, answering Marbois's questions involved more than just sending off a pamphlet or two, accompanied by the official road map and an article from the World Book Encyclopedia. Most of the information Marbois was looking for was simply not available anywhere in 1781, and most of what was available was scattered in a thousand different places. (Not to mention the fact that the United States was, at the time, still at war with Great Britain, and the officials to whom Marbois directed his queries might, understandably, have been preoccupied with other matters, too busy to undertake the massive effort that would be required to respond adequately to any of Marbois' questions, let alone to all of them.)

But with correspondent number 13, Marbois hit the jackpot. Jefferson, in what the historian Donald Jackson nicely calls his "dogged way," took Marbois's request as a golden opportunity:

I had always made it a practice, whenever an opportunity occurred of obtaining any information of our country which might be of use to me in any station public or private, to commit it to writing. These memoranda were on loose papers, bundled up without order, and difficult of recurrence when I had occasion for a particular one. I thought [Marbois's

---

7. The number of its Inhabitants.
8. The different Religions received in that State.
9. The Colleges and public establishments. The Roads Buildings &c.
10. The Administration of Justice and a description of the Laws.
12. The present State of Manufactures Commerce interior and exterior Trade.
13. A notice of the best Sea Ports of the State and how big are the vessels they can receive
14. A notice of the commercial productions particular to that State.
15. The weight measures and the currency of the hard money.
16. The public income and expences.
17. The measures taken with regard to the Estates and Possessions of the Rebels commonly called Tories.
18. The condition of the Regular Troops and the Militia and their pay.
19. The marine and Navigation.
20. A notice of the Mines and other subterranean riches.
21. Some samples of these Mines and of the extraordinary Stones. In short a notice of all what can increase the progress of human Knowledge
22. A description of the Indians established in the State before the European Settlements and of those who are still remaining. An indication of the Indian Monuments discovered in that State.

request] *a good occasion to embody their substance, which I did in the order of Mr. Marbois' queries, so as to answer his wish and to arrange them for my own use.*

"Just pullin' together some stuff I've got lyin' around." His response, delivered to Marbois in December 1781, was actually a veritable encyclopedia about the New World: more than two hundred pages of text with responses to all of Marbois's questions, containing information on everything from the length and navigability of Virginia's rivers to a description of the different languages spoken by the Native American inhabitants, from the location of all known veins of gold, iron, lead, copper, coal, marble, granite, limestone, salt, and sulfur to a comprehensive list of Virginia's native plants (divided into four categories: *medicinal, succulent, ornamental, and useful for fabrication,* with *the scientific and popular name of each*), from the quantity and dollar value of Virginia's trade in tobacco, wheat, Indian corn, tar, pelts, flax seed, sturgeon, brandy, and whisky to the historical rainfall patterns across the Virginia Piedmont, from the number of inhabitants in each of Virginia's counties to the enactments of the English parliament relating to the colonization of the New World and the history of the Constitution of Virginia.

Who else, then or now, could possibly have pulled it off? Marbois, surely, could not reasonably have expected anything remotely like it, and one can only imagine his reaction when he received it.[4]

Jefferson kept a copy of his responses to Marbois's questions (no small task in those pre-photocopying days) for his own use. He spent the next few years revising and expanding and updating the material, finally publishing the whole thing in 1785—anonymously, in a private printing of two hundred copies—as *Notes on the State of Virginia.* It was one of only two books he would publish during his lifetime.[5]

---

4   For the "What Goes Around Comes Around" file: Jefferson's generous act of providing Marbois with this storehouse of information about the new country to which Marbois was traveling did not go unrewarded. Twenty years later it was none other than Marbois, at that time the French Minister of Finance under Napoleon, who negotiated the sale of the Louisiana Territory to the United States—which was led by then-president Jefferson. One can only speculate on whether residual feelings of goodwill had anything to do with the almost unbelievably good bargain that the Americans obtained in those negotiations.

5   The other "book" Jefferson published was the pamphlet he published in 1812 bearing the catchy title *The Proceedings of the Government of the United States, in Maintaining the Public Right to the Beach of the Missisipi* [sic], *adjacent to New Orleans, against the Intrusion of Edward Livingstone*—"dry legal argument not at all suited to popular reading," historian Dumas Malone called it. It was an expanded version of the legal brief he wrote in response to a lawsuit filed against him by Edward Livingstone, a somewhat shadowy character living in New Orleans, involving some actions Jefferson had taken while serving as president in regard to boundary lines in New Orleans. (The episode is described in Dumas Malone, *The Sage of Monticello* [1981].)

BOX P.2 THE VIEW AT HARPER'S FERRY

My personal favorite passage in *Notes* is Jefferson's description of *one of the most stupendous scenes in nature,* the confluence of the Shenandoah and "Patowmac" (Potomac) Rivers near what is now Harper's Ferry, West Virginia:

> *You stand on a very high point of land. On your right comes up the Shenandoah, having ranged along the foot of the mountain a hundred miles to seek a vent. On your left approaches the Patowmac, in quest of a passage also. In the moment of their junction they rush together against the mountain, rend it asunder, and pass off to the sea. The first glance of this scene hurries our senses into the opinion that this earth has been created in time, that the mountains were formed first, that the rivers began to flow afterwards, that in this place particularly they have been dammed up by the Blue ridge of mountains, and have formed an ocean which filled the whole valley; that continuing to rise they have at length broken over at this spot, and have torn the mountain down from its summit to its base. The piles of rock on each hand, but particularly on the Shenandoah, the evident marks of their disrupture and avulsion from their beds by the most powerful agents of nature, corroborate the impression.*
>
> *But the distant finishing which nature has given to the picture is of a very different character. It is a true contrast to the fore-ground. It is as placid and delightful as that is wild and tremendous. For the mountain being cloven asunder, she presents to your eye, through the cleft, a small catch of smooth blue horizon, at an infinite distance in the plain country, inviting you, as it were, from the riot and tumult roaring around, to pass through the breach and participate of the calm below. Here the eye ultimately composes itself; and that way too the road happens actually to lead. You cross the Patowmac above the junction, pass along its side through the base of the mountain for three miles, its terrible precipices hanging in fragments over you, and within about 20 miles reach Frederic town and the fine country round that.*

This scene is worth a voyage across the Atlantic.

Like everything Jefferson wrote, it contains prose of great majesty and beauty. But, in truth, not that much of it. *Notes on the State of Virginia* is a pretty dull read; even Jefferson, it turns out, can't make data on rainfall and wind velocity, or the relative sizes of European and American tree squirrels, sing in the ears of the reader.

It is, though, where he answered the question: What's it really like over there in the "new world"? What does someone trying to understand it need to know about it?

And what about that moose?

PARIS, 1787: THE MOOSE ARRIVES

Is not the Caribou and the Black Moose one and the same animal?

Is not the grey Moose and the Elk one and the same Animal and quite different from the former?

What is the height of the grey Moose at the weathers, its length from the Ears in the root of the Tail, and its circumference where largest?

Has it a Sollid or Cloven Hoof?

Do their feet make a loud ratling as they run?

Is the under part of the Hoof covered with Hair?

Are they a Swift Animal?

Do they sweat when hard run or only drip at the tongue?

At what season do they shed their Horns, and when recover them?

Has the Doe Horns as well as the Buck?

How many young does She produce at a time?

What is their Food?

How far southward are they known?

Have they ever been tamed and used to any purpose?

JEFFERSON TO GOVERNOR JOHN SULLIVAN OF NEW HAMPSHIRE, 1783

1787 was a truly remarkable year in human history. On one side of the Atlantic, delegates were gathering in Philadelphia to begin deliberating over a new constitution for the recently formed United States of America. On the other, rioting to protest the rising cost of food had begun in the streets of Paris, signaling the opening chapter in a complex and bloody chain of events that would tear European society to pieces and fundamentally alter the course of the modern world.

Jefferson, recently installed as the Minister Plenipotentiary to France, was probably the only person with close links to both events, the one central node in a transatlantic network of revolutionaries. He was a kind of virtual participant in the Philadelphia convention; he didn't actually attend any of the sessions (he didn't return to the United States until 1789), but his ideas were surely there, largely because James Madison, his disciple and close friend, was there and ended up playing a critical role in formulating the structure of the new government.[6]

---

6 The relationship between the elder Jefferson and the younger Madison—who, in the words of Jefferson biographer Joseph Ellis, "probably knew Jefferson as well or better than anyone else alive"—was one of the more extraordinary collaborations in American history; John Quincy Adams would later call it "a phenomenon, like the invisible and mysterious movements of the magnet in the physical world." While Jefferson was stationed in Paris, he and Madison had kept up a lively stream of correspondence about matters great and small—constitutional theory, the price of food, political developments, Virginia's weather, the prospects for a European war, how Jefferson's children were getting on, etc.—and it

And in France, when, in the winter of 1787, a beleaguered King Louis XVI, his government bankrupt and the French economy in free fall, convened a special gathering of the French nobility—the so-called Assembly of Notables[7]—for the purpose of securing funds from the nobles to prop up the regime and stave off financial collapse, Jefferson found himself—put himself—at the center of events. He attended most of the assembly sessions, and he was there when the Marquis de Lafayette—a member of Jefferson's inner circle in Paris and a leader of what came to be known as the "Patriot Party," with whom Jefferson had forged close ties and for whom he was serving as unofficial advisor[8]—stood up and demanded a true National Assembly,

---

was to Jefferson that Madison turned for help, in 1785, when he began formulating his ideas about the structure of a new government for the United States. Recalling Jefferson's earlier offer to *procure me such books as may be either old and curious, or new and useful,* Madison sent Jefferson "a catalogue of my wants": "treatises on the ancient or modern federal republics, the law of Nations, and the history natural and political of the New World," along with "such of the Greek and Roman authors where they can be got very cheap, as are worth having and are not on the common list of School classics."

Jefferson, who needed few excuses to buy books in prodigious quantities, sent back more than 250 volumes: the collected works of David Hume and Voltaire, the first 37 volumes of Diderot's *Encyclopedia*, De Solis's *Conquest of Mexico*, Smith's *History of New York*, and many others. It wasn't just books, too; the complete list of the items that Jefferson sent to Madison from Paris includes such things as the newly invented phosphorous matches (*by having them at your bedside with a candle,* Jefferson wrote his friend, *the latter may be lighted at any moment of the night without getting out of bed!*); a pedometer; a new kind of oil-burning lamp (the "Argand cylinder lamp," *thought to give light equal to six or eight candles*), pamphlets on ballooning and animal magnetism, a pocket compass, a wristwatch, and a telescope fitted inside a hollow cane (for use on Madison's country rambles).

In what Douglass Adair nicely called "the most fruitful piece of scholarly research ever carried out by an American," Madison took this "literary cargo" and distilled it into two essays, "Notes on Ancient and Modern Confederacies" and "Vices of the Political System of the United States," outlining his thoughts on the defects of the government under the Articles of Confederation and the possible remedies for those defects. These essays, which he sent to Jefferson for review and comment during the winter and spring of 1787 (accompanied by "a few Peccan nuts" from his Virginia farm for Jefferson to nibble on, in case he was feeling homesick) contained Madison's first tentative sketch of what he called the "foundation of the new system" that he would champion at the Constitutional Convention.

7   The Assembly of Notables, Lafayette wryly noted in a letter to George Washington, was composed primarily of people "not able" to do much of anything.

8   Famously, Jefferson collaborated with Lafayette on the draft of a "Charter of Rights" for the French government, which would serve as the basis for the "Declaration of the Rights of Man" that Lafayette presented to the National Assembly in 1789.

a representative body constructed along the lines of the British House of Commons or the U.S. Continental Congress.[9]

As earth-shaking as these events proved to be, they were hardly the only things on Jefferson's mind in 1787. He was working hard to negotiate a new trade pact that would reduce France's prohibitively high tariffs on imported American goods (notably, tobacco, fish, and whale oil), and to organize collective military action against the Barbary pirates, who were then plundering American and European vessels along the coast of North Africa. There were also negotiations with the bankers to keep him busy. Obtaining credit for the newly formed United States was of the gravest importance in the 1780s; many believed then and many historians believe now that the very survival of the new nation was at stake, that without an additional infusion of cash the new nation was about to go bankrupt. The debts incurred to pay for the War of Independence—loans from the French and Dutch governments, and from various private interests, including a syndicate of Amsterdam bankers who negotiated a deal with John Adams in 1782 to float a 5 million florin ($1.5 million) note on behalf of the United States—were coming due, and the new government was having problems coming up with the cash.[10] And just to top things off, he had

---

9   The king, upon receipt of Lafayette's demand, promptly dissolved the Assembly of Notables and sent everyone home. It is one of history's truly delightful coincidences that on the very day that the king dissolved the Assembly—May 25, 1787—delegates to the Constitutional Convention in Philadelphia convened their opening session.

10 *Among the debilities of the government of the [Articles of] Confederation*, Jefferson wrote later, *no one was more distressing than the utter impossibility of obtaining, from the States, the monies necessary for the payment of debts, or even for the ordinary expenses of the government. Some contributed a little, some less, & some nothing, and the last furnished at length an excuse for the first to do nothing also.*

From the moment he arrived in Paris, Jefferson found himself

daily dunned by a company who had formerly made a small loan to the U S., the principal of which was now become due. Our bankers in Amsterdam had notified me that the interest on our general debt would be expected in June, [and] that if we failed to pay it, it would be deemed an act of bankruptcy and would effectually destroy the credit of the U S. and all future prospect of obtaining money there.

Rumors that the new government of the United States was insolvent, unable to pay off even the debt previously accumulated, let alone new credit, were widespread (and, in retrospect, not that far off the mark). The official depositary of U.S. funds in Paris—the bank belonging to Emperor Ferdinand the Great of Prussia—began refusing Jefferson's requests for funds to cover his expenses.

The moment of paying a great sum of annual interest was approaching. There was no money on hand; the board of treasury had notified [us] that they could not remit any, and the progress of the loan which had opened [in Amsterdam], had absolutely

fallen in love—with Maria Cosway, the wife of British painter Richard Cosway, with whom he carried on a pretty torrid affair during 1786 and '87.

But in the midst of it all, Jefferson managed to have the complete carcass and skeleton of an American moose, seven feet tall at the shoulders and with skin and antlers attached, shipped to him in Paris and reassembled and installed in the entrance hall of his residence, the elegant Hotel de Langeac in the center of town.[11]

What, as they say these days, was up with that? It's not as if he had a lot of time on his hands, and getting a moose from the North American woods to Paris in 1787 was an awfully difficult business—as it would be, come to think of it, even today. You can't just shoot it, stuff it in an envelope, and send it off by overnight express. The whole thing had to be skinned, dismembered, and cleaned; a preservative had to be

---

stopped. Our bankers there gave me notice of all this, and that a single day's failure in the payment of interest would have the most fatal effect on our credit.

To make matters worse, in 1787 John Adams, Jefferson's counterpart as U.S. ambassador to England, announced that he would be returning to the United States the following year, throwing Jefferson into something of a panic. The details of banks, bonds, refinancings, and the like were never Jefferson's strong suit—*the money negotiations in Holland,* he wrote to James Madison, *is a business for which I am the most unfit person living; I do not understand bargaining nor possess the dexterity requisite to make them.* He was well aware that he lacked Adams's talents in this regard, and he wrote to him for help: *Your knowledge of the subject enables you to give the best opinion, and your zeal for the public interest, and, I trust, your friendly dispositions towards me, will prompt you to assist me with your advice on this question.*

The two arranged to meet in the Hague in the spring of 1787, on Adams's way home, and to travel together to Amsterdam to meet with the bankers:

The danger of our incurring something like a bankruptcy in Holland, which might have been long, and even fatally, felt in a moment of crisis, induced me to take advantage of Mr. Adams's journey to take leave at the Hague, to meet him there, get him to go on to Amsterdam, and try to avert the impending danger. A consultation with [Adams] *was indispensable, while we could yet avail ourselves of his powers, for when they would be gone, we should be without resource.*

The mission was a success; the two were able to persuade the bankers to execute an additional loan for 500,000 florins—in effect, rolling over their existing debt by advancing them additional money to retire the previous debts that had then come due. It was probably, for Jefferson, the most significant achievement of his years in Europe.

11 Jefferson's residence—"luxurious," his daughter Patsy would write, "even for Paris!"—was a new and magnificent structure, designed by the architect of the new tower on the nearby church of Saint-Sulpice, with modern amenities like running water, a lovely view of Paris, and surrounded by fine gardens. Jefferson, typically, began a major remodeling project immediately after moving in.

applied to the skin to keep it from decomposing; the whole thing—bones, skin, and antlers—had to be placed in boxes strong (and watertight) enough to survive a long ocean journey in the hold of a sailing vessel; ocean transportation to Le Havre had to be secured, along with ground transportation from Le Havre to Paris; and finally, someone in Paris had to reassemble it all. It had taken him years and considerable personal expense—*the experiment,* he wrote later, *was expensive to me, having cost me hunting, curing, and transporting, 60 guineas* (roughly equivalent to several hundred dollars today)—to get the thing done.[12]

What was he up to? This is not, after all, some randomly chosen eighteenth-century eccentric we're talking about here; this is the author of the Declaration of Independence and the Summary View of the Rights of British America, the soon-to-be secretary of state and later the third president of the United States. Even allowing for hyperbole, what could possibly have made a moose skeleton, of all things, *an acquisition more precious than you can imagine*? Was he serious?

So here's my plan. I want to put Jefferson's ideas to work. I want to use them to help think about cyberspace. I'll try to follow his blueprint—asking the questions he

---

12 In 1786 Jefferson had written to Governor John Sullivan of New Hampshire:

> *The readiness with which you undertook to endeavour to get for me the skin, the skeleton, and the horns of the Moose ... emboldens me to renew my application to you for those objects, which would be an acquisition here more precious than you can imagine. Could I chuse the manner of preparing them, it should be to leave the hoof on, to leave the bones of the legs and of the thighs if possible in the skin, and to leave also the bones of the head in the skin with the horns on, so that by sewing up the neck and belly of the skin we should have the true form and size of the animal. However I know they are too rare to be obtained so perfect; therefore I will pray you to send me the skin, skeleton and horns just as you can get them.*

Sullivan went to work. The first specimen he procured for Jefferson was unsatisfactory; it would not "meet your Expectations," he wrote to Jefferson, because "the bones not being left in the skin, or proper Care taken to preserve and dress the skin with the hair on, ... no proper resemblance of the Animal could be had."

Sullivan's second moose was only marginally better; by the time it reached him in Portsmouth, New Hampshire, the "remaining flesh [was] in a state of putrefaction." But, he told Jefferson,

> Every Engine was [then] set at work to preserve the Bones and Cleanse them from the remaining flesh, and to preserve the skins with the hair on, with the hoofs on and Bones of Legs and thighs in the skin without putrefaction, and the Jobb was both Expensive and Difficult, and such as was never before attempted, in this Quarter. But it was at Last Accomplished exactly agreable to Your Directions ... I am much mortifyed and no doubt you will be greatly surprized at the Expence of what I now send.

asked about his complicated, strange place to help us understand ours: Notes on the State of Cyberspace. Along the way, we'll keep our eyes out for any moose we see along the side of the road.

Cyberspace, of course, is not Virginia; its moose won't look exactly like Jefferson's moose, a Jeffersonian natural history of cyberspace won't look exactly like Jefferson's natural history of Virginia—and I, needless to say, am not Jefferson. If I am not up to this task, so be it; I'm not sure anyone is really up to this task, but one has to start somewhere. The goal is to explore, to try to understand something about the way life proceeds there, so that we can begin the process of imagining, and perhaps bringing into being, the new structures and institutions that can help to govern it wisely and well.

BOX P.3

Landing on this great continent is like going to sea....We must have a compass, some friendly directing needle; or else we will uselessly err and wander for a long time, even with a fair wind.

JEAN DE CRÈVOCOEUR, *LETTERS FROM AN AMERICAN FARMER* (1782)

When it finally arrived in Paris, it was, Jefferson reported back to Sullivan, *all in good enough condition*, except that *a good deal of the hair had fallen off*. What remained, though, was *still enough to give a good idea of the animal*. Jefferson was a bit disappointed that the *horns are remarkably small*, and he asked Sullivan to keep his eyes open for a better specimen; *should a pair of large horns of the Moose fall into your way by accident I would thank you to keep them till some vessel should be coming directly from your nearest port to Le Havre, for I understand they are sometimes enormously large indeed.*

But *please—I would ask these things only on condition they should occasion you no trouble, and me little expense.*

NOTES ON THE STATE OF CYBERSPACE
PART I: CHAOS

I consider...the idea of preparing a new copy of [Notes on the State of Virginia] *as not to be entertained. The work itself...is nothing more than the measure of a shadow, never stationary, but lengthening as the sun advances, and to be taken anew from hour to hour. It must remain, therefore, for some other hand to sketch its appearance at another epoch.*
TJ TO JOHN MELISH, DECEMBER 10, 1814

Suppose—just suppose—that the Web is a new world we're just beginning to inhabit. We're like the early European settlers in the United States, living on the edge of the forest. We don't know what's there and we don't know exactly what we need to do to find out. Do we pack mountain climbing gear, desert wear, canoes, or all three? Of course, while the settlers may not have known what the geography of the New World was going to be, they at least knew that there was a geography. The Web, on the other hand, has no geography, no landscape. It has no distance. It has nothing natural in it. It has few rules of behavior and fewer lines of authority. Common sense doesn't hold there, and uncommon sense hasn't yet emerged....We don't yet even know how to talk about a place that has no soil, no boundaries, no near, no far.
DAVID WEINBERGER, *SMALL PIECES LOOSELY JOINED* (2002)

I find impossibly difficult the range of new questions raised about [cyberspace] ...these are hard questions because in an important sense, they are new questions....In this context, what we need [is] permission to work things out freely. We need a space where we can experiment with ideas without condemnation reigning down around us....[T]his is cyberspace, where no one has the right to declare truth is on their side; and where no one should claim the right to condemn. This is a space where we need the space to try out different, and even heretical, ideas. In this space, the heroes will be lunatics...or crazies.
LAWRENCE LESSIG, *CODE AND OTHER LAWS OF CYBERSPACE* (1999)

CHAPTER ONE

MAPPING THE TERRITORY
THE GEOGRAPHY OF NOWHERE

On arriving at a town, the first thing is to buy the map of the town, and a book noting its curiosities. Walk round the ramparts when there are any, or go to the top of a steeple to have a view of the town and its environs.

TJ TO JOHN RUTLEDGE, JUNE 3, 1788

We need to get our bearings before we set out. Jefferson, helpfully, provided the reader of *Notes on the State of Virginia* with a map of the place (see following page).

It's a good place to start, to get the lay of the land, as it were. A good map always tells us some useful things, and this one is no exception.[1]

Jefferson's map shows us, for instance, that the "Virginia" of 1781 was a lot bigger than the Virginia of today, stretching north all the way up to the Ohio River and west all the way to the Mississippi, encompassing the current states of Virginia and West Virginia in their entirety as well as much of what is now Kentucky and

---

1   Jefferson didn't include a map of the New World in his initial response to Marbois's queries in the winter of 1781. It was an excusable omission, surely; good maps of the New World were few and far between at that time, the state of knowledge about the New World and the state of cartography being what they were, and even an educated European or American in the late eighteenth century was unlikely to have ever laid eyes on such a thing.

Jefferson, however, was something of a map freak, possessing a deep love for maps and for map-making. He had, in Donald Allen's words, an "easy mastery" of the tools of the cartographer's trade:

the ability to view the world at different scales and to work easily up and down the hierarchy from the local to the global and back again, the tendency to seek concepts that help make sense of the complicated spatial patterns that make up the world's natural and cultural mosaic, the ability to convert the map view into a view of the real world, [and] the understanding that geography is a point of view, a way of looking at things, rather than a study of any particular thing.

He came by it naturally; his father, Peter Jefferson, was himself a mapmaker of some renown, having made a small but important contribution to the history of map-making in the New World. As the younger Jefferson put it in his *Autobiography*:

FIGURE 1.1 Jefferson's 1786 Map. *A map of the territory from Albemarle Sound to Lake Erie, and from Philadelphia to the mouth of the great Kanawha, containing Virginia, Delaware, and Pennsylvania, a great part of Maryland, and a part of North Carolina.* Courtesy of the Tracy W. McGregor Library of American History, Special Collections, University of Virginia Library.

My father's education had been quite neglected; but being of a strong mind, sound judgment, and eager after information, he read much and improved himself, insomuch that he was chosen, with Joshua Fry, Professor of Mathematics in William and Mary College,... to make the first map of Virginia which had ever been made.... They possessed excellent materials for so much of the country as is below the Blue Ridge; little being then known beyond that ridge.

This map—known as the "Jefferson-Fry" map—was completed in 1751 and was the first map of Virginia based upon actual ground survey data.

Over the course of his lifetime, Jefferson was to amass a prodigious personal collection of more than 100 printed and manuscript maps and 350 atlases. One of the first things he

Tennessee—*An area, somewhat triangular, of 121,525 square miles, one third larger than the Islands of Great Britain and Ireland.* We see that it is a well-watered place, with a number of large rivers—the Delaware, Susquehanna, Patowmac, Rappahannock, James—all wending their way from the interior to the coast. We see that the mountains *are not solitary and scattered confusedly over the face of the country,* [but] *commence at about 150 miles from the sea-coast, are disposed in ridges one behind another, running nearly parallel with the sea-coast though rather approaching it as they advance north-eastwardly.*

The map lets us gauge the distance between different places—both relative distance and, once we know the scale (one inch = twenty miles in the original engraving), absolute distance as well. Philadelphia is closer to the mouth of the Delaware

---

did when he entered the White House in 1800 was to install a special map case (of his own design) into the wall of his study; it allowed for the storage of a number of maps, any one of which could be pulled down and remain suspended for study, at a time. (You might be familiar with Jefferson's map holder, as many school classrooms in the United States still use map holders of basically the same design.) And in 1816, when he was seventy-three years old and long retired from public life, perched on his hilltop at Monticello, he wrote a remarkable twelve-page letter to Virginia governor Wilson C. Nicholas, lobbying for a new law authorizing preparation of the first complete map of Virginia to be *based on an accurate chart of each county.* He describes in detail the work that would be required to carry out the plan and shows his easy familiarity with the technique of "barometric admeasurement," with the use of a "table of amplitudes" to correct for the deviation of magnetic North and true North, and with the proper use of the "theodolite," the "Hadley," the "Circumferenter," the "equatorial," the "sliding Nonius," and the other mysterious tools of the cartographer's trade. When the bill became law later that year, Jefferson helped to secure the labors of John Wood to supervise the necessary county surveys, and his efforts bore fruit in the year of his death, 1826, with publication of another small cartographic monument, the "Map of the State of Virginia Constructed in conformity to Law from the Late Surveys Authorized by the Legislature and Other Original and Authentic Documents."

So back in 1786, when he was preparing *Notes on the State of Virginia* for publication, he got to work. He embarked on one of his more feverish book-buying sprees, purchasing *everything I can lay my hands on which related to any part of America*—Jonathan Carver's *Travels in the Interior of North America,* Pierre Charlevoix's *Histoire et Description Generale de la Nouvelle France* [*History and General Description of New France*], Thomas Jeffrey's *American Atlas,* Thomas Hutchins's *Topographical Description of Louisiana and the Floridas* as well as his *New Map of the Western parts of Virginia, Pennsylvania, Maryland and North Carolina,* Louis Hennepin's *Description of Louisiana,* Henri Tonti's *Late Discoveries in North America,* and numerous others. With these, and with the maps (including his father's map, the Jefferson-Fry Map) in his own personal collection close at hand, he spent several weeks at the drafting table and put together what was, at the time, the most accurate pictorial depiction of this territory available anywhere.

River than it is to the mouth of the James; Norfolk is closer to the mouth of the James than it (or Philadelphia) is to the mouth of the Delaware; Alexandria is closer to Fredericksburg than it is to Roanoke.

Useful stuff, all of it.

We also see—or at least we sense—some kind of wilderness out there, west of the mountains, where the details of the map give way to a vaguer, more indeterminate place. It's as though our mapmaker were standing on the Atlantic Coast, looking west—which in a sense, of course, he was—and only able to capture the nearer features with any accuracy. He's not quite sure what's out there beyond the Alleghenies, although what he can make out seems tantalizing and even a bit bizarre: The "Great Meadows" out near the Monongahela River, the "Large Rock" on the Ohio River, "Mahonings Salt Springs" on Big Beaver Creek, and—my personal favorite—the massive "Buffalo Swamp" in Central Pennsylvania.[2]

A good map of cyberspace, then, will help us get started.

We need to be a little clearer about what it is we are calling "cyberspace" in order to provide one. Whatever else it may be, cyberspace is, at bottom, just a network, linking computers together so that information, in the form of electronic pulses (on/off, one/zero), can be transmitted from one to another. There are thousands upon thousands of such networks out there—millions, probably, by now: local area

---

2   There are some other strange things on Jefferson's map. For one thing, he put the "prime meridian"—the line of zero degrees longitude—running right through the center of downtown Philadelphia. Pretty cheeky! This was, he wrote, *in accordance with common usage*, but I take it that's just some kind of cartographer's in-joke; Jefferson knew full well that this was not, in fact, "common usage," that no other mapmaker of the time placed the prime meridian anywhere near Philadelphia, and that there really wasn't any "common usage" at all in the 1780s regarding the proper location for the prime meridian—different maps put it in different places (depending, usually, on the nationality of the cartographer). Placement of the prime meridian was something of a political and scientific football in the nineteenth century; in 1816, the United States actually passed a law declaring it to be the line of longitude running through the White House in Washington, D.C. In 1884, however, an international convention agreed to use the line of longitude passing through the British Royal Observatory in Greenwich, England, to represent the line of zero longitude, and thus it remains to this day. Jefferson, one suspects, would have been a tad disappointed.

   Jefferson also, rather audaciously, added five new states to the Union: "Kentuckey" (for the western part of Virginia), "Frankland" (for the territory most of which would ultimately become Tennessee), and three others that, rather forlornly, were given no names ("A New State," he labels each of them). Kentucky did not actually become a state until 1792, Tennessee in 1796, and the other states west of the Alleghenies still later. Was our mapmaker's imagination carrying him away?

networks (LANs), wide area networks (WANs), home networks, office networks, interoffice networks, wireless networks, intranets, extranets.

One of those networks stands out. It is, among other things, the largest, by far, of all of them. It has a name—"the TCP/IP network"—referring to the specific set of networking rules (or "protocols") it uses to move information around (TCP/IP, the Transmission Communication Protocol/Internet Protocol (about which I'll have a great deal more to say in chapters 4–6). It is not just a network linking individual computers together, but an inter-network, or "internet," linking whole networks of computers together. There are thousands upon thousands of internets out there, too: the internet that connects the network at my law school with the network at the university's Department of Computer Sciences, for instance, or the internet that connects the network at the Boston warehouse of Joe's Shoes with the Chicago warehouse, or the thousands of other instances all around us. The big one is known as **the** inter-network, or, more simply, "the Internet."[3]

It looks like this:

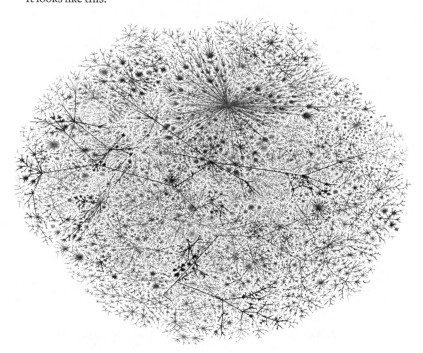

FIGURE 1.2 The "Peacock Map" of the Internet. Created by Hal Burch and Bill Cheswick; Courtesy of the Lumeta Corporation.

3 "The Internet." There is a small de-capitalization crusade under way these days, under which we would refer to the global TCP/IP inter-network henceforth not as "the Internet" but as "the internet." Proponents say that because it is now a part of everyday life, we can, as with "television" and "radio," dispense with the distinction of the initial capital letter.

This map (known as the "Peacock Map" because its creators, Hal Burch and Bill Cheswick, thought it looked like "a peacock smashed on a windshield" when printed in full color) depicts what the engineers call the Internet's "physical layer." Each line represents a physical connection between the individual networks (shown as points)—fiber-optic cable, usually, though it may be anything over which electronic messages can travel, such as ordinary telephone wire, or even a portion of the electromagnetic spectrum.[4]

Personally, I prefer "the Internet." It doesn't much matter what we call it—Edgar, or RX&7-42—as long as we don't obscure the fact that when we refer to Edgar, or RX&7-42, or "the Internet," we are referring to one particular inter-network among many thousands of such inter-networks. **The** Internet. Distinguishing **this** inter-network—the big, globe-spanning one, the one that we can get "on" from pretty much any place on the planet—from all the others is useful if we are to ask questions like: Why did this one get to be so big, so fast? The initial capital letter serves that purpose—reminding us that this is a proper name, that it refers to a particular "internet," the one known as "the Internet" (much the way we would preserve the initial capital when referring to that geological formation in Arizona as "the Canyon," or the collection of astronomical objects of which we are a member as "the Galaxy," in order to distinguish them from other canyons and other galaxies).

So "the Internet" it is—at least, in my book.

4 Burch and Cheswick constructed the Peacock Map by sending messages from a single computer in the United States—located in Murray Hill, New Jersey, to be precise—to each of the more than 100,000 individual networks linked together on the Internet, using a little software program known as "traceroute." Traceroute attaches itself to a message and compiles information about each intermediate "hop" the message takes as it makes its way from sender to recipient; when the message finally reaches the recipient, Traceroute automatically sends the list of intermediate hops back to the original sender.

You can, in fact, try this at home. When you're connected to the Internet, open up a window that allows you to run MS-DOS programs, and type in

C:\>tracert www.cybergeography.com

Or, instead of www.cybergeography.com, you can type in the name of any World Wide Web server—www.google.com, or www.temple.edu, or the like. You should see, popping up on your screen, something that looks like this:

Tracing route to www.cybergeography.com [209.8.64.161] over a maximum of 30 hops:

1. 10 ms <10 ms <10 ms cisco-2.bart.ucl.ac.uk [128.40.59.245]
2. 10 ms 40 ms 10 ms 128.40.255.53
3. <10 ms <10 ms <10 ms 128.40.20.254
4. <10 ms <10 ms <10 ms atmr-ulcc.lonman.net.uk [194.83.100.62]
5. <10 ms <10 ms <10 ms atmr-ulcc.lonman.net.uk [194.83.100.62]
6. <10 ms 70 ms 40 ms tglobe-gw2.ja.net [193.63.94.80]
7. 91 ms 90 ms 90 ms Teleglobe.net [207.45.215.201]

It certainly makes for a lovely picture. The Internet looks like some kind of strange organic being—there's something almost biological about it, like a connected mass of nerve fibers in the brain, or capillaries in the skin, or veins in a leaf.

But it doesn't really do what we want a good map to do. For one thing, it doesn't really show us what the Internet looks like, because **it has no scale.** The lines connecting networks together on the Peacock Map are of completely arbitrary length; they don't correspond to actual, physical distance between the linked networks. Networks that appear "close together" on the map, in network space—i.e., networks connected directly to one another, or through a relatively small number of intermediate "hops"—may actually be quite far apart from one another (in real-space), and vice versa.[5] There's no vantage point from which one could look down over the physical connections between Internet networks and have them actually look like what is shown on the Peacock Map.[6]

More important, it doesn't really orient us to the territory nearly as well as Jefferson's map does. That Philadelphia was closer to Wilmington than to Richmond

---

8. 80 ms 90 ms 101 ms Teleglobe.net [207.45.215.2]

9. 90 ms 130 ms 110 ms gin-nyy-ac1.Teleglobe.net [207.45.199.233]

10. 110 ms 110 ms 110 ms gin-nyy-bb1.Teleglobe.net [207.45.201.33]

11. 111 ms 120 ms 170 ms gin-maee-bb1.Teleglobe.net [207.45.223.2]

12. 150 ms 121 ms 140 ms mae-east.cais.com [192.41.177.85]

13. 120 ms 120 ms 111 ms hssi12-0.mch.cais.net [209.8.159.26]

14. 110 ms 120 ms 120 ms 209.8.64.161

Trace complete.

Burch and Cheswick went through this procedure hundreds of thousands of times, compiled all of the information on all of the connections from one intermediate hop to another, and then plotted the accumulated information in two dimensions to produce the Peacock Map.

5 So, for instance, to take two examples at random from the Peacock Map, the CAMPUS.CEGS. ITESM.MX network (which belongs to the Instituto Technologico de Monterrey in Monterrey, Mexico) and the SYD.HEALEY.COM.AU network (which belongs to a service provider in New South Wales, Australia) are closer to one another in **network** distance than either is to ATT.NET (belonging to AT&T, Inc., and located in Murray Hill, New Jersey).

6 "[T]he Web is a space without distance, at least in the usual sense. You could play with [the Peacock] map of the Net until the router placements correspond to their placement on the earth, and then you could overlay a grid on top of that. But that would be a map of where the Web's hardware is housed. That might be useful; it could remind you to be careful when digging up your backyard, for example, but it wouldn't be a map of the Web. To achieve this grid, we've had to reduce the Web to a set of computers. But that's precisely what's not interesting about it. (David Weinberger, *Small Pieces Loosely Joined*)

mattered, and it mattered a great deal, because the speed at which people and goods and information could travel between these points was dependent to a significant extent on the distances between them. But "network distance," so nicely displayed in the Peacock Map, doesn't really matter very much at all on the Internet. On the inter-network, all points are effectively equidistant from all other points; information travels around the network as pulses of electrical energy—on-off, one-zero—moving at the speed of light, and it can get from any point to any other point on this vast inter-network in the blink of an eye, irrespective of the number of "hops" it has to make along the way. That it takes (infinitesimally) less time for a message to travel between networks that are "close together" (in network space) than between networks that are "far apart" (in network space) is invisible to network users; you can reach anyplace, from anyplace, equally easily and equally quickly.[7]

So while we could, in theory, put a **"you are here"** sticker onto the Peacock Map, showing exactly where your office network, or your Internet Service Provider's network, is located relative to other networks,[8] that won't tell you anything that you really need to know in order to get around, to communicate with others, or to use the global inter-network. From the user's perspective, the Internet is more like a gigantic circle or sphere (a circle or sphere, you recall from high school geometry, being a way of portraying the set of all points that are equidistant from any single point): You (or, more precisely, your network) in the center, and *all* of the Internet's other networks on the perimeter of the circle (or the surface of the sphere), equidistant from you.

But that's not to say that we can't learn some important things about this network from the Peacock Map. We can see, for instance, that the Internet is, literally, "decentralized." Most computer networks—including most of the constituent computer networks that are connected together to make up the Internet—look more or less like the network in figure 1.3, opposite.

Your office network, for example, probably takes this shape—centralized around a single central point on which all paths converge and through which all messages

---

7   It's not strictly correct to say that network distance is completely irrelevant on the Internet. There are, in fact, measurable differences in the time it takes messages to get from one point on the Internet to another, depending largely on the number of intermediate hops it must take. The differences, though, are measured in milliseconds, and, generally speaking, are of little concern to anyone using the inter-network.

8   In theory. The network through which you access the Internet is almost certainly not on the Peacock Map, only because a complete map of the Internet would require, as we'll see in the next chapter, more than 500 million points, and no map could come close to displaying that much information in one place.

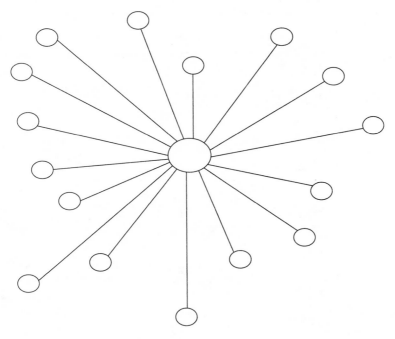

FIGURE 1.3 A Simple Centralized Network.

must travel, a single central "server" to which all machines must be connected if they are to be "on the network."

The Internet, though, doesn't look like that. It doesn't have a single central point through which all paths run, no single central machine or network of machines to which all others must be connected and through which all messages must travel. Some of its constituent networks do have (many) more connections than others; the network is decidedly "clumpy," in that sense. But there are multiple pathways that messages can take to get from one point of the inter-network—some network down there in the "southwest" corner of the map—to another (up in the far "northeast").

And while we're on the subject of what the Internet doesn't look like, it also doesn't look like the network in figure 1.4 on the next page.

It did look like that, once—as it says, in December 1969. Figures 1.2 and 1.4 depict the same network: "the Internet."⁹

---

9 It's not quite correct, technically speaking—and we are, after all, technically speaking—to say that the two maps depict the "same" network. The network shown in 1969 in figure 1.4 would grow, over the next decade or so, to comprise several hundred machines. This

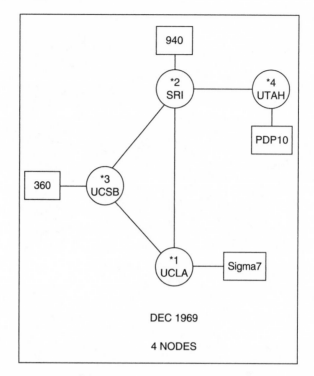

FIGURE 1.4 The Internet, c. 1969.

What happened? How did this little four-node network become this gargantuan thing?

network, too, had a name—DARPANet (or sometimes ARPANet—at two hundred or three hundred machines, it wasn't really important enough for people to get too finicky about what it was called), standing for the "Advanced Research Project Agency" in the U.S. Defense Department that had funded much of its development to that point. By the late '70s, it had become—or it was showing signs of becoming—unmanageable; it was starting to clog up, becoming overly cumbersome to use. Several years of discussion and debate among the cadre of engineers working on this project ensued, and on January 1, 1983, all the machines on the DARPANet, by pre-arrangement, switched over from the set of networking protocols they had been using (known as "Internet Protocol") to a new, and fundamentally redesigned, set—the TCP/IP protocols, still in use today.

The two networks shown in figures 1.2 and 1.4, then, are the same insofar as they are in the same lineage: there's an unbroken, continuous chain of intermediates connecting the network in figure 1.4 with the network in figure 1.2. At the same time, they're different networks in the sense that they have different DNA—different rules for moving information from one point on the network to another.

CHAPTER TWO

POPULATION

As to repressing our growth, [the British] *might as well attempt to repress the waves of the ocean.*

TJ TO JOHN MELISH, DECEMBER 10, 1814

Have you seen the new work of Malthus on population? It is one of the ablest I have ever seen....Several important questions in political economy are treated with a masterly hand.

TJ TO JOSEPH PRIESTLY, JANUARY 29, 1804

Before we look at how and why this network got to be so big, we should ask: How big is it, exactly?

Here are the numbers:

TABLE 2.1 NUMBER OF INTERNET HOST MACHINES (DATA FROM THE INTERNET SYSTEMS CONSORTIUM, WWW.ISC.ORG)

DATE	# OF HOSTS
December-69	4
April-71	23
June-74	62
March-77	111
August-81	213
May-82	235
August-83	562
October-84	1,024
October-85	1,961
February-86	2,308
November-86	5,089

(continued)

TABLE 2.1 CONTINUED

DATE	# OF HOSTS
December-87	28,174
July-88	33,000
October-88	56,000
January-89	80,000
July-89	130,000
October-89	159,000
October-90	313,000
January-91	376,000
July-91	535,000
October-91	617,000
January-92	727,000
April-92	890,000
July-92	992,000
October-92	1,136,000
January-93	1,313,000
April-93	1,486,000
July-93	1,776,000
October-93	2,056,000
January-94	2,217,000
July-94	3,212,000
October-94	3,864,000
January-95	5,846,000
July-95	8,200,000
January-96	14,352,000
July-96	16,729,000
January-97	21,819,000
July-97	26,053,000
January-98	29,670,000
July-98	36,739,000
January-99	43,230,000
July-99	56,218,000
January-00	72,398,092
July-00	93,047,785

January-01	109,574,429
July-01	125,888,917
January-02	147,344,723
July-02	162,128,493
January-03	171,638,297
January-04	233,101,481
July-04	285,139,107
January-05	317,646,084
July-05	353,284,187
January-06	394,991,609
July-06	439,286,364
January-07	433,193,199
July-07	489,774,269
January-08	541,677,360

and figure 2.1 shows what the numbers look like when displayed graphically.

Put aside, for the moment, any questions you may have about precisely where these numbers come from or how they were obtained; counting the number of computers on the Internet at any one time is a tricky business, for reasons we'll take

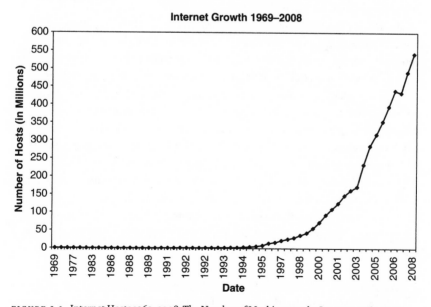

FIGURE 2.1   Internet Hosts 1969–2008: The Number of Machines on the Internet, 1969–2008.

a look at shortly. But for now, we can take these as roughly accurate counts of the number of machines connected together on the global TCP/IP network, with no reason to suspect that they systematically overstate the number of those machines or the rate of growth of that population of machines.

So there's our answer: **541,677,360** computers on the Internet as of January, 2008.

––––––––––

In responding to Marbois's question about "the number of Virginia's inhabitants," Jefferson began by gathering together as much information as he could get his hands on in civil and church records—tax accounts and parish population records, primarily—to produce an answer: **567,614.**

Merely pulling the information together this way was a real accomplishment, given the scattered nature of the information involved, and he could, presumably, have stopped there.

He didn't stop there, however, because the answer (567, 614) was more than a little disturbing. Only half a million or so people? Fewer than in metropolitan London or Paris, in an area 30 percent larger than Great Britain and Ireland put together? Less than one-tenth the population ($\approx$ 9 million) of Great Britain alone, and less than one-fortieth the population of France ($\approx$ 24 million) (which was only about twice Virginia's size)?

Where was everyone? Europeans had been in the New World for a long time— more than 160 years, longer than the period that has elapsed since the beginning of the Civil War to the day I'm writing these words. After all that time, it had fewer than six hundred thousand inhabitants?

It is a little difficult for us to appreciate, from our twenty-first-century perch, just how troubling these questions would have been for Jefferson and his eighteenth-century contemporaries. Under the conventional wisdom of the time, bigger societies were better societies; population size was seen as an indicator of how well a society was managing its affairs, a kind of litmus test for judging how well-organized and well-run it was. It made sense, at least in a world in which the overwhelming majority of people were perched precariously at the edge of survival, in which infant death was commonplace, and in which starvation and disease ravaged populations with alarming regularity. An abundant population was the mark of a society that had somehow ordered its affairs so as to solve the basic problems of human survival, and to allow its people, in the biblical phrase, to "be fruitful and multiply."

We know better now, of course; we no longer think that bigger is necessarily better when it comes to human populations, or that population size is an indicator of good governance or a well-ordered society.[1]

––––––––––

1   We "know better" because we know more—more about how and why human populations expand or contract. When Jefferson penned this chapter of *Notes on Virginia*, what we would today call "demography"—the systematic study of the growth and distribution of human

But Jefferson and his contemporaries took this all very, very seriously. By this conventional Bigger-is-Better standard, 567,614 was a failing grade; the mark, surely, of a society in trouble. If this New World is such a great place—and if these "Americans" know what they're doing—why aren't there more people there?

It was a serious ideological challenge, calling into question the entire American experiment in nation-building and self-governance to which Jefferson was so deeply committed. It was also a serious practical problem as well. As we saw earlier, one of Jefferson's primary tasks while he was in France in the mid-1780s was to persuade the European bankers to lend additional money to the United States. It was a tricky proposition under the best of circumstances; the United States had not even begun to pay off the millions of dollars it had previously borrowed, from these same bankers, to pay for the War of Independence. The bankers were not stupid, nor were they prone to tossing money around out of sympathy for the cause of democracy and self-government. They wanted assurances that the United States was going to make good on its promises to pay them back, and a widespread view that things were not going well on that side of the Atlantic would not make that task any easier.

He needed to do something. So, having answered the question Marbois had asked, he went on to ask a question of his own, one Marbois had not asked: **How fast is Virginia's population growing?**

BOX 2.1

When you consider the character which is given to our country by the lying newspapers of London, & their credulous copyers in other countries; when you reflect that all Europe is made to believe we are a lawless banditti, in a state of absolute anarchy, cutting one another's throats, & plundering without distinction, how can you expect that any reasonable creature would venture among us?

TJ TO MARIA COSWAY, OCTOBER 12, 1786

---

populations—hardly existed; the word itself was not coined until the nineteenth century, because prior to that there was no such field of study requiring separate designation. Questions like "Is the population of Europe increasing or decreasing in size?" "Why (or why not)?" "How do people spread themselves out over different kinds of territory?" "How densely are different countries populated, and what might account for the differences?" hadn't even begun to be systematically attacked. And we "know better" because things have happened, and the world has changed, during the last 225 years or so, and we know about things that nobody could possibly have known about in the 1780s—the Industrial Revolution, the "demographic transition" (a sharp downturn in growth rates at some point as societies become wealthier), the development of sophisticated birth control technologies, and the like.

His answer: **really, really fast**. "Geometrically," in fact.[2]

He prepared a simple table showing the *intermediate enumerations, a census of inhabitants at different periods, extracted from our historians and public records*—what modern-day demographers would call the "time series" for Virginia's population:

TABLE 2.2 VIRGINIA'S POPULATION (FROM *NOTES ON THE STATE OF VIRGINIA*)

YEAR	POPULATION SIZE
1654	7,209
1700	22,000
1748	82,100
1759	105,000
1772	153,000
1782	567,614

These data, he went on, *enable us to calculate, with a considerable degree of precision, the rate at which we have increased.* They showed that there had been *a duplication once in every 27 ¼ years*—i.e., that Virginia's population had been doubling in size every twenty-seven years or so, equivalent to a geometric growth rate of around 2.5 percent per year.

2   You probably covered this in high school algebra, but just to refresh your recollection: a population is said to be growing **linearly** when it adds a fixed **number** of individuals (whether 4, or 400, or 4 million) each year:

$$N(t+1) = N(t)+X$$

where N(t) stands for the population size at some arbitrary time ("t"), and N(t+1) stands for the population size at the **next** period ("t+1").

A population is growing **geometrically** when it adds a fixed **percentage** (R%) of individuals per year.

$$N(t+1) = N(t) + R \times N(t)$$

where N(t) is again the population size at time "t," N(t+1) the population size at the next time period (period t+1), and R is the growth rate.

A little algebra lets us simplify Equation 1 a little:

$$N(t+1) = N(0) \times [1+R]^{t+1}$$

That is, the size, at time (t+1), of a population that is growing geometrically at rate R is equal to the starting population multiplied by a constant [1+R] raised to the t+1th power. (The exponent in the above equation is why geometric growth can also be called "exponential" growth.)

Compound interest is probably the most familiar example of geometric growth. If you start with a "population" of $100, and a growth rate of 5 percent a year, you'll have 100 × $(1.05)^t$ after t years ($105 after 1 year, $162.88 after 10 years, $13,150.13 after 100 years), and the amount of money in the account increases by increasing amounts each year (by $5 the first year, $5.25 the second, $5.51 the third, $8.15 in the 10th, $657.50 in the 100th, etc.).

Good news!

Should this rate of increase continue, we shall have between six and seven millions of inhabit-ants within 95 years [and] there will then be 100 inhabitants for every square mile, which is nearly the state of population in the British islands.[3]

Exactly how he figured out, from these data, that Virginia was growing at 2.5 per-cent per year is an interesting story in and of itself. He doesn't describe his methods of calculation in any detail, and the answer doesn't exactly jump off the page, does it? It looks like an especially nasty SAT question: "How fast is the population in Table 2.2 growing?" But it's not too difficult to reconstruct what he did: He assumed that Virginia's population had been growing geometrically over the entire period, and then he confirmed that the observed data was consistent with the assumption.[4]

3   Those of you paying **really** close attention might be wondering if Jefferson got his math-ematics right here. As we saw in chapter 1, Jefferson's own figures showed that Virginia comprised an area of 121,525 square miles. If that's the case, when it reaches a population of *between six and seven million inhabitants* it will not have 100 per square mile (as Jefferson would have it), but more like 50 or 60. What was going on?

A lot, as it turns out. The early 1780s were a time of complex (and often incomprehen-sible) maneuverings between and among the newly independent states (and between the individual states and the newly created "United States of America") to define and rear-range state boundaries. Jefferson and Madison were, at the time, spearheading an effort to get Virginia to give away thousands of square miles of its territory to the United States, an effort that involved persuading the new federal Congress to accept the gift. Oddly enough, it had been rejected several times. "Nothing so fantastic," historian Claude Bowers has writ-ten of the episode, "is to be found in American history."

When he was calculating Virginia's future population density, Jefferson incorporated this territorial giveback in his calculations. The Virginia of the future, he assumed, would be a considerably smaller Virginia than the one existing in 1781; its western boundary would not be the Mississippi River (as it was in 1781) but *the meridian of the mouth of the Great Kanha-way* [River]—i.e., on a north-south line running approximately through modern-day Point Pleasant, West Virginia. *64,491 square miles*, he calculated; thus, six to seven million future inhabitants would yield a population density of around 100 per square mile.

Remember the "New States" he added in the western portion of Virginia? Well, Jeffer-son had some big plans for this new territory.

4   His calculations appear to have proceeded as follows. He calculated the average amount of time it took Virginia's population to double in size between 1654 and 1772 (having first eliminated the data from the 1782 census because it had been generated by a "census of inhabitants"—an *enumeration of all inhabitants, slave and free, male and female, of any age*—while each of the other five data points came from a "census of tithes" that included only *the free males above 16 years of age, and slaves above that age of both sexes*.) In those 118 years (1654–1772), the original population had doubled in size once (to go from 7,209 to 14,418), twice (to 28,836), three times (to 57,672), four times (to 115,344). And it was approxi-mately one-third of the way to completing its fifth doubling.

We can be pretty certain where he got that assumption of geometric growth (though again, he does not say so explicitly); it came from the work of Benjamin Franklin, who had made the same assumption of geometric growth some thirty-five years earlier.[5]

It was really just a guess, in other words—Franklin's guess turned into Jefferson's hypothesis—but it turns out to have been an inspired one. The assumption of geometric growth (at a rate of 2.5 percent per year) fits the actual observations almost perfectly (see fig. 2.2). Or, as Jefferson himself put it, *the intermediate enumerations taken in 1700, 1748, and 1759, furnish proofs of the uniformity of this progression.*

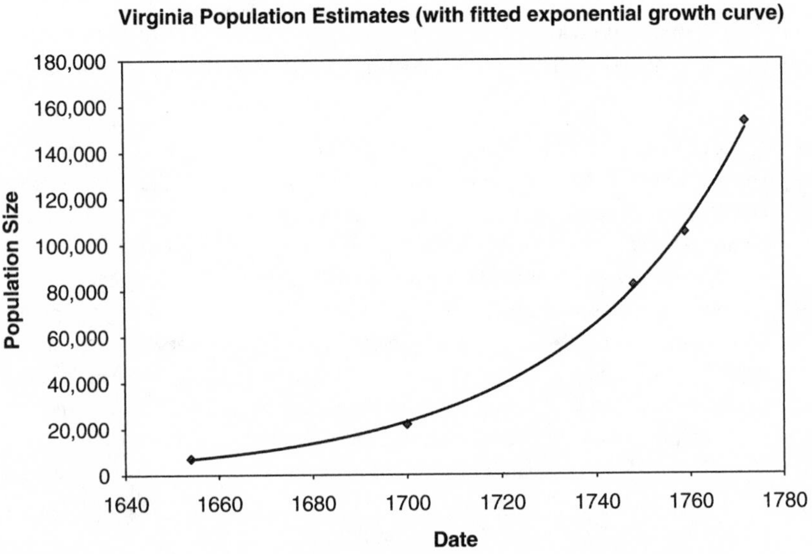

Virginia Population Estimates (with fitted exponential growth curve)

FIGURE 2.2 Jefferson's Virginia Population Estimates (with fitted exponential growth curve).

So: four and one-third doublings over 118 years, or an average of one doubling every 118/4.33 = 27.25 years. Bingo—*a duplication once in every 27 ¼ years.*

His calculation of "average doubling time" is the tip-off that he's assuming geometric growth. Geometrically growing populations double in size in a fixed amount of time; they take the same amount of time to go from 4 to 8 as from 400 to 800 or from 4 million to 8 million. So "average doubling time" is a meaningful statistic for geometrically growing populations. By contrast, a population growing linearly takes longer and longer to double in size as it gets larger; you can still calculate an "average doubling time" for such a population, but it doesn't mean anything, because it is an estimate of a characteristic of the population that is constantly shifting.

5   Franklin's reputation has suffered, quite unfairly, over the last two hundred years (a trend that is, one hopes, in the process of being reversed, helped along by the publication of several excellent recent biographies). We seem often to regard him as a quasi-comical

It was, strangely enough, a pivotal moment in the history of human ideas—though nobody (including Jefferson) realized it, or could possibly have realized it, at the time. It is the first time, as far as I can tell, that anyone had ever actually demonstrated, with real data, that a human population had grown geometrically for a

---

figure—fat and jolly, flying his kite in the thunderstorm, writing the clever homilies of *Poor Richard's Almanack*. In fact, he was one of the great scientists of the eighteenth century. His theoretical work in what we now call physics—electricity, magnetism, optics, and allied fields—was groundbreaking, and his practical engineering acuity was profound—the lightning rod, the "Franklin" stove, and bifocal eyeglasses were among the century's most important inventions, improving the lot of common people beyond measure.

Jefferson's admiration and love for Franklin, his predecessor as U.S. ambassador at the Court of Louis XVI and his elder by thirty-seven years, was life long and deeply held. He called him once *the most amiable and the greatest of men, the ornament of the age and country in which he lived.* Replacing him as ambassador to France, Jefferson wrote, had been *an excellent school of humility:*

> On being presented to anyone as the minister [from] America, the commonplace question was: "Is it you, Sir, who replace Doctor Franklin?" I generally answered: "No one can replace him: I am only his successor."

Of all the extraordinary political figures with whom Jefferson was to become acquainted over his lifetime—Washington, Hamilton, Lafayette, Burr, Adams, Madison, Monroe, etc.—Franklin was one of only two (Madison being the other) for whom he never seemed to have had an unkind or critical word.

In 1751 Franklin published a small pamphlet titled *Observations Concerning the Increase of Mankind, Peopling of Countries, etc.* He concludes a discussion about the ways that land ownership systems, labor supply, marriage and contraception practices, disease, and the like affect population size and growth, with these words:

> There is . . . no Bound to the prolific Nature of Plants or Animals, but what is made by their crowding and interfering with each other's Means of Subsistence. Was the Face of the Earth vacant of other Plants, it might be gradually sowed and overspread with one Kind only, as, for instance, with Fennel; and, were it empty of other inhabitants, it might in a few ages be replenished from one nation only, as, for instance, with Englishmen. . . .
>
> Thus, there are suppos'd to be now upwards of one million English souls in North America (tho' 'tis thought scarce 80,000 have been brought over Sea) . . . **This million doubling, suppose but once in twenty-five years**, will, in another Century, be more than the People of England, and the greater number of Englishmen will be on this Side of the Water.

As far as we can tell, Franklin was just guessing; he doesn't provide any actual population data in his pamphlet, nor does he explain the basis for his supposition that the average doubling time for the population of the New World was twenty-five years. It was, though, remarkably, almost eerily, prescient. The first U.S. census, taken in 1790 (the year, coincidentally, that Franklin died) reported a population of 3,939,214. If that population were

sustained period,[6] and it brought the world substantially closer to unlocking one of the truly fundamental laws of nature, the law of evolution by natural selection.

Geometric growth has one unnerving characteristic: it is, literally, explosive. As Albert Einstein is reported to have said, compound interest is the most powerful force in the universe.[7] Once it gets rolling, it really takes off, and it can reach astronomical, unimaginable, and unrealizable numbers in a great hurry.[8] Jefferson was correct when he stated that Virginia's population would reach 6 or 7 million inhabitants within ninety-five years or so if it continued to grow geometrically at its then-current rate. What he didn't mention—perhaps because he didn't think about it—was that if it kept growing at that rate, doubling every twenty-seven years or so, it would have 152 million people in another 100 years (1982), 1.2 billion in 2082, 16.3 billion by 2182, and so on. (See fig. 2.3.) Or that if it continued for another thousand years or so, there would be more people in Virginia than there are atoms in the universe.

---

to double every twenty-five years, we would predict a population in 1890 of 62,947,424. Unbelievably enough, the actual census count in 1890 was 62,947,714—off by 290, or .0004 percent!

It is, of course, just a coincidence—but, as the historian Conway Zirkle observed, "Major prophets have the exasperating habit of being right."

6   Jefferson continued to find the geometric growth of the New World's population of interest throughout his life. In his first "Annual Message to Congress as President of the United States," in 1801, he delivered the results of the 1800 census of the United States, which showed that the United States had grown an astounding 35.1 percent during the preceding decade:

> I lay before you the result of the census lately taken of our inhabitants, to a conformity with which we are to reduce the ensuing rates of representation and taxation. You will perceive that the increase of numbers during the last ten years, **proceeding in geo-metrical ratio, promises a duplication in little more than twenty-two years**. [Emphasis added.] We contemplate this rapid growth, and the prospect it holds up to us, not with a view to the injuries it may enable us to do to others in some future day, but to the settlement of the extensive country still remaining vacant within our limits to the multiplications of men susceptible of happiness, educated in the love of order, habitu-ated to self-government, and valuing its blessings above all price.

7   See the "urban legends" page at www.snopes.com/quotes/einstein/interest.asp for a dis-cussion of whether Einstein actually said this. If he didn't actually say it, he probably should have.

8   The Parable of the Chessboard:

> The shepherd boy was called before the king. The king spoke thus to him: "You shall tend my flocks in the mountains; here are 100 pieces of silver for your troubles." "I will tend your flocks," the boy replied, "but I do not want your silver." Pointing to a nearby chessboard, the boy said, "Instead of the silver, place a grain of rice on the first square of the chessboard. Tomorrow, put two grains on the second square. The next day, put four grains on the third square. And every day thereafter, until the sixty-four squares

Exponential Growth Projections for Virginia

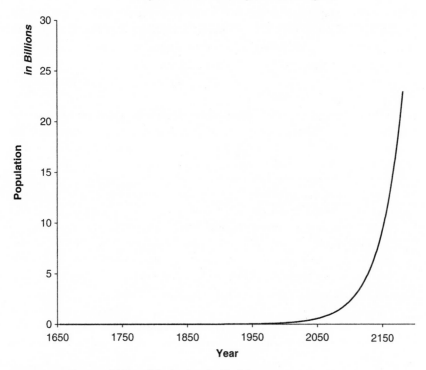

FIGURE 2.3 Exponential Growth Projections for Virginia.

That observation, though, set off a spark in the mind of an obscure Scottish preacher named Thomas Malthus, becoming the focal point for his *Essay on the Principle of Population As It Affects the Future Improvement of Society*, published (anonymously) in 1798—probably among the two or three dozen most influential books

---

are covered, place two grains on the next open square for each grain you placed on the board the preceding day. That shall be my payment." The king, amused by the shortsightedness of a peasantry that preferred rice to silver, readily agreed. Before the month was up, and long before the chessboard squares were filled, the boy owned all of the riches of the kingdom.

The king, of course, is undone by geometric growth: a population of rice grains with a doubling time of 1 day:

2^0 (=1) grain on day 1,
2^1 (=2) grains on day 2,
2^2 (=4) on day 3,
2^3 (=8) on day 4,
and so on.

ever written, a foundational document for the development of the modern disciplines of demography, economics, and statistics—no mean achievement that, for any one book. If human populations could grow geometrically—and the New World data showed, for the first time, that they could—then "the power of population is indefinitely greater than the power in the earth to produce subsistence."[9]

On day thirty-three, the king will need more than 4 billion grains of rice—2^{32} =4,294,967,296, to be precise—and he's only halfway there! By the sixty-fourth (and last) day, the king would have to place 2^{63} grains on the board—a bit more than 9 thousand trillion grains of rice, or 9 billion bags holding a million grains each.

9 We know that Malthus had read Franklin's book on population (see n. 5); it's not known whether he had seen Jefferson's chapter on Population in *Notes* confirming Franklin's hypothesis prior to writing his *Essay*. "It is observed by Dr. Franklin," Malthus wrote "that there is no bound to the prolific nature of plants or animals but what is made by their crowding and interfering with each other's means of subsistence...." For humans, however, the situation was less clear. "No country has hitherto been known [where] the power of population been left to exert itself with perfect freedom. But:

> In the United States of America, where the means of subsistence have been more ample, the manners of the people more pure, and the checks to early marriages fewer than in any of the modern states of Europe, **the population has been found to double itself, for above a century and a half successively, in less than twenty-five years.** [Emphasis added.]

This, then, "we will take as our rule, and say, that population, when unchecked, goes on doubling itself every twenty-five years or increases in a geometrical ratio."

Malthus, famously, went on: if human populations could "increase in a geometrical ratio [when] allowed to do so by fortunate circumstance" (as in the New World), they will quickly outstrip the supply of available food:

> The rate according to which the productions of the earth [i.e., the supply of food] may be supposed to increase it will not be so easy to determine. Of this ... we may be perfectly certain—that the ratio of their increase in a limited territory must be of a totally different nature from the [geometric] ratio of the increase of population. **A thousand millions [of people] are just as easily doubled every twenty-five years by the power of population as a thousand. But the food to support the increase from the greater number will by no means be obtained with the same facility.** [Emphasis added.]

In other words: if human populations can grow geometrically, disaster loomed. Human populations will quickly expand to the limit of their subsistence, and then be held there—by famine, war, disease, "vice" (which included, for Malthus, contraception), and "misery."

> The power of population is so superior to the power of the earth to produce subsistence for man, that premature death must in some shape or other visit the human race. The vices of mankind are active and able ministers of depopulation. They are the precursors in the great army of destruction; and often finish the dreadful work themselves.

Population, when unchecked, increases in a geometrical ratio. Subsistence increases only in an arithmetical ratio. A slight acquaintance with numbers will show the immensity of the first power in comparison of the second.

Geometric growth of population, linear growth ("arithmetical ratio") of the food supply on which that population has to subsist. Uh-oh.

Malthus's idea, in its turn, itself sparked an idea in the minds of a couple of young British naturalists, Charles Darwin and Alfred Russell Wallace. Co-discoverers of the principle of natural selection, both Darwin and Wallace, remarkably enough, pointed to Malthus's *Essay* as the key that unlocked for them their understanding of the origin and evolution of life on the planet.[10]

> But should they fail in this war of extermination, sickly seasons, epidemics, pestilence, and plague, advance in terrific array, and sweep off their thousands and tens of thousands. Should success be still incomplete, gigantic inevitable famine stalks in the rear, and with one mighty blow levels the population with the food of the world.

Things, we know now, are a bit more complicated than that. Malthus simultaneously underestimated both the human capacity to devise better and better means of food production, and our ability to keep our populations in check short of the point of famine and misery.

10 That Charles Darwin and Alfred Russell Wallace, 10,000 miles apart from one another and in complete ignorance of each other's work, came more-or-less simultaneously to the theory of evolution by natural selection is one of the classic tales in the history of science. It is, along with the simultaneous invention of calculus by Isaac Newton and Gerhard Leibniz, the textbook example of "independent development," the way that brilliant insights that have escaped all of those who have been searching for them for so long can, all of a sudden, pop up in two (or sometimes more) places independently at virtually the same moment.

Darwin, actually, had the idea first. He was a generation older than Wallace, and he had conceived of the fundamental principle of natural selection upon his return to England from his voyages aboard the *Beagle* in the late 1830s, when Wallace was still in grammar school, The idea, as David Quammen puts it, "remained Darwin's secret insight, his carefully guarded intellectual treasure," until the day in 1858 that he

> received a manuscript in the mail from a young, obscure naturalist named Wallace— and the Wallace manuscript, to Darwin's horror, contained his own precious concept. Wallace had found his way to it independently. For a brief heartsick period, Darwin believed that the younger man had eclipsed him and preempted his life's work by staking a just claim to priority. As things developed, however, . . . Wallace and Darwin announced the concept [at a meeting of the Royal Society of London] simultaneously. For a variety of reasons, some good and some shabby, Darwin received most of the recognition; and Wallace, in consequence, is famous for being obscure.

Both men describe the theory of natural selection as having come to them in a single insightful, almost revelatory, flash, immediately upon reading Malthus's *Essay*. "You are right," Darwin wrote in a letter to Wallace in 1887, "that I came to the conclusion that

Not bad—two degrees of separation between the observation that the population of the New World was growing geometrically to the principle of evolution by natural selection.

It just goes to show you, I suppose: you never know you will find, or what will happen, when you ask good questions. There was something new in this New World after all, something that would change our view of the world forever.

The Internet, like Virginia, has been growing geometrically (see fig. 2.4), at a rate of just under 5 percent **a month** (about 80 percent per year), yielding an "average doubling time" of about fourteen months.

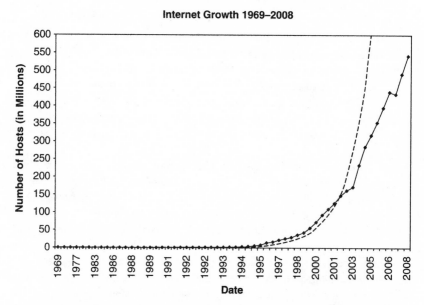

Internet Growth 1969–2008

FIGURE 2.4 Internet Growth 1969–2008. The solid line connects the actual census results; the dashed line represents the "best fit" of the geometric growth curve to these data.

Selection was the principle of change from study of domesticated productions; and then reading Malthus I saw at once how to apply this principle." He put it this way in his *Autobiography*:

> In October 1838, that is fifteen months after I had begun my systematic enquiry, I happened to read for amusement Malthus on Population, and being well prepared to appreciate the struggle for existence which everywhere goes on from long-continued observations of the habits of animals and plants, it at once struck me that under these circumstances favourable variations would tend to be preserved and unfavourable ones to be destroyed. The result of this would be the formation of new species.

The geometric growth curve (the dashed line in fig. 2.4) fits the Internet census data extremely well, statistically speaking, although the fit is not nearly as good as it was for Virginia's population.[11] (Compare figure 2.4 with figure 2.2.) Unlike Virginia, where growth appeared to be geometric at a more-or-less constant rate throughout the period—*the intermediate enumerations furnish proof of the uniformity of the progression*—there appears to be a kink, a slowdown in the growth rate, for the Internet around about 1999 or 2000. There has been considerable commentary about this apparent slowdown in growth. It occurred, presumably not coincidentally, just at the time the dot-com investment bubble burst, and many have speculated on the extent to which the one was a consequence, or a cause, of the other.

But the interesting thing isn't the slowdown. It couldn't have gone on for too much longer at the rate it was going in any event; at 5 percent a month, there would have been around 1.35 billion machines on the network by 2005, 25 billion by 2010, 165 trillion in the year 2025—more than a thousand Internet-connected computers for everyone on earth!

The interesting thing is that it occurred at all, and for so long. There's not much else on the planet that grew exponentially for this long a period, and nothing—at least, nothing I can think of—that did so at this astonishing rate. If some living organism, or some population of organisms, had managed to grow exponentially in size over the past thirty-five years at the rate the TCP/IP network did, we'd surely want to understand what was going on, and how it managed to do that.

So how did this network do that? How did the network linking a few hundred machines together in the early 1980s manage to grow so fast for so long? How and why did it become "the Internet"—**the** dominant global communications platform, connecting together hundreds of millions of individual machines (and, sitting behind those machines, probably more than a billion people)? Why **this** network?

It is easy to forget—perhaps you never knew in the first place—that the world of long-range computer communications in the late 1970s and early 1980s was awash (as it is still, today) with dozens, even hundreds, of different networking schemes and systems. A gathering of computer networking specialists in, say, 1985, would have been filled with talk about any number of different networking protocols.

"Here, then, I had at last got a theory"—the principle of natural selection—"by which to work."

Wallace wrote in *his* autobiography that he was resting from an attack of fever when something recalled Malthus' *Essay* to his memory. He, too, was struck, as if by a revelation: "it suddenly flashed upon me that this self-acting process would improve the race, because in every generation the inferior would inevitably be killed off and the superior would remain—that is, the fittest would survive."

11 The assumption of geometric growth applied to these data accounts for over 95 percent of the statistical "variance" in the data.

There would surely have been a workshop or two devoted to discussion of the "X.25" and "OSI" (Open Systems Initiative) protocols developed during the late 1970s by two of the most influential standards-setting organizations in the world of telecommunications at the time: the CCITT—the International Telegraph and Telephone Consultative Committee (*Comittée Consultatif International Téléphonique et Télégraphique*), a UN-affiliated institution whose roots trace back to the 1920s and which had responsibility by international treaty for the management of the international telephone and telegraph networks—and the International Organization for Standards (ISO), an organization comprised of representatives from the national standards bodies of 157 member countries. The major computer manufacturers, for their part, would have set up their booths in the entry hall to push their own private, proprietary networking protocols—IBM alone had dozens of different networking protocols, including its highly-touted "Systems Network Architecture" (SNA) standards, first introduced in 1974; Xerox had its Xerox Network Services; Digital Equipment Corp. had its DECNET protocols, and so forth. And a whole afternoon would probably have been devoted to discussion of the Ethernet protocols, a set of networking rules that was already, by 1985, coming to dominate the world of short-distance networking (Local Area Networks).

And there was also, of course, TCP/IP.

On your mark. Get set. Go.

During the ensuing two decades, it was TCP/IP that triumphed, the TCP/IP network that outgrew them all. Why? **It didn't grow so fast or become so big because it was "the Internet"; it became "the Internet" because it grew so fast and became so big.**

How, and why, did that happen?

CHAPTER THREE

NETWORKS

We must know at once whether we can acquire New Orleans or not.... The future destinies
of our country hang on the event of this negotiation
TJ TO ROBERT LIVINGSTONE, FEBRUARY 3, 1803

One thing that helped the fledgling TCP/IP network become "the Internet" was that it had a head start—and when it comes to networks, head starts can make a big difference.

They can make a big difference because the conventional wisdom of the 1780s— that bigger is better—is actually pretty much on target when it comes to networks. Bigger networks, all other things being equal, are better, just because they're bigger. In network-speak: Network value scales positively as a function of network size; as the latter increases, so does the former.

Network engineers have a number of different "laws" that express this principle of "bigger-is-better" scaling, depending on the kind of network you're talking about. They're not really "laws" in the sense of Newton's Laws of Motion, or the Second Law of Thermodynamics, or Ohm's Law—they're more like rules of thumb. They only hold **on average**, all other things being equal; they express general tendencies, not invariable relationships.

For instance, "Sarnoff's Law" (credited to radio broadcasting pioneer David Sarnoff) holds that the value of a **one-way** communications network—like a radio or television broadcast network, in which communication goes in only one direction, from source to recipient—is proportional to N, the number of network members.

$$\text{Network Value} \sim N$$

Bigger, on average, is better.

"Metcalfe's Law" states that, on average, the value of networks that permit **two-way** communication—networks on which each participant can be both a source and recipient (like the postal network, or the telephone network)—scales **geometrically** with the number of participants on the network

$$\text{Network Value} \sim N^2$$

because each member of a two-way network with N members can connect to (N-1) others,[1] making the number of interconnections equal to

$$N \times [N-1] = N^2 - N.$$

And finally, there's "Reed's Law," named for David Reed, an important figure in the development of TCP/IP whom we will meet again later in the book, which holds that the value of a "group-forming network"—like the Internet, a network that allows not just two-way communication among individual members but multi-way communication among groups of various sizes—scales even faster than that. Hyper-geometrically, the mathematicians call it:

$$\text{Network Value} \sim 2^N$$

because the total number of possible groups in a network of N members—groups of 2, 3, 4,…all the way up to a single group of size N containing everyone on the network—is proportional to 2^N.

And scaling by a factor of 2^N is a **lot** faster than N^2, as you can see here:

TABLE 3.1

N	N^2	2^N
1	1	2
10	100	1024
50	2500	1,125,899,907,000,000
100	10000	126,765,600,000,000,000,000,000,000,000,000

You get the idea.

It makes for a potentially dizzying positive feedback loop: As networks get bigger, they become more valuable; as they become more valuable, more people want to join; as more people join, they get bigger; as they get bigger, they get even more valuable; that makes even more people want to join…and so on.

That's why head starts are of such significance for networks: For a network, a good strategy for getting bigger is to be big. The bigger the network, the more likely (all other things being equal) that it will get even bigger.

---

1 A two-way network with 3 members (A, B, and C) has 6 (= 3 × 2) possible interconnections (A-B, A-C, B-A, B-C, C-A, C-B); a 4-member network has 12 (= 4 × 3) possible interconnections (A-B, A-C, A-D, B-A, B-C, B-D, C-A, C-B, C-D, D-A, D-B, D-C); a 5-member 20 (= 5 × 4) possible interconnections, etc. A 30-member network, therefore—a network **10** times larger than one with 3 members—has 870 (= 30 × 29) possible interconnections, more than **100** times more than the 3-member network.

Imagine that you're back in 1985; there are thirty, or forty, or one hundred different inter-networks out there, each with anywhere from a handful to a couple of hundred members. Someone asks you: "Which one of those will sweep the globe to become 'the Internet'?" Your answer: "How would I know? But if I have to guess, and knowing nothing else about them except their size, I'll bet on the one that is, at this moment, the biggest." The smart money's on the front-runner—the one with the head start.

Although these network scaling laws weren't coined until the latter part of the twentieth century, the idea that networks can get more valuable as they get bigger (and bigger as they get more valuable) would not have surprised Jefferson; the United States is a story, in small but not insignificant part, of network engineering, and Jefferson was a network engineer (before anyone called it "network engineering") of great skill and considerable achievement.

The "network" on which Jefferson focused his attention was the network that mattered in eighteenth-century America: the network of rivers. Water transportation in the 1780s was, by many orders of magnitude, the most efficient way to move people and goods from one place to another. (At least downstream or on the oceans; we're talking, remember, about a time not merely pre-railroad, and pre-automobile, and pre-telegraph, but pre-steamboat).[2] This was especially true in the New World, where, not having had the benefit of Roman occupation several millennia prior, the roads were in particularly abysmal condition; it was considerably easier and cheaper to ship a ton of goods from Philadelphia to London than from Philadelphia to Lancaster, Pennsylvania, a mere sixty miles away.[3] Rivers, not roads, formed the backbone for the network(s) of communication and commerce over which goods and people and information could flow in the New World, and it was riverine topography—the location, size, and navigability of the New World's rivers—that

---

2   Speaking of steamboats...Jefferson was a big admirer (and frequent correspondent) of Robert Fulton's. *I rejoice at your success in your steamboats,* Jefferson wrote to Fulton, *and have no doubt they will be the source of great wealth to yourself and permanent blessing to your country.* Their correspondence covered the usual odd and diverse Jeffersonian landscape—fireplace construction, the use of torpedoes, and the design of plows–and when, in 1808, Jefferson was looking to borrow a dynamometer (a device, recently invented by the Frenchman Edmier Regnier, for measuring force, working versions of which were very hard to come by in the States), Fulton loaned him his. (Jefferson needed the dynamometer to test the efficiency of a new plow he had invented—more on that later.)

3   Late eighteenth-century American roads were, in most cases "hardly more than trails choked with stumps," as Joel Achenbach put it; a typical backcountry road

   didn't have a uniform surface, [and was] often...just a tunnel in the vegetation. A traveler endured diabolical combinations of holes, mires and tree stumps. When a state government got around to chartering a road, it would specify how high the stumps

defined the architecture of those networks, and that would play a crucial role in determining who, and what, could go where.

And Jefferson was really into rivers.[4] They loomed large in his life, and he devoted more space in *Notes on the State of Virginia* to answering Marbois's question about "rivers [and] rivulets, and how far are they navigable?" than to practically any other subject (in contrast to the single paragraph devoted to Virginia's roads). He described thirty-four separate streams, from large (the James, the "Patowmac" and the "Missisipi") to small (the Nansemond, the Chickahominy, and the Piankatank), often in jaw-dropping detail. A typical entry:

> *York River, at York town, affords the best harbour in the state for vessels of the largest size. The river there narrows to the width of a mile, and is contained within very*

---

could be. The more a road was traveled by horses and wagons, the more the surface became chewed up and rutted.... Roads were not self-healing, and eventually, the track through the woods would not really be a road at all, just a linear bog.

Jefferson devoted only a single paragraph in *Notes on the State of Virginia* (in Query 15, "Colleges, Building, and Roads?") to Virginia's roads—this in an area of 121,000 square miles!

> *The roads are under the government of the county courts, subject to be controlled by the general court. They order new roads to be opened wherever they think them necessary. The inhabitants of the county are by them laid off into precincts, to each of which they allot a convenient portion of the public roads to be kept in repair. Such bridges as may be built without the assistance of artificers, they are to build. If the stream be such as to require a bridge of regular workmanship, the court employs workmen to build it, at the expense of the whole county. If it be too great for the county, application is made to the general assembly, who authorize individuals to build it, and to take a fixed toll from all passengers, or give sanction to such other proposition as to them appears reasonable.*

4 His very first public act, as a young man of twenty-two fresh out of William and Mary College, involved organizing his Albemarle County neighbors to remove the loose rocks and other debris that were obstructing navigation from their main local stream (the Rivanna) through to the James River (and therefore from the James to the Atlantic, through Richmond and Williamsburg).

> *The Rivanna had never been used for navigation; scarcely an empty canoe had ever passed down it. Soon after I came of age, I examined its obstructions, set on foot a subscription for removing them, got an Act of Assembly passed, and the thing effected, so as to be used completely and fully for carrying down all our produce.*

For a generation or so thereafter much of the produce of Albemarle County traveled to market this way. It was an accomplishment of which Jefferson was immensely proud; when, later in life, he composed "A Memorandum: Services to My Country"—an attempt, as he put it, to figure out *whether my country is the better for my having lived at all*—clearing the Rivanna was the first thing he listed, right above authorship of the Declaration of Independence.

high banks, close under which the vessels may ride. It holds 4 fathom water at high tide for 25 miles above York to the mouth of Poropotank, where the river is a mile and a half wide, and the channel only 75 fathom, and passing under a high bank. At the confluence of Pamunkey and Mattapony, it is reduced to 3 fathom depth, which continues up Pamunkey to Cumberland, where the width is 100 yards, and up Mattapony to within two miles of Frazer's ferry, where it becomes 2 1/2 fathom deep, and holds that about five miles. Pamunkey is then capable of navigation for loaded flats to Brockman's bridge, 50 miles above Hanover town, and Mattapony to Downer's bridge, 70 miles above its mouth.

Only somebody who was really into rivers would have known (or cared) that the York River holds four fathoms of water at high tide up to the mouth of the Poropotank (wherever that is), but only three fathoms at the confluence of the Pamunkey and the Mattapony (wherever they are).[5]

Over the course of a busy lifetime Jefferson devoted considerable energy to re-engineering this network, to make it bigger and therefore more valuable for all. His program: Eliminate physical obstacles to navigation; build interconnectivity with canals; gain control over the Mississippi-Missouri watersheds; and find the Northwest Passage connecting the latter with the Pacific. And, amazingly enough, he accomplished a great deal of it.

---

5 At the time Jefferson was writing, all of Virginia's major towns, as you might expect, were located along the backbone of its river network, and when listing those towns for Marbois, Jefferson grouped them according to the rivers along whose banks they sat:

Our towns, but more properly our villages or hamlets, are as follows.

- *On James river and its waters, Norfolk, Portsmouth, Hampton, Suffolk, Smithfield, Williamsburgh, Petersburg, Richmond the seat of our government, Manchester, Charlottesville, New London.*
- *On York river and its waters, York, Newcastle, Hanover.*
- *On Rappahannoc, Urbanna, Portroyal, Fredericksburg, Falmouth.*
- *On Patowmac and its waters, Dumfries, Colchester, Alexandria, Winchester, Staunton.*
- *On Ohio, Louisville.*

And in case you missed the point, he added: *There are other places at which, like some of the foregoing, the **laws** have said there shall be towns; but **Nature** has said there shall not, and they remain unworthy of enumeration* [emphases are Jefferson's own].

The same pattern held true, at a larger scale, for the United States as a whole; all of the cities with populations over 10,000 in the first U.S. census in 1790 (New York, Philadelphia, Boston, Charleston, and Baltimore) were located along navigable waterways, and the pattern would continue throughout the nineteenth century (as Pittsburgh, New Orleans, St. Louis, Memphis, etc. were added to the list) and well into the twentieth.

Nature had already endowed the New World's river networks with a substantial degree of interconnectivity; by happy accident of topography, its rivers already had outstanding connections to the global inter-network, i.e., to the Atlantic Ocean. *No ports but our rivers and creeks*, as Jefferson put it; the New World's best seaports (Baltimore, New York, Philadelphia, Boston, Norfolk, Charleston) were

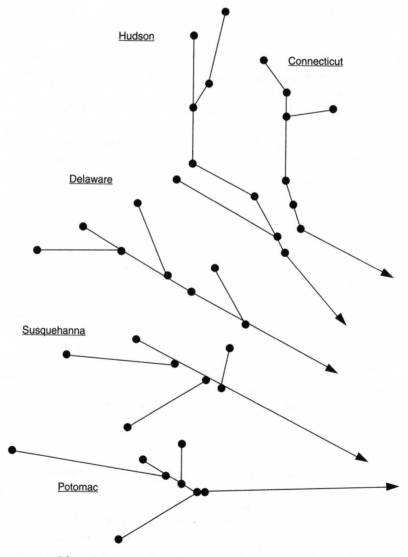

FIGURE 3.1 Schematic Representation of Eastern U.S. River Networks.

all located at the mouths of large, navigable rivers,[6] and, conversely, its great river systems—the Hudson, the Delaware, the Susquehanna, the James, the Mississippi—all entered the ocean at places suitable for ocean-going vessels.[7] So instead of something that looked like figure 3.1, the New World networks looked more like this:

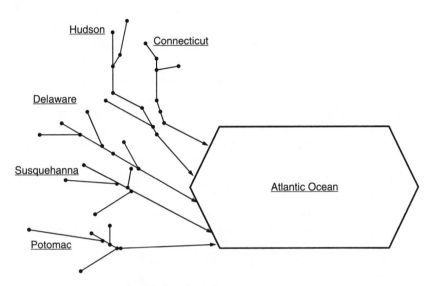

FIGURE 3.2   Interconnections via the Atlantic Ocean.

Jefferson had big plans to make this a bigger, and a better, network. He was, you will perhaps not be surprised to learn, one of the world's leading experts on canal technology and design.[8] He had especially ambitious plans for *a canal of no great expence between the Cayahoga River and Big Beaver* [Creek] that might unite the sources of the Ohio and Potomac rivers. Opening a canal between those two water-courses, he wrote to President Washington,

> *would be the most important work in that line which the state of Virginia could undertake.* [By] *uniting the navigations of L. Erie and the Ohio, it will infallibly turn thro' the Patow-mack all the commerce of lake Erie and the country West of that, except what may pass down the Missisipi itself.*

6   This is, by the way, not necessarily the case; many of the world's great ocean ports—Dover, England, for example, or Sydney, Australia—are not at river mouths.

7   The chapter following "Rivers," titled "Sea-ports," is the shortest in *Notes on the State of Virginia,* consisting of a single sentence: *Having no ports but our rivers and creeks, this Query has been answered under the preceding one.*

8   On vacation in southern France in the late winter of 1787, Jefferson spent eight days aboard a barge traversing the Canal du Languedoc, one of the engineering marvels of the age,

And, he added, *it is important that it be soon done, lest that commerce should in the meantime get established in another channel.*[9]

It was, it turned out, mostly wishful thinking on his part. The canal was never built; the portage between the Ohio and the Potomac—forty miles of very mountainous road—remained almost impassable, the falls along the Potomac (*fifteen*

---

connecting the Mediterranean and Atlantic watersheds. As was his wont, he kept copious notes of all he saw; as the historian George Shackleford has written, he was

> more interested in the machinery for opening and closing the locks than in its traffic.... He estimated that the system of operating the lock gates was so inefficient that it added a day to the transit. With plenty of time to make calculations, he suggested to officials that the canal company should install *gates turning of a pivot lifted by a lever like a pump handle, aided by a windlass and a cord*. The officials promised to consider his plan. A manual system somewhat similar to the one Jefferson proposed operates the locks today.

9   The "other channel" to which Jefferson referred was the Hudson. He was expecting that there would be a *competition between the Hudson and Patowmac rivers for the residue of the commerce of all the country westward of Lake Erie, on the waters of the* [*Great*] *lakes, of the Ohio, and upper parts of the Missisipi*—all of the stuff that, for one reason or another, wouldn't travel down the Mississippi—and he thought that the Potomac had some crucial natural advantages over its rival. For one thing, it was far closer to the Mississippi watershed than the Hudson. Once goods coming from the upper Mississippi region reached the Great Lakes, they would be *brought into Lake Erie*; and once in Lake Erie they could *coast along its southern shore, on account of the number and excellence of its harbours, the northern* [coast], *though shortest, having few harbours, and these unsafe*. For another, it was closer, in network distance, to the ocean via the Potomac; from the southern shore of Lake Erie, *to proceed on to New-York* [via the Hudson] *they will have 825 miles and* **five** *portages*, while from the same spot in lake Erie it was *but 425 miles to Alexandria* [at the mouth of the Potomac], *with but* **two** *portages* (one between the Cayahoga and Bigbeaver Creek, the other between the Ohio River and the Potomac). The Potomac route could therefore reduce not only *the expence occasioned by frequent change of carriage,* but also the *increased risk of pillage produced by committing merchandize to a greater number of hands successively.* Not to mention that

> *the Hudson's river is shut up by the ice three months in the year, whereas the channel to the Chesapeake leads directly into a warmer climate* [*and*] *vessels may pass through the whole winter, subject only to accidental and short delays.*

And finally,

> *that in case of a war with our neighbours the Anglo-Americans or the Indians, the route to New-York becomes a frontier through almost its whole length, and all commerce through it ceases from that moment.*

He was worried, though, because the Hudson had the head start:

miles in length, and of very great descent, and the navigation above them for bateaux and canoes, is so much interrupted as to be little used) were never cleared, and the Potomac would never carry more than a tiny fraction of the volume of goods transported down the Ohio or down the Hudson.[10]

He had more success when it came to the Mississippi. To Jefferson's eye, the network diagram of the New World actually looked more like this:

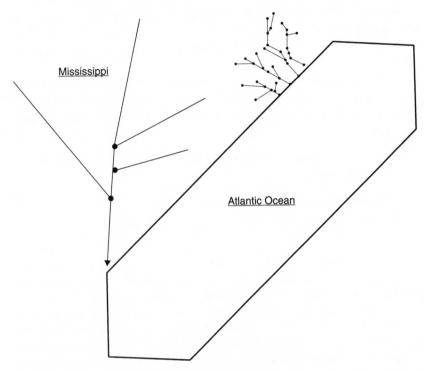

FIGURE 3.3 The Mississippi River and the Eastern River Network.

> *The channel to New-York is already known to practice; whereas the upper waters of the Ohio and the Patowmac, and the great falls of the latter, are yet to be cleared of their fixed obstructions.*

10 The whole canal-building enterprise, in fact, never amounted to a great deal. Jefferson was a very smart guy, but he was no prophet; he couldn't foresee the network of railroads that would be crisscrossing this territory within fifty years or so, eliminating many of the advantages of water transportation (and thereby eliminating exclusive reliance on the river networks and their canal interconnectors for the movement of goods). Or the invention of dynamite, either, which would change forever the processes of road-building; or the internal combustion engine, fueling vehicles to travel over those roads.

A glance at the map—and Jefferson, as we saw earlier, was forever glancing at the map—shows that the Mississippi River watershed dominates the landscape; *the country watered by the Missisipi and its eastern branches constitutes five-eighths* of the United States—and that's just the **eastern** branches of the Mississippi (e.g., the Ohio, the Tennessee, the Kanaway, the Illinois), not counting any territory **west** of the Mississippi River itself, none of which was yet part of the United States. The Mississippi, Jefferson saw, would *become one of the principal channels of future commerce for the country westward of the Alleghaney* [Mountains]; *from its fertility it will ere long yield more than half of our whole produce, and contain more than half of our inhabitants.*[11] All of it flowing through New Orleans, and from there into the global inter-network.

There was one small problem; New Orleans, and most of the Mississippi itself, and virtually the entire Mississippi watershed, were all, literally, foreign soil, claimed at various times and at various places by Great Britain, France, and Spain. This spelled trouble:

> *There is on the globe one single spot, the possessor of which is our natural and habitual enemy. It is New Orleans*

Jefferson, of course, would help take care of **that**.[12]

---

11 Consider Pittsburgh, or Fort Pitt, as it was known at the time Jefferson was writing. A lonely and often endangered frontier outpost in the 1780s, it was clearly destined for greater things, lying there at the confluence of three great river systems—the Allegheny, flowing from up near Lake Erie in the north, the Monongahela, from the mountains of Virginia in the south, and the Ohio, flowing westward into the Mississippi. Pittsburgh was (and of course remains) in the Mississippi watershed; a drop of rain falling in Pittsburgh flows to New Orleans, and from there to the Gulf of Mexico and the Atlantic. Pittsburgh is therefore actually closer, in "network distance" terms, to New Orleans than it is to Philadelphia (though the former is more than 1,500, and the latter less than 300, miles away as the crow flies). Goods and people in the eighteenth century followed the raindrops; they could more easily make their way from Pittsburgh to the sea through New Orleans, and from there to the world markets beyond, than through any of the eastern sea-ports. (And, indeed, by the early nineteenth century, Pittsburgh had a thriving trade in ocean-going vessels, built on the shores of the Ohio and floated down to New Orleans and sold for the transatlantic trade.)

12 Jefferson first became actively entangled with the history of New Orleans in 1792, when, as secretary of state in President Washington's first cabinet, he began negotiations for United States access to the Mississippi and to New Orleans. Spain was, at the time, the overlord of all of "Louisiana," including New Orleans, and the negotiations eventually produced the 1795 Treaty of San Lorenzo; under the terms of the treaty, Spain guaranteed full and free access to the Mississippi River for U.S. boats (even below the 31st parallel, where Spain laid claim to **both** banks of the River), and a "right of deposit" for U.S. vessels and commerce in New Orleans (guaranteeing the right to unload goods on the New Orleans docks and to reload them onto ocean going vessels).

And the final piece of the network puzzle, the Missouri River, also loomed large in Jefferson's imagination and in his life (though he was never to have the privilege of actually laying eyes on it, either). Jefferson hoped for many things from the Lewis and Clark expedition, but first and foremost, as he reminded Lewis in the final "Instructions" from the White House as the expedition was about to set out on its journey, *the object of your mission is to explore the Missouri River, & such principal stream of it, as, by it's course & communication with the water of the Pacific Ocean, may offer the most direct & practicable water communication across this continent, for the purposes of commerce.* In short: Find the (or at least "a") Northwest Passage from the Missouri to the Pacific.

It was all network engineering of the highest order, and it was without question one of the great accomplishments in a career laced with great accomplishments. Each part of the river network becomes more valuable as the network grows larger, and more interconnected: Metcalfe's Law. Pittsburgh (and Erie, and Louisville, and Cincinnati,

---

Just as he was assuming the presidency, in 1801, news reached the capital that Spain had ceded all of Louisiana, including New Orleans, to the French. *It was very ominous to us,* he wrote to James Madison.

> *Spain might have retained it quietly for years. Her pacific dispositions, her feeble state, would induce her to increase our facilities there, so that her possession of the place would be hardly felt by us, and it would not, perhaps, be very long before some circumstance might arise, which might make the cession of it to us the price of something of more worth to her.*

> *Not so can it ever be in the hands of France ... circumstances render it impossible that France and the United States can continue long friends, when they meet in so irritable a position. They, as well as we, must be blind if they do not see this; and we must be very improvident if we do not begin to make arrangements on that hypothesis.*

Things got more ominous when, in 1802, the French-appointed governor ("Intendant") of New Orleans suspended the right of deposit in New Orleans for U.S. vessels, effectively closing the docks to U.S. boats:

> *Nothing since the revolutionary war has produced more uneasy sensations through the body of the nation; the agitation of the public mind is extreme. The suspension by the Intendant of New Orleans of our right of deposit there, without which the right of navigation* [*on the Mississippi*] *is impracticable, has thrown this country into such a flame of hostile disposition as can scarcely be described.*

We must know at once, he wrote to Robert Livingstone, U.S. ambassador to France, in early 1803, *whether we can acquire New Orleans or not.* And he sent his protégé James Monroe to join Livingstone in Paris with instructions *to procure cession of New Orleans and the Floridas to the United States.* Monroe and Livingstone were authorized to offer up to $6 million for the whole package (though Jefferson *hoped that less would do*), or up to $4.5 million (75 percent of the total authorized) for New Orleans alone.

and St. Louis…) are all suddenly more valuable, more able to support large aggregations of population, because each is now connected to the others, and each to New Orleans, and each thereby to Santo Domingo, and to Liverpool, and to Le Havre.

———————

TCP/IP's head start was courtesy, in large part, of the U.S. taxpayer. The TCP/IP protocols were developed over a twenty-year period (from around 1964 to 1983) largely as part of a networking research project under the auspices of, and funded by, the U.S. Department of Defense's Advanced Research Projects Administration (which is why the network was called "DARPANET," or "ARPANET," up until the early 1980s). Money was funneled through DARPA to an initially small, and then ever-widening, number of major U.S. research institutions, which formed the early adopters of the developing protocols; those first four Internet nodes, for example, were located at UCLA, UC Santa Barbara, Stanford, and the University of Utah.

The money itself was chump change; total public spending on the Internet during this twenty-year period was probably less than $100 million, making the Internet surely one of the most, if not the most, productive public investments in human history.

It did, though, give this network a leg up on the competition at an early stage in its development. As more groups of researchers at more universities came on board, it became increasingly easier to convince others to do so, so as to have access to and communication with those who were already members—**especially** when the government was offering to pay for and support the connection. By the time the general public got wind of what was going on—in the late 1980s and early '90s, with the first demands to open up what was then called "NSFNET," the giant academic network that ARPANET had evolved into—there were already hundreds of thousands of computers on the network and a whole lot of really interesting stuff already going on there.

This head start, important though it was, is not the whole story. Having a head start is great; it puts you in position to ride those positive feedback loops, to grow

————————

Livingstone and Monroe, of course, would considerably overshoot the mark, in terms of both money and land. The crucial moment comes on the night of April 12, 1803, when the French Finance Minister—incredibly enough, it's our old friend Monsieur Marbois, for whom Jefferson had written *Notes on the State of Virginia* two decades earlier! Quelle coincidence!—drives up to Livingstone's house and offers up for sale not just New Orleans, but **all** of the land claimed by France in North America (including the **entire Mississippi watershed**, on **both** sides of the River). Livingstone and Monroe seize the opportunity, eventually agreeing to take it all for around $17 million—or, as James Lewis puts it, "agreeing to spend two-and-a-half times what they had been authorized to spend to buy a province that they had never been instructed to buy."

geometrically. But to take advantage of the position, you have to be able to handle the numbers, to function as efficiently with 100 million users as with 100, to add 5 million new users in a month as easily as you added 50.

To become the Internet, the TCP/IP network had to be able to handle the numbers; it had to solve the problem(s) of scale. How it did so is one of the great (and under-appreciated) achievements in the history of information processing and human communication.

CHAPTER FOUR

JEFFERSON'S MOOSE AND THE PROBLEM OF SCALE I

A mouse and a mammoth derive their dimensions from the same nutritive juices. . . . But all the manna of heaven would never raise the mouse to the bulk of the mammoth.

TJ, NOTES ON THE STATE OF VIRGINIA

Turning Small into Big can be a tricky proposition indeed, because scaling problems—the problems that arise solely as a consequence of increasing size or increasing numbers—can be profound, and profoundly difficult to solve.

Scaling problems are ubiquitous in the natural world, and biologists and zoologists have long understood that size affects nearly every aspect of an organism's structure and function. "It is only a slight overestimate," biologist G. A. Bartholomew wrote, "to say that size is the most important attribute of an animal, both physiologically and ecologically." Large and small organisms inhabit completely different worlds, and their design has to take very different constraints and forces into account.

In large part, it's a simple consequence of three-dimensional geometry: As objects get larger, their **surface area** increases less rapidly than their **volume**, because surface area is roughly proportional to length squared, while volume is proportional to length raised to the third power.[1] A small object, therefore, has more surface area per unit of volume than the same object blown up to larger size

---

1   Consider the simplest possible object: a simple sphere, like a ping-pong ball. The amount of area on the surface of a ping-pong ball of radius = r is given by the formula:

$$\text{Surface Area} = 4 \pi r^2$$

The ball's volume is given by the formula:

$$\text{Volume} = (4/3) \pi r^3$$

So a ping-pong ball with a radius of 1 inch (r = 1) has

$$4 \times \pi \times (1)^2 \approx 12.5 \text{ square inches}$$

and, conversely, the large object has more volume per unit of surface area than the small one.

The consequences of this simple geometric rule for the design of the world around us are profound. Take gravity, for example. It's largely irrelevant to small organisms; you can drop a beetle, or even a small mouse, down a thousand-foot mine shaft, and it will walk away unharmed; try this with your Labrador retriever and you'll have a mess on your hands. The force pulling downward (gravity) is proportional to an object's **volume**, while the force pushing back and slowing the descent (air resistance) is proportional to its **surface area**. Small animals (like the beetle and the mouse) have enough surface area relative to their volume to enable the air resistance to counteract the downward pull of gravity; Fido, alas, does not.

Small organisms can therefore pretty much ignore gravity as they go about their daily lives, just as a simple consequence of being small. At the same time, the force that really matters to them—surface tension—is one that we (and our dogs) hardly ever need to think about. When you or I step out of the bathtub, surface tension causes a thin film of water, about 1/50th of an inch thick and weighing about 400 grams, to cling to our skin. It's hardly worth noticing; because we have so little surface area relative to our volume, it amounts to under 1 percent of our total weight. Get a mouse soaking wet, though, and its weight doubles, because of its greater relative surface area; and a soaking wet beetle is usually a dead beetle, because so much water clings to it (relative to its volume) that its weight increases tenfold, and it is unable to move around at all. As the great English biologist J. B. S. Haldane put it, "an insect going for a drink of water is in as great danger as a man leaning out over a precipice in search of food," which is why most insects have evolved a long snout, or "proboscis," for the purpose of drinking, enabling them to avoid the need to get too close to water sources and the deadly clutches of surface tension.

Large organisms are not and cannot be simply small organisms blown up to larger size, because increase in size brings with it a different set of constraints on, and

---

on its surface, and contains

$$4/3 \times \Pi \times (1)^3 \approx 4.2 \text{ cubic inches.}$$

Now imagine that we make the ball larger—increasing its radius from 1 inch to 10 or 100 inches. As it gets larger, its surface area increases with the square of the radius ($1^2=1$, $10^2=100$, $100^2=1,000$, etc.); but its volume increases by the cube of the radius ($1^3=1$, $10^3=1,000$, $100^3=1,000,000$, etc.). A giant 100-inch ping-pong ball has 10,000 times more surface area than the ball we started with ($r^2 = 100 \times 100 = 10,000$), but it has **1,000,000** times more volume ($r^3 = 1,000,000$).

As it gets bigger, in other words, **the ratio of its volume to its surface area increases**, and it does so exponentially (at a rate proportional to $r^{3/2}$ or $r^{1.5}$).

requires new solutions to, the fundamental problems all organisms face: obtaining energy, avoiding predators, and reproducing.[2]

Strangely enough, the longest chapter in *Notes on the State of Virginia*—the subject about which Jefferson apparently had the most to say in regard to the New World—is about scaling in the natural world, specifically the relative sizes of animals in the Old World and the New.

---

2   This simple surface area/volume scaling principle also helps explain, for instance, why there are no six-foot-long mosquitoes. Insects, like most living things, obtain oxygen through their surface—in the case of insects, through little holes ("tracheae") on the surface of their bodies. The amount of oxygen they can take in is, therefore, a function of the amount of surface area they have. The amount of oxygen they need, however, is a function of their volume—the total number of cells packed inside their bodies that need to be supplied with oxygen to keep functioning. So insects can only get so big; at a certain point, they don't have enough surface area to take in the oxygen needed to keep their cells stoked with energy. They can't scale up; the largest known insect, the Goliath Beetle, is only about five inches long. To get any bigger than this requires a fundamental redesign.

Natural selection has been breathtakingly successful at solving that redesign problem; the largest organisms on the planet are, incredibly enough, more than **twenty-one orders of magnitude**—that's 10^{21}, or one trillion billion times—larger than the smallest. Trees, for instance, produce specialized structures with lots and lots of extra surface area to suck in oxygen—"leaves." Human beings (and many other organisms) have specialized organs whose internal foldings and branchings produce the same surface-area-increasing effect: lungs. Fish have gills, which accomplish the same thing. Without leaves or lungs or gills or something equivalent to them, life couldn't have scaled up.

But natural selection's had a few billion years to work, and it's a very efficient problem-solving mechanism—and even so, some scaling problems remain unsolved; it hasn't (yet) devised a solution to the problem of "scaling up" the mosquito or the ant.

This decreasing ratio of surface area to volume as organisms increase in size also affects, quite dramatically, an organism's ability to absorb and retain energy. The amount of heat that an organism absorbs from the surrounding atmosphere (or dissipates to it) is (largely) a function of its surface area, while the amount of heat that it produces is (largely) a function of its volume (the number of cells it has). So small organisms, with more surface area per unit volume than large animals, absorb heat from the atmosphere (and dissipate heat *to* the atmosphere) much more rapidly than large ones. That's why mice and birds don't hibernate in winter and bears do; a mouse has to eat constantly in winter because its high surface area/volume ratio means that it is losing (through its surface) proportionally more of the heat its cells are producing than the bear. If a small animal takes a nap in the snow, it quickly freezes to death, while the bear can put its whole heat-making system on "Low" and still have enough to make it through the winter, because it loses heat through its surface so much more slowly. In a hot climate, the problem is reversed; large animals have a harder time than small ones getting rid of all of the heat that their cells are producing.

That chapter (Chapter 6, "Productions Mineral, Vegetable, and Animal") focuses on what seems, at first glance, to be another one of those silly-in-retrospect scientific debates in which Jefferson always seemed to find himself embroiled. There was a theory gaining prominence in late eighteenth-century scientific circles, which held that animals in the New World were smaller-sized, scaled-down versions of their Old World counterparts, that **something** (in the atmosphere, perhaps? or arising from the nutritive properties of New World plants?) was causing nature to become *less active, less energetic on one side of the globe than the other, with a tendency to belittle her productions on this side of the Atlantic.*

The theory was championed by the great French naturalist George Louis Leclerc Buffon in his magisterial and spectacularly influential forty-four-volume (!) *Natural History of Animals—***the** great zoological treatise of the age.[3] *Lending the theory his vivid imagination and bewitching language,* Buffon gave scientific respectability to the notion that, as Jefferson summarized it:

1. *The animals **common** both to the Old and New Worlds are smaller in the latter;*
2. *Those animals **peculiar to** the New World are on a smaller scale* [than those in the Old World];

Decreasing surface area/volume ratios also explains why there are no birds the size of bears. Flight requires surface area ("wings"), and volume makes you heavy; that exponentially increasing ratio catches up to you eventually, and natural selection hasn't figured out a way to make a bear-sized flying machine. (We have, of course, done so, using internal combustion engines to generate speed, which increases the effective surface area of an airplane's wings).

3 Buffon's name is probably unfamiliar to you, but he was a towering figure in eighteenth-century scientific circles, one of the great naturalists of the Enlightenment. His treatise on the *Natural History of Animals,* the first volume of which appeared in 1761 while Jefferson was a student at the College of William and Mary, occupied him for more than twenty years and was prodigiously influential—William Peden called it the "premier contribution to the hottest field in biology at the time, the study of animal and plant classification." The *celebrated Zoologist,* Jefferson called Buffon in *Notes on the State of Virginia: I think him the best informed of any naturalist who has ever lived; I render every tribute of honor and esteem to [him], who has added, and is still adding, so many precious things to the treasures of science.*

Buffon was among the first naturalists to suggest that living things changed over time, through a process that appeared to have something to do with their adaptation to local environmental conditions—temperature, humidity, available food supply, rainfall, etc. He got the details of that process all wrong—it wouldn't be for another hundred years that Darwin and Wallace would figure that out—but it was an enormously impressive achievement nonetheless.

And just to complete the circle: several scholars, following Gilbert Chinard, have suggested that it was Buffon who drafted the questions that Marbois sent to Jefferson and which formed the basis for *Notes on the State of Virginia.*

3 *Those animals which have been domesticated in* **both** *the Old and New Worlds have degenerated in America; and*

4 *That on the whole, the New World exhibits fewer species than the Old.*

The explanation Buffon offered for these phenomena was that the New World was cooler and wetter than the Old—that *the heats of America are less, and more waters are spread over its surface by nature, and fewer of these drained off by the hand of man*—and that *heat is friendly, and moisture adverse, to the production and development of large quadrupeds.*

Jefferson was convinced that it was hogwash—*as true as the fables of Aesop,* as he put it[4]—and he took it upon himself, in *Notes on the State of Virginia,* to demonstrate just what hogwash it was.

It took a peculiarly Jeffersonian brand of intellectual chutzpah to take on the world's most celebrated naturalist—and on the latter's home field, as it were. After all, Jefferson had no formal training whatsoever in zoology or natural history, having studied law at the College of William and Mary in Williamsburg, Virginia, an institution which Buffon had surely never even heard of and which had only been formed a few decades before. (To put things in perspective, the Sorbonne in Paris had, by this time, been in existence for more than five hundred years). A little backwater academy in the wilds of Virginia would hardly have been regarded by educated Europeans as a suitable training ground for a scientist capable of challenging Buffon.

But challenge him he did, point by point, page after eye-glazing-over page. To modern eyes, chapter 6 of *Notes on the State of Virginia* is almost unreadable; no magnificent Jeffersonian prose here in his discussions of the relative weights of the flying squirrel in America (4 lbs.) and Europe (2.2 lbs.).

He drew up "A Comparative View of the Quadrupeds of Europe and of America"—three separate tables displaying estimates of the weights of

(a) species common to America and Europe (26 species),

(b) species unique to Europe (18 species) or to America (74 species), and

(c) domesticated species appearing on both continents (8 species)

along with notations showing whether the weights listed were (a) the *actual weights of particular subjects,* (b) *conjectures furnished by judicious persons well acquainted with the species saying what the largest individual they had seen would* **probably** *have* weighed, or (c) taken from Buffon's own data.

The tables taken all together showed that the New World species were, on average, actually **larger** than their European counterparts, and that there were **more of them:**

---

4 Although he deferentially added: *The wonder is not that there is something in* [Buffon's] *great work to correct, but that there is so little.*

Of 26 quadrupeds common to both countries, 7 are [found] to be larger in America, 7 of equal size, and 12 not sufficiently examined. So that the first table impeaches [Buffon's] assertion that of the animals common to both countries, the American are 'without exception' smallest. That the last part of [Buffon's hypothesis], which affirms that the species of American quadrupeds are comparatively few, is erroneous is evident from the tables taken all together. It appears that there are an hundred species aboriginal of America. Buffon supposes about double that number existing on the whole earth. Of these Europe, Asia, and Africa, furnish suppose 126; that is, the 26 common to Europe and America, and about 100 which are not in America at all. The American species then are to those of the rest of the earth, as 100 to 126, or 4 to 5. But the residue of the earth being double the extent of America, the exact proportion would have been but as 4 to 8.

Take that, M. Buffon!

Jefferson's fascination with animal scale in general, and with large mammals in particular, can only be described as boundless and perhaps even bizarre. He also included in chapter 6 of *Notes on the State of Virginia* a lengthy disquisition on the woolly mammoth—*an animal six times the cubic volume of the elephant*—having convinced himself that they still roamed *on the Ohio, and in many parts of America further north* (though in truth it had been extinct for several thousand years). Jefferson would later be ridiculed by his political opponents for this idea—the great American Philosopher-King, Mr. Big-Genius, and he thinks there are still woolly mammoths in Ohio![5] In 1796, when he was chosen to succeed Franklin once again, this time as president of the American Philosophical Society—*the most flattering incident of my life,* he called it, and this **after** he had already been elected governor of Virginia and vice president of the United States—he offered, as his inaugural act, a scientific paper he had written describing a new species of giant American lion—*as preeminent*

---

5   Jefferson was frequently pilloried, as Paul Semonin recounts in *American Monster: How the Nation's First Prehistoric Creature Became a Symbol of National Identity,* for his obsession with mammoths and enormous prehistoric animals of all kinds. Semonin quotes a poem written by William Cullen Bryant, age thirteen, in 1807:

Go, wretch, resign thy presidential chair,
Disclose thy secret measures, foul or fair,
Go search with curious eyes for horned frogs,
'Mid the wild wastes of Louisianian bogs;
Or Where the Ohio rolls his turbid stream
Dig for huge bones, thy glory and thy theme.

Of all the charges brought against me by my political adversaries, Jefferson later wrote, *the charge of 'possessing some science' has done them the least credit. Our countrymen are too enlightened themselves to believe that ignorance is the best qualification for their service.*

over the lion in size as the Mammoth is over the elephant—which he named *Megalonyx*. (Wrong again!)[6]

In all of the data that Jefferson compiled in *Notes on the State of Virginia*, there was nothing on the animal that was in fact the largest of all (nonextinct) American quadrupeds, the American moose. You wouldn't think it would have mattered all that much—but to Jefferson, apparently, it did, and in the spring of 1787 the moose carcass and skeleton (antlers included) arrived at his living quarters in the center of Paris. He wrote to Buffon, inviting him to come and see it:

> *I had the honour of informing you some time ago that I had written to some of my friends in America, desiring they would send me . . . the complete skeleton, skin, & horns of the Moose, in such condition as that the skin might be sewed up & stuffed on it's arrival here. I am happy to be able to present* [it] *to you at this moment,* [along with] *the horns of the Caribou, the elk, the deer, the spiked horned buck, & the Roebuck of America. They all come from New Hampshire & Massachusetts. I give you their popular names, as it rests with yourself to decide their real names . . .[7] I really suspect you will find that the Moose, the Round horned elk, & the American deer are species not existing in Europe. The Moose is perhaps of a new class.*

6   The individual specimen Jefferson described in his paper was not, it turned out, from a new species of giant carnivore but rather an extinct Giant Sloth from the genus *Megatherium*, a close relative of modern tree sloths, armadillos, and anteaters. *Megatherium*, unique to the New World and extinct for around 8,000 years, had itself been a truly astonishing creature—up to fifteen feet long and weighing as much as an African elephant—but it was, alas, no lion.

And to Jefferson's further embarrassment, it was also not entirely "new." *Megatherium* had been named and described just a year before Jefferson wrote his paper, in a 1796 paper by the French paleontologist Georges Cuvier, based on specimens brought over to France from Patagonia. Jefferson saw a copy of Cuvier's paper only a few weeks before he was to present his own paper to the American Philosophical Society. He realized his mistake (and corrected his paper) right away—which is, to my eyes, the most remarkable part of the whole remarkable story (recounted in delightful detail in both the Boyd and Semonin references listed at the end of the book), having myself, while a graduate student in physical anthropology, spent many hours staring at teeth and bones, and drawings of teeth and bones in published papers, and trying to compare the two, with precious little success.

7   What **is** the "real name" of the moose?! Jefferson was, of course, presumably referring to its "scientific" name, its name within the system of zoological nomenclature, though he doesn't say, perhaps out of politeness, which system of nomenclature he had in mind.

The world of zoological nomenclature in the 1780s was a bit like the world of internetworking protocols in the 1980s, with any number of competing systems that we don't hear much about any more because one of them triumphed so completely over the others—in this case, the Linnaean system, still used today, first propounded by the great Swedish naturalist Carl Linnaeus in his *Natural Systems* (*Systema Naturae*), published in the 1730s. Jefferson and Buffon were on different sides of the nomenclatural debate, as both men were

I wish these spoils, Sir, may have the merit of adding [something] *new to the treasures of nature which have so fortunately come under your observation, & of which she seems to have given you the key. They will in that case be some gratification to you, which it will always be pleasing to me to have procured.*

It does seem a little ridiculous in retrospect—both Buffon's notion that animals were actually shrinking in the degenerate and fetid atmosphere of the New World, and Jefferson's positively Herculean efforts to show that it was not so.

But, once again, it was—or at least it turned out to be, later—of the profoundest significance. The Buffon-Jefferson colloquy was part of a worldwide argument about the origin of species, though neither man—certainly not Jefferson—really knew that, at the time. The Buffon-Jefferson debate was repeated, over and over again, dozens and dozens of times, as the data from the great nineteenth-century naturalists poured in from the New Worlds—not just the United States but also from what is now Brazil, and Kenya, and Australia, and Indonesia, and Hawaii. The worldwide community of scientists, centered in Great Britain and continental Europe, pored over it and scratched its collective head, cataloguing and comparing and looking for patterns of size increase (or decrease), of increasing species richness (or impoverishment), and for the environmental factors that might account for those patterns.

It turns out that animal size, and the relative numbers of different species, **do** systematically vary from one place to another, and a great deal of the formative evolutionary thinking in the nineteenth century (including, again, Darwin's and

---

well aware; Buffon used a system of his own devising for classifying and naming plants and animals, while Jefferson was a staunch supporter of the Linnaean scheme—not because it was necessarily better, but because it was, as it were, bigger. *The most important consideration*, he wrote, was to *unite all nations under one language in Natural History, which had been happily effected by Linnaeus.*

> *Ray had formed one classification, Klein adopted another, Brisson a third, and other naturalists other designations, till Linnaeus appeared. Fortunately for science, he conceived, in the three kingdoms of nature, modes of classification which obtained the approbation of the learned of all nations. Linnaeus' method was received, understood, and conventionally settled among the learned, and was even getting into common use, uniting all in a general language. To disturb it was unfortunate…*
>
> *I do not mean to insinuate that Linnaeus's method is intrinsically preferable to those of Blumenbach and Cuvier* [or others]. *But I adhere to the Linnaean…mainly because it has got into so general use that it will not be easy to displace it, and still harder to find another which shall have the same singular fortune of obtaining the general consent.* ***My reluctance is to give up an universal language of which we are in possession, without an assurance of general consent to receive another***. [Emphasis added.]

Wallace's) was driven by attempts to explain these related biogeographical phenomena.[8] Scale really **does** matter. Buffon had been wrong—Jefferson, too; animals in the New World are neither systematically larger or smaller, more numerous or less, than those in the Old. But they were asking the right questions, and the study of animal scaling that they helped provoke was to yield unimaginable dividends long after both men were gone from the scene.

Communications networks, it turns out, have profound scaling problems of their own—not the same as the moose's, but not unrelated to them, either. Understanding the Internet means understanding something about how it solved (and continues to solve) them. Networks, of course, don't have to obtain energy or avoid predators or reproduce; but they do have to get messages reliably from one place to another, and that gets a lot harder to do as they grow in size.

To see why, let's build a simple network. We'll start with ten machines. Our goal is simply to enable each of them to exchange one message each day—"Good morning!"—with each of the others.

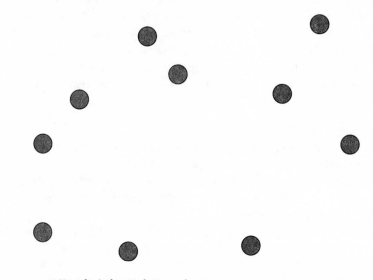

FIGURE 4.1 A Hypothetical 10-Node Network.

8 Islands, it turned out, were the key—who knew?—to unlocking these patterns. Animal species do change size when they move from mainland ecosystems to nearby islands, some getting larger, and some getting smaller ("midgets and giants, behemoths and runts," a "confusing welter of upscaling and downscaling," as David Quammen puts it in *The Song of the Dodo*), and islands also tend to have systematically fewer species than areas of equivalent size on the mainland. Understanding these patterns was of central importance to the development of a theory of natural selection; it is no coincidence that both Darwin

There are lots of ways to do this, of course. To illustrate the scaling problem, let's put all of the required processing into a single machine—a network "server"; concentrating all tasks in one place will make it easier to see how much processing is required to get messages where they're supposed to go, and how that processing workload increases as the network grows in size. Each of the ten machines must be connected to the server. The server's job is to keep track of who everybody is and where everybody is, so that when it receives a message directed to a particular machine, it can direct it to the right place. Each network participant will have to have a "name"—some unique designation ("A", "B", "C", or "1," "2," "3," or even "Alice," "Bob," Charlie," etc.) that serves to identify it and to distinguish it from all others on the network; the designators have to be unique, because if they're not—if there are two machines named "Charlie" and four named "Lois"—confusion will obviously ensue, as the server won't know where to deliver a message addressed to "Charlie" or to "Lois."

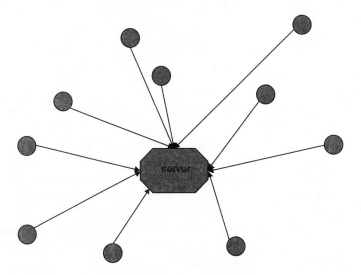

FIGURE 4.2 A Hypothetical 10-Node Network with Central Server.

The server will need an "addressing protocol" to be able to determine where each message is supposed to go. On a network on which all information is in digital form, the addressing protocol has two components: first, some code (like the familiar ASCII Code) to translate the 1s and 0s that are being transmitted to the server into machine names (Alice = 10010011, Bob = 0011100, Charlie = 10110110, etc); and

---

and Wallace spent years collecting and analyzing data from island ecosystems, Darwin in the Galapagos Islands and Wallace up and down the Indonesian and Malay archipelagos. "Under peculiar conditions evolution decrees peculiar specifications for survival. Islands provide those peculiar conditions. Size change . . . is one signal of this fact."

second, some rule about where in the stream of digits the recipient's name is to be found (like "PUT THE NAME OF THE INTENDED RECIPIENT IMMEDIATELY AFTER THE 'START-MESSAGE' STRING"]. The server and the network members all have to use the same code and the same rule, of course, or things will get hopelessly out of whack.

The server will also need to keep track of the location of all network machines. Once it determines that a message is for "Charlie," it has to flip the right switch, so that the message can be sent to the right machine. It needs to have what network engineers call a "routing table," a simple list or database that contains the names of all machines alongside the location of each of them.

TABLE 4.1

NAME	LOCATION
Machine A	wire 44C
Machine B	wire 11
Machine C	wire 221.3
...	...

Every time a message reaches the server, the server has to read the address so that it can figure out which machine is the intended recipient ["This is a message for 'E'"] and then it has to find out where E is located by performing what engineers call a "lookup" operation—searching through that routing table to find E's location [" 'E' is on wire #39"], and then it has to flip the right switch to send the message on its way.

It's a perfectly sensible way of doing things. Many communications networks work more-or-less this way. See Box 4.1.

It's going to be hard to scale up, however. Look at what happens as the network grows; fasten your seatbelts. With 10 members, each of whom sends out 9 messages a day (one message to each of the others), a total of 90 messages pass through the server. (N, the number of machines on the network, multiplied by (N-1), the number of other machines to which each sends a message). Each of those 90 messages requires a "lookup"—a search through a database with 10 separate entries.[9] So,

---

9 Every message requires a search through the same 10-entry routing table because our server—like all computers—is fundamentally very stupid. At least, stupid in the sense that while it can do some things incredibly fast, it doesn't get faster or better at doing those things the more it does them. If the server were a human being, he/she would be able to throw away the routing table after the first fifty or so times through it. "This message is for Ed—I remember where Ed lives." Or "Here's another message for Alice—I just had a message for Alice a moment ago and looked up her address, so I don't have to look it up again." But computers can't really do that—or not nearly as well as we can. Every time a message comes in bearing the 01100010 address, it has to search for a match in order to flip the correct switch.

BOX 4.1 THE POSTAL NETWORK

This is, more or less, how the post office works. If we're connecting people, instead of machines, together:

FIGURE B4.1A

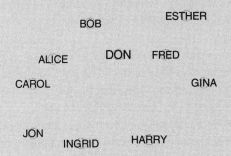

...and we were designing a system to move letters, rather than electronic impulses, from anyone "on the network" to anyone else, a post office would function like our "server."

FIGURE B4.1B

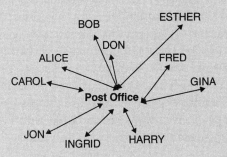

The post office does all of the "routing." It has to know where everyone is (so that letters can be delivered to them). The individuals on the network don't have to know where **anyone** is; they just have to (a) have a connection to the post office, and (b) know how to address their letters in a manner that the post office can read. Everything will work smoothly from there.

roughly speaking, the number of operations that the server needs to perform in order to move messages on this network around is equal to

$$\text{Number of Operations} \approx N \times (N-1) * N = N^3 - N^2$$

So with 10 machines, our server needs to perform 900 operations ($10 \times 9 \times 10$).

Now suppose everyone on the network invites one friend to join—doubling the size of the network (from $N = 10$ members to $2N = 20$). With 20 members, 380 messages (20×19) pass through the server, and each lookup requires searching through a database with 20 entries instead of 10. The total number of operations is now 7,600 ($20 \times 19 \times 20$).

A **twofold** increase in size, in other words, leads to a roughly **eightfold** (2^3) increase in the number of operations the server has to perform. A tenfold increase in network size (from 10 to 100) increases the number of operations roughly a thousand-fold (10^3) ($100 \times 99 \times 100 = 990,000$), and so on.

Geometric growth! The number of operations is increasing roughly as the **cube** of the number of machines on the network. Those exponents will catch up to you, eventually. Remember the parable of the chessboard! (See chap. 2.) Each time the network grows by a factor of 10, the number of operations the server has to perform grows roughly 1,000-fold. If this network grows to 100 times its original size, the server will have to perform about a million times more work. If it grows 100 million-fold (as the Internet actually did, from 4 to 400 million), the number of operations it has to perform will grow roughly by a factor of (100 million)^3—10 trillion trillion. That's a 10 with 24 zeroes after it.[10]

So there's our scaling problem. It's a kind of double-exponential whammy: The amount of work that the network has to do is an exponential function of the number of machines and the number of messages, which are themselves growing exponentially. Even if each operation takes a billionth of a second—what the hell, even if each operation takes a trillionth of a second—it will take 10 trillion seconds (roughly, a million years) to accomplish **one day's** worth of processing![11] Or put it another way: If our network needs one server to handle the workload when it has one hundred members, we will need a thousand servers when the network has a thousand members, and a trillion servers—a thousand billion—when it has (only) a million members.

---

10 And it's probably even worse than that. If we allow network members to form **groups** of different sizes—David Reed's insight (see chap. 3)—then we're really in a pickle. The total number of possible groups in a network of N members is proportional to 2^N. So if we would like our network to enable all members to send "Good Morning!" messages not merely to every other machine on the network but to every possible group of machines of which it might be a member, we reach truly astronomical processing requirements in a hurry.

11 Assuming the universe to be 15 billion years old, there have only been around 10^{17} seconds since the beginning.

Somehow, the TCP/IP network has managed to solve this problem; it has managed to grow by a factor of 100 million and still get all the necessary work done. How does it do that? We know that it doesn't use this central server design—but how then do messages get where they're supposed to go? Without a central server to keep track of who everybody is and where everybody is, who keeps track? Who's got the routing table? Who is responsible for getting messages to the right place?

To manage this problem, TCP/IP uses something called "distributed routing," and it's quite a neat little feat of engineering. It works, roughly, like this. To form a TCP/IP network out of our ten machines, we can connect them together any which way.

Like this:

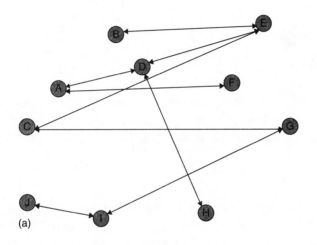

(a)

Or this:

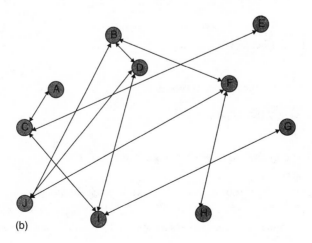

(b)

Or this:

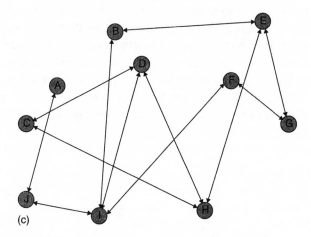

(c)

We can then let our Good Morning messages bounce around at random. A message from, say, C to E, for example, is sent to **any** machine to which C is connected—machine D, say. Machine D has to read the address on the message ("TO: E"), and then follow one simple rule:

Routing Rule:

- If you are the designated recipient (i.e., if the message is addressed "To: D"), **Stop**.
- If you are not the designated recipient (i.e., if the message address says anything **other** than "To: D"), **Send** (i.e., re-transmit the message to any machine to which you are connected).

D applies the rule and re-transmits the message—to I, say. The process is repeated:

- If the address label says "To: I," Stop
- If not, re-transmit.

I sends to B, and the process is repeated:

- If the label says "To: B," Stop
- If not, re-transmit.

… until eventually the message lands at the "correct" machine (i.e., B sends to E, and E stops).

The actual TCP/IP routing rules don't work precisely this way, to be sure. To begin with, TCP/IP doesn't use letters of the alphabet ("A," "B," "C," and so on) to designate individual machines; it uses a numerical identifier known as an "Internet

Protocol Address" (or "IP Address"),[12] and messages don't actually bounce around from machine to machine entirely at random. But this is, fundamentally, how TCP/IP gets messages—by the billions and hundreds of billions—from one place to another. It splits the work of routing into pieces, and parcels it out—distributes it—among the network machines themselves. Instead of having a central server subjecting every message to a **series** of questions—searching through the entire routing table and asking "Is this a message to A?" "Is this a message to B?" "Is this a message to C?" until it finds the correct entry—in a distributed system the network **as a whole** subjects every message to a series of questions, one machine at a time: "Is this message addressed to me?" "Is this message addressed to me?" "Is this message addressed to me?" The aggregate

12 An IP Address is just a number—4253, or 11, or 4444444, or 19828383, etc.—expressed as a string of binary digits ("bits"), 32-characters long:

00101001010100010101110100101111, or

10010100010100010101110100101111, or

00000000000000000000000000101011

Every machine on the TCP/IP network has to have a unique IP Address. Whenever you (or anyone else) "logs on" to the Internet, your computer must have its own unique 32-bit IP Address. In a later chapter we'll look at just how, and from where, it gets that IP Address; for now, it is sufficient to note that without it, you're not "on" the network, because without it the network can't "find" you (i.e., direct messages from the other machines on the network to you).

To simplify matters (though simplification, like beauty, is often in the mind of the beholder, and you may find this making things more, rather than less, complicated), IP Addresses are usually written out as four-item decimal strings, i.e., as

155.153.127.44

instead of

10011011100110010111111100101100

They're precisely equivalent representations of the same number. To convert the original 32-bit string into this form, you:

(a) Break the 32-bit binary string into four units, each 8 bits long. Thus, the string

10011011100110010111111100101100

becomes:

10011011 10011001 01111111 00101100

(b) Convert each of these 8-bit sequences—known as "bytes"—into decimal form:

$10011011 = ([1 \times 2^7] + [0 \times 2^6] + [0 \times 2^5] + [1 \times 2^4] + [1 \times 2^3] + [0 \times 2^2] + [1 \times 2^1] + 1 \times 2^0])$

$\qquad\qquad = 128 + 0 + 0 + 16 + 8 + 0 + 2 + 1$

$\qquad\qquad = \mathbf{155}$

$10011001 \qquad = \mathbf{153}$

$01111111 \qquad = \mathbf{127}$

$00101100 \qquad = \mathbf{44}$

So the original 32-bit IP address

10011011100110010111111100101100

can be expressed by the "octal" **155.153.127.44**

work—reading the addresses on the messages and making some decision about where to send it—still gets done, but it has been split up into pieces and spread around.

It wasn't obvious, at the time the early TCP/IP networks were being cobbled together in the 1970s and early '80s, that it would work; no other networking protocol worked like this, and the engineering involved, I'm told, is a lot trickier than in my hypersimplified example above. But, obviously, it does work; the Internet itself is, in that sense, "proof of concept." Messages can (and routinely do) make their way from any point down there in the corner of the Peacock Map (see chap. 1) to any other point, finding their way among the 500 million or so potential recipients by bouncing from one machine to another like that. All machines are locatable, even though nobody has the information about where everybody is located (i.e., even though there's no master routing table). Even though each machine has information concerning only the location of the machines to which it is connected—its "local" neighborhood—messages can indeed get where they are supposed to go anywhere on the network.

We can see why a distributed system like TCP/IP scales better—manages the problems associated with geometrically increasing workload—than networks built along centralized lines. The math is complicated—too complicated for me to master, to be honest, let alone to recapitulate here. But even in our simplified model network, we can see that arranging it into a distributed system divides the total workload (increasing as N^3) among the (N) machines. The total work **per machine** is only (!) increasing by N^2 (=N^3/N).

It's a start, anyway—geometric growth, but at a much slower rate. A nice little competitive advantage for distributed networks (whose workload is increasing by N^2) over their centralized cousins (N^3). It doesn't make the scaling problem go away—it just makes it about two-thirds as overwhelming, changing all those millions back into thousands, the billions back to millions, the trillions to billions, etc. Imagine two network administrators, one running a TCP/IP network and the other a centralized network; every time the former submits a request for a hundredfold increase in processing power to cope with the growth of the network, the latter's request is for a thousandfold increase. Whose job would you rather have? It's as though distributed routing makes the network's "volume"—ordinarily proportional to the **cube** of size—scale like its "surface area" (proportional to the square of network size). It's a neat trick; you could probably build yourself a pretty amazing giant flying mosquito if you could do that with real physical objects.

Notice, too, that distributed routing lets TCP/IP networks **grow from any point**. Centralized networks grow radially—outward from the center, like a starfish; there's only so fast they can grow, because the center has to "keep up" with the whole network. But a TCP/IP network grows like a bush, each of whose terminal twigs can sprout new twigs, or like a coral reef; every machine already on the network—every point on the Peacock Map—can serve as the point of attachment for a machine or machines joining the network. New entrants can join the network at any point. Because every machine already on a TCP/IP network can perform its part of the critical network function—getting messages to and from anyone on the network—new machines can join a TCP/IP network anywhere, i.e., by connecting to **any** machine that is itself already on the network.

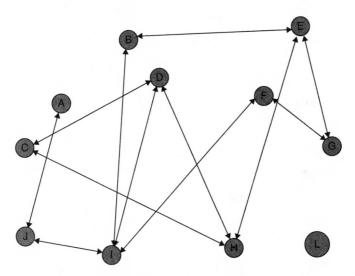

FIGURE 4.4   New Entrant ("L") to the TCP/IP Network.

A new machine—machine L—can join this network by finding one connection point to an existing network member; it just needs the "permission" of **one** existing network member to become a network member. There are therefore as many points of attachment and growth as there are existing machines on the network. The following figure shows alternate ways of connecting the new entrant to the existing TCP/IP network:

Like this:

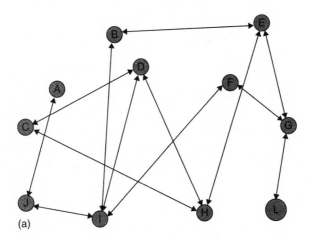

(a)

Or this:

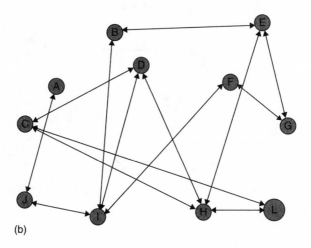

(b)

Or this:

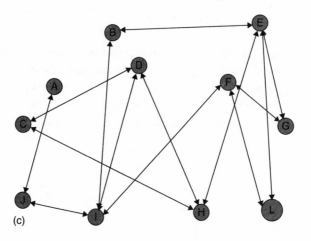

(c)

So as the TCP/IP network grows and the number of machines increases, the number of points to which others can attach themselves also increases; as the network grows, its **ability** to grow grows.

So while you were reading the preceding few pages, a dozen, or a hundred, or a thousand computers could have joined the global TCP/IP network, connecting to any of the hundreds of millions of machines already on the network. And each of

those new machines—each of the ones that came "on" the network during the past fifteen minutes—can itself become an attachment point for others to get on the network. And so on. Positive feedback; Malthusian growth.[13]

13 Now you can see why I said earlier that it's tricky to figure out how many machines are on the Internet at any one time. On a centralized network, census-taking is easy; you just "ask" the server, i.e., look at the server's routing table, count the number of machines listed there, and there's your answer.

But there is no master routing table in a TCP/IP network. What the netwizards.org folks actually did to come up with the data shown in Table 2.1 above is something like this: they sent a message to every possible IP Address (0.0.0.1 to 255.255.255.255) saying, in essence: "Reply when you get this," and then they counted the number of replies. (It's a little more complicated than that. Sending a message to all 4,294,967,296 possible IP Addresses and recording whether or not there's a response is no mean feat, even for high-speed computers; even if it takes only, say, 1/1000th of a second to do each one, it will take more than fifty days to complete the task [and, as we saw, the Internet could have grown substantially in those fifty days, making the estimate less useful]. So the folks who conduct these surveys take samples from among all possible addresses and then extrapolate to get an estimate of the total population.)

CHAPTER 5

THE PROBLEM OF SCALE II

There's a lot more to the TCP/IP scaling story than this, however. The Internet could grow as fast as it did also because it is a very stupid network, thanks to a principle known as "end-to-end" (or "e2e") design.

To see how e2e works (and to see just how stupid the Internet is), it's helpful to think about networks, as the engineers do, as performing their work in different "layers" of a "protocol stack." It's an idea, as Tim Wu put it, that can be "difficult to grasp at first, yet is so clever that it merits understanding."

The good old-fashioned postal system, for instance, has two "layers" of processing:

> Consider what happens when one lawyer uses the postal system to mail a legal argument to another lawyer. The postal system is structured so that no one in the postal system needs to understand law (the language of the lawyers) for the message to be successfully delivered. And, similarly, neither lawyer need do anything more than understand the rules on addressing and postage. This makes for a simple two-layer network. The function of understanding the contents of the letter has been delegated to a "higher" layer (in this case lawyers), and the function of delivering the letter has been delegated to a "lower" layer (the postal system).

Each layer has its own functions, and its own rules (protocols) for carrying out those functions. The Transport Layer moves letters from one place to another, and its own set of rules and procedures for getting that done—rules about how letters are sorted, and about when they are moved by air and when by truck and when by human carrier, about delivery routes and delivery schedules, and all the rest. The Interpretation Layer governs the interpretation of the text of the letters;

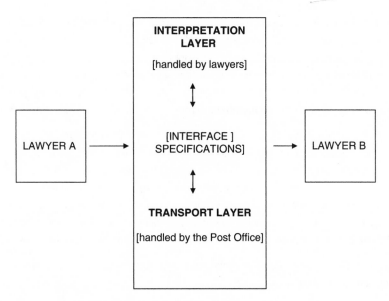

FIGURE 5.1 A Simple Two-Layer Communications System.

Interpretation Layer rules include the ordinary rules of English (assuming the message is written in English), as well as the specialized rules of legalese—"res ipsa loquitur," "estoppel," "jurisdiction in personam," and the like. And there are "Interface Specifications" between the two layers; the lawyers don't have to understand anything about how the Transport Layer protocols work, but they do have to format their letters in such a manner that the Transport Layer protocols can operate correctly on them—i.e., they have to put the recipient's address on the outside of the envelope, they have to include a zip code in the lower right-hand corner, etc.

The Transport Layer is "lower" than the Interpretation Layer in several senses. First, the lawyers need it, but it doesn't need the lawyers. That is, if the Transport Layer protocols break down, lawyers can't send mail to one another; but if the lawyers' Interpretation Layer protocols break down, the Transport Layer is entirely unaffected, and the system can continue to transport mail perfectly well for doctors, scientists, and (as Wu puts it) "other interpreters of strange lingo." Second, the Transport Layer is "lower" in the sense that it is more fundamental; Interpretation Layer protocols have to comply with Transport Layer rules, but the reverse is not true. If the Transport Layer protocols change ("Only 5×5 blue envelopes accepted from now on"), all users of higher-level protocols (lawyers, doctors, French-speaking network engineers, Chinese-speaking auto designers) must comply with the new rules or their letters will not get delivered to the correct places. On the other hand, if the lawyers change their Interpretation Layer protocols ("You may end sentences with prepositions," or "the doctrine of estoppel no longer means what it used to mean"), the Transport Layer protocols don't have to change in response. (That's why law firms and doctors' offices and automobile distributorships all have mail rooms, filled with people whose job it is to make sure that the firm's communications over the postal network comply with the Transport Layer protocols, but post offices don't have lawyer-rooms or doctor-rooms or auto-distributor-rooms to ensure that messages are in compliance with **higher**-level protocols.) Here's Tim Wu again:

> The Transport Layer can focus on one task: delivering mail without regard to the content or meaning of any of the messages it delivers. The system is very flexible: The Transport Layer can carry any type of message, and the communication will be successful, provided that the person on the other side understands it. This makes the postal network useful for a wide variety of applications. Finally, the layers are modular: Were the Transport Layer to begin using spaceships to deliver its mail, the lawyers would be unaffected so long as the rules for postage and writing addresses remained the same.

The Internet uses a similar layering of functions, with a "Network Layer" running beneath an "Applications Layer."

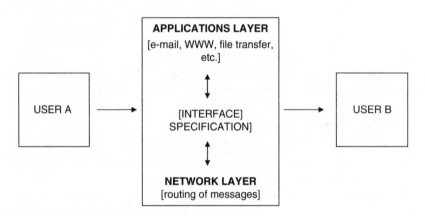

FIGURE 5.2 The Internet as a Two-Layer System.

Network Layer protocols control the processing of messages as they move **through** the network from sender to recipient; they're the equivalent of the postal system's Transport Layer rules and procedures. The distributed routing procedures discussed in the previous chapter are part of the Network Layer, determining how messages get from one place to another across the network. Applications Layer protocols control the processing of messages by senders/recipients; like the rules of English (and Legalese), these consist of the rules applied to messages that have already been processed by the Network Layer, and which have therefore been delivered to the right place (we hope). Like the rules of English and Legalese, these are interpretive protocols; they take the bit-streams handed over by the Network Layer and they process them so as to turn then into "email messages," or "web pages," or "pictures," or "music files," etc.[1]

With these layers of the protocol stack in mind, the e2e principle can be stated as: PUSH AS MUCH PROCESSING **UP** THE PROTOCOL STACK AND **OUT** TO THE PERIPHERY OF THE NETWORK AS POSSIBLE. LET THEM DO THE WORK.

In an e2e network, the Network Layer does the **minimum number of tasks required** to get messages from one place to another. Network Layer protocols in e2e networks are stripped down and simple—at least, as simple as the engineers can get them to be—and they do nothing **except** message routing and transport. Everything else is left for the applications running on the machines at the network periphery, for the sender(s) and the recipient(s) of the messages to work out, as it were, for themselves.

To appreciate the significance of e2e design, consider all of the things the Network Layer protocols (or the postal service) could do to messages as they travel over the network in addition to merely getting them to go wherever

---

1   The Internet, actually, is usually described as having three layers—see fig. 5.3 in the appendix—with a third layer, usually referred to somewhat confusingly as the "Transport Layer" or the "Control Layer," squeezed in between the Network Layer and the Applications Layer. To understand the role of the Transport Layer protocols, TCP/IP networks are "packet-switched" networks—that is, messages (like the one from Lawyer A to Lawyer B) are first broken up into small segments ("packets") before they are transported over the inter-network. So a message from Lawyer A to Lawyer B might be broken up into 500 separate packets, each of which is routed to Lawyer B **independently of all the others**; that is, the recipient's address is placed on each little piece of the original message, and each packet then bounces around in a different way among the routing machines on the Internet before they all eventually reach the same destination. As a consequence, they will arrive at Lawyer B at different times, and out of order. The Transport Layer protocols are responsible for this "reassembly" process; they specify how the individual pieces of each message are to be reassembled, they check to see whether any packets have gotten lost, or damaged, while in transit (a not-at-all-unlikely occurrence), and they arrange for any necessary retransmission in the event of lost or damaged packets.

Every one of the billions upon billions of messages traveling over the Internet in any given hour is treated this way—broken up into packets, bounced around the network, reassembled in proper order, checked for errors, and presented to the recipient. If you're thinking "It can't possibly work that way!" you're not alone; many, many people did not believe that "packet-routing" like this could reliably deliver messages from one place to another over a network; when Paul Baran presented the idea in the early 1960s to management at AT&T, he was, literally, laughed out of the room.

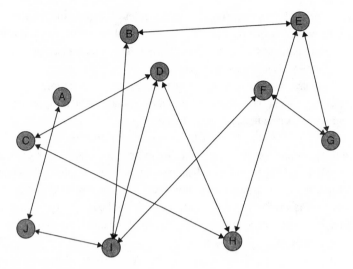

FIGURE 5.4 A Simple TCP/IP network.

they're supposed to go. Recall the simple network we looked at in the previous chapter. (See fig. 5.4.)

As a message makes its way from, say, C to E, the Network Layer protocols **could** process the message to accomplish many other goals besides just moving the message to the correct place. For instance:

- **Authentication and verification.** The string of bits appears to come from C; but did it really? Intermediate machines (like D) could perform various tests to verify that the message it received was actually sent by C before sending it on its way. For instance, D could send a message to C requesting confirmation: "I have just received a message that indicates it has come from you, and is to be delivered to machine E. Please verify that you did, indeed, send this message."

- **Error-Checking.** Bits travel over the network in the form of electrical pulses, whose on/off patterns represent strings of ones and zeroes, and transmission errors ("noise" in engineering parlance) will inevitably occur. Noise is an immense headache for network engineers, and they have developed a dazzling variety of what are called "Quality of Service" procedures to detect errors as messages move from one place to another, and to rectify those errors. The Network Layer protocols could require machine D to perform various procedures to insure that the message it (D) received was **precisely** the one sent to it (and, if it isn't, to request retransmission, or take some other corrective action).

- **Translation.** Messages traveling over the network may have been composed using applications running on the sending machines that are not present on the recipient's machine. Someone has to have the responsibility for translating these messages into code that the recipient machines can understand, a task that could be given to the intermediate routing machines.

- **Checking for Hostile Code**. The network layer protocols could require all intermediate machines to scan all messages for destructive code—viruses of some kind, for example—before sending them on their way.
- **Tracing**. D could send a message back to C: "I have just received a message that appears to have come from you, and that indicates that it is to be delivered to machine E. The message has been routed to machine I. Have a nice day." As C received messages from each of the machines to which the original string of bits was routed, it could easily keep track of the message's progress as it moved through the inter-network.
- **Discrimination**. There are many reasons we might want the network to discriminate among messages—in the nonpejorative sense of placing messages into categories for differential treatment of some kind or other. For example, we might want the network to have the ability to route certain kinds of messages (those deemed, for whatever reason, the most "critical") more rapidly than others (i.e., to process them ahead of others when they are received at intermediate machines), or we might want to apply particularly intensive error-checking or hostile-code-detecting algorithms to certain types of messages but not others.

These are all important and useful functions. The Network Layer protocols could perform any or all of them.

But, on e2e networks, they don't. All of that additional processing (and more) is pushed up and out, to the Applications Layer and to the network periphery. The Network Layer is stripped down to its essentials; it does **only what is necessary** to get bit-strings where they are supposed to go. All other functions are left for the senders and the recipients, the network end-points: "Work all of those things out for yourselves, end-to-end." The Network Layer gets the message to E, and then—figuratively speaking—it says: "Here's a message for you. I don't know what it says, or what it means, or what you're supposed to do with it. As far as I am concerned, it's just a bunch of ones and zeroes with an address on it. It was addressed to you, so here it is." Everything required to turn these 1s and 0s into things that mean something, or do something, to interpret them and to turn them into "web pages," or "music files," or "email messages," or file transfer requests, or search results, all the processing required to check that they arrived in the same form as they were sent, to scan them for viruses . . . all that is left for the senders and the recipients to work out for themselves. End to end. As long as messages are formatted in accordance with the Network Layer addressing rules, the Network Layer protocols will get them to the right place; what happens next is none of its concern, any more than what those lawyers are saying to one another is of any concern to the postal system's Transport Layer. Many different applications can use the same Network Layer protocols for moving bits around from one place to another, just as English-speaking lawyers and French-speaking doctors and Chinese-speaking auto parts distributors can all use the same postal system to deliver mail.

Smart machines, connected to a dumb network. Complicated and sophisticated applications, and a network doing nothing more than moving bits around as directed by those applications. That's the Internet. All the interesting stuff is at the edges—the network just gets the bits there, as quickly and efficiently as possible.[2]

It's worth keeping this in mind the next time you read something like "the Chinese government is cracking down on the Internet," or that "the Internet is transforming retail operations in the [fill in the blank] industry," or about "Internet gambling," or "Internet pornography," or even "Internet law" or "Internet governance." This "Internet" that everyone is talking about is, fundamentally, nothing more than a gigantic global machine designed to move zeroes and ones from one place to another.

End-to-end design is not the same as decentralization. The postal network, for example, is a **centralized** e2e network; a single institution (the post office) is given the responsibility for implementing the Transport Layer protocols (centralization), and those protocols focus on a single task: getting messages reliably from point A to point B across the network (e2e). Users don't have to know anything about the Transport Layer protocols in order to communicate with one another, as long as they comply with the simple addressing rules imposed by the lower-level rules. Conversely, as long as messages are addressed properly, the Transport Layer protocols can do their job without regard to what the messages they're moving around might "mean."

The Internet, though, is both decentralized and end-to-end. To appreciate how remarkable a thing that is, consider its opposite: the good old telephone

---

2   Mark Lemley and Lawrence Lessig put it this way:

> [End-to-end] counsels that the "intelligence" in a network should be located at the top of a layered system—at its "ends," where users put information and applications onto the network. The communications protocols themselves (the "pipes" through which information flows) should be as simple and as general as possible.

> Or, in the words of a prominent networking textbook:

> Put simply, [e2e means] that the final decisions should always be made by the users themselves, that trying to supplement them by intelligence **inside** the network is redundant, and that the networking functions should thus be delegated as much as possible outside the network.

network. Though different countries built their own telephone networks differing in some details, the basic structure was always the same: telephone networks link **dumb machines to a smart network**. The dumb machines, of course, are "telephones," which were, for most of the one hundred years or so during which the telephone network came to dominate global communications, the dumbest machines imaginable—not much more, really, than a microphone and a speaker glued together. The network, though, was really smart—it had to be, because those machines were so dumb. All of the information-processing "intelligence" required to connect two machines together over the telephone network is concentrated **inside** the network, in the Network Layer, where a zillion little switches get flipped all across the network, the effect of which is to connect a single wire leading from one telephone to the other.[3]

It, too, is a neat little bit of engineering—something of a marvel, when you think about it. But on a smart network like this, innovation itself is centralized; new services (conference calling, say, or call forwarding) can come only from inside the network itself, via reprogramming of all those switches, and only those who have access to the (very, very complicated) software that controls the switches can design new services without messing up the network.

---

3   This is probably as good a place as any to try to clarify the often-confusing relationship between two very different networks—the Internet, on the one hand, and the global telephone network (sometimes called the PSTN [Public-Switched Telephone Network], or sometimes POTS—Plain Old Telephone Service) on the other.

It's confusing, in part, because the two networks exist side-by-side (you and I can easily talk over the PSTN network while simultaneously exchanging email over the Internet), and they even, at times, share the same physical infrastructure—the same cables and wires—for transmitting messages. And to make matters even more confusing, it's quite easy to jump between networks; many people, for example, access the Internet via "dial-up" Internet service, which involves a crossover between the two networks: (a) A places an ordinary telephone call to her Internet Service Provider over the PSTN network; (b) A's ISP takes the information transmitted by A during the telephone call—a message intended for B, for example—and sends it over the Internet to its intended destination. In reverse, A's ISP sends to A messages it receives from elsewhere on the Internet that are addressed to A over their PSTN connection. (See fig. 5.5 in the appendix.)

Although they operate side by side and pass information back and forth this way, the two networks could hardly be more different in terms of what goes on inside those clouds, i.e., how they move information from place to place.

The Internet, we saw, uses "distributed routing" to get messages where they are supposed to go. Each packet constituting A's message to B bounces around from one machine to the next until it reaches its destination.

Paradoxically (or perhaps not so paradoxically), being stupid helped that little TCP/IP network become "the Internet." Because the network layer protocols are kept so simple, needing only to know the address of the machine to which each string of bits is to be sent, it doesn't matter (to the network) what language was used to create the string of bits, what language should be used to interpret it, or what it might "mean"; the machines at the end-points can figure all of that out. All that matters when a machine attempts to join the Internet (see fig. 5.6) is that, whatever else it may be doing, it uses the correct Network Layer addressing rules—the Internet Protocols—when it delivers bit-strings to the network for processing. This is why, as I mentioned earlier, TCP/IP makes it easy to link whole **networks** together into inter-networks. For all the TCP/IP network knows (or cares), a new participant might itself be part of, or even the hub of, a whole network of its own, using some operating system(s) totally foreign to everyone else on the network. (See fig. 5.6.) It doesn't matter, for purposes of joining the TCP/IP network, what machine L is doing in its spare (i.e., off-network) time—what language(s) **it** uses to communicate with the members of its own *sub*-network (i.e., its own internal networking system protocols), what applications it runs, or what operating system(s) it uses. The only thing that matters is that when L communicates over the TCP/IP network—when it sends something to machine H for distribution over the inter-network—it addresses the message properly (i.e., in accordance with the TCP/IP rules).

———————

Instead of Internet-style distributed packet-routing, the PSTN uses a technique known as "circuit-switching" to get information from one point on the network to another. When two parties—A and A's ISP in fig. 5.5, for instance, or you and your uncle Al in Fargo, North Dakota—communicate over the telephone network, the network sets a series of internal switches so that there is a single, direct path between the two parties, a single circuit connecting the two parties that is kept "open" for the entire duration of the call. All of the information moving between the two parties travels over this single circuit and through these switches, which serve those two users and **only** those two users until the call is terminated, at which point they can be reset to connect other users together.

It's a complicated bit of engineering, and it's all concentrated inside the network itself, in the software and processing that controls those switches; the network's end-points are just dumb telephones. Smart in the center, dumb at the edges. (It's also a far less efficient use of the available transmission capacity than packet-routing; keeping the circuit open and unavailable to other callers for the duration of a call, though convenient for billing purposes, means that a single set of switches can support one and only one connection at a time; during any pause in the conversation, they're just sitting idly by, waiting, doing nothing in particular.)

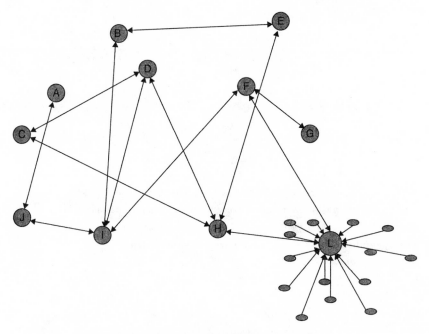

FIGURE 5.6 A New Network Entrant ("L") to the TCP/IP Inter-network.

So a TCP/IP network can not only add new members **anywhere** (thanks to distributed routing, see chap. 4), it can add **anyone** (thanks to e2e design).

In a world in which there are hundreds of thousands, or millions, of individual networks, each of which may consist of dozens, or hundreds, or thousands of individual machines, and each of which uses any one (or possibly more) of several dozen different available networking protocols, **being able to add any of them to an existing network at any point on that network** sounds like a good way to grow big in a hurry.

And when it comes to networks, remember, bigger is (all other things being equal) better.

CHAPTER SIX

CONNECTIONS

Doubt is wisdom.... Ignorance is preferable to error. He is less remote from the truth who believes nothing, than he who believes what is wrong.... The wise know too well their weakness to assume infallibility; he who knows most, knows best how little he knows.

TJ TO MARQUIS DE CHASTELLUX, JUNE 7, 1785/TJ *NOTES ON THE STATE OF VIRGINIA*

It takes something—courage? insensitivity? obtuseness? all of the above?—to expose one's ignorance to the world in print. It's embarrassing to keep pointing out things you don't understand; it undermines one's credentials as an "expert," and it can be unsettling to readers, who, one assumes, don't want to know what you don't know but what you do know. "Focus on what you do understand and can explain," one imagines them saying; "save what you don't and can't for your **next** book, after you've figured it out."

Whatever it takes, Jefferson surely had it, in spades. I know of no other writer more willing to utter the words "I don't understand this" than he. For someone who knew so much, who had so much information about the world at his fingertips—someone who could write *Notes on the State of Virginia*—he is remarkably candid about his own ignorance; *Notes* is as much a catalogue of the things Jefferson did **not** understand as of those he did.[1]

In a sense, this was the whole point of the intellectual enterprise, for Jefferson—identifying those things that are, with our current understanding, inexplicable. *He who knows most, knows best how little he knows.* Nobody believed more fervently than

---

1   Among the many questions Jefferson asked but could not answer in *Notes on the State of Virginia*: Why was there pumice—a rock of volcanic origin—floating in the Mississippi River? [Query 4] Why was there water inside "Madison's cave" in western Virginia, and where did it come from? [Query 5] What causes "blowing caves" (Query 5) and "siphon fountains" (Query 6)? Were there really (as some had reported) marble deposits in Kentucky? What

Jefferson that the important intellectual action is always at the frontier, the place where collective knowledge and understanding butt up against ignorance, the border between The Land of What We Know and The Land of What We Don't Know. And nobody believed more fervently than Jefferson that science and human knowledge would, over time, push that boundary "outward," converting territory within Not-Known to Known. *The general spread of the light of science*, he called it in the very last letter he ever wrote:

> *When I contemplate the immense advances in science and discoveries which have been made within the period of my life, I look forward with confidence to equal advances by the present generation, and I have no doubt they will consequently be as much wiser than we have been as we than our fathers were, and they than the burners of witches.*

insects live in Virginia? Do medicinal springs actually work? If so, how? Are long moss, reed, myrtle, swamp laurel, holly, and cypress absent from the Virginia highlands because it's too cold there, or for some other reason? [all from Query 6]

My two favorites: first, Jefferson's account of an optical illusion that really had him scratching his head, a *phenomenon that seamen call "looming."*

> *Rare at land, though frequent at sea, its principal effect is to make distant objects appear larger, in opposition to the general law of vision, by which they are diminished. I knew an instance, at Yorktown … wherein a canoe with three men, at a great distance, was taken for a ship with its three masts. I am little acquainted with the phenomenon as it shows itself at sea; but at Monticello it is familiar. There is a solitary mountain about 40 miles off, in the South, whose natural shape, as presented to view there, is a regular cone; but, by the effect of looming, it sometimes subsides almost totally into the horizon; sometimes it rises more acute and more elevated; sometimes it is hemispherical; and sometimes its sides are perpendicular, its top flat, and as broad as its base. In short it assumes at times the most whimsical shapes, and all these perhaps successively in the same morning.*

And in Query 7, he sinks his teeth into an even tougher (and, as it turns out, more profound) question: *Why are there sea-shells in the mountains?*

> *Near the eastern foot of the North mountain are immense bodies of Schist, containing impressions of shells in a variety of forms. I have also received petrified shells of very different kinds from the first sources of the Kentucky, which bear no resemblance to any I have ever seen on the tide-waters. It is said that shells are found in the Andes, in South-America, fifteen thousand feet above the level of the ocean.*

Another terrific Jeffersonian question. How **did** they get there? It would take over a century before we had an answer (based on an understanding of the movement of continental plates, the geological processes of mountain-building, and the sheer immensity of geological time, none of which was understood in the slightest degree in 1787).

And he had an almost mystical belief in science's power to improve, slowly but inexorably, the human condition.[2]

So here's an odd observation for you. As I said earlier, members of a TCP/IP network can connect themselves together "any which way." It turns out that something remarkable happened when they did. As the 500 million or so machines connected themselves together over the past several decades, a striking regularity in the pattern of their connections emerged. If we take a big sample of several hundred thousand of those machines and count the number of connections per machine, the results look like this:

---

2 Advances in human knowledge, and the spread of freedom and liberty, were, for Jefferson, two sides of the same coin, *grounds for hope that the general spread of the light of science would allow people to assume the blessings and security of self-government by bursting the chains under which monkish ignorance and superstition had persuaded them to bind themselves.*

> *I brand as cowardly the idea that the human mind is incapable of further advances. This is precisely the doctrine which the present despots of the earth are inculcating, & their friends here re-echoing & applying especially to religion & politics: that it is not probable that any thing better will be discovered than what was known to our fathers. We are to look backwards then & not forwards for the improvement of science, & to find it amidst feudal barbarisms and the fires of Spital-fields!*
>
> *But thank heaven the American mind is already too much opened, to listen to these impostures. While the art of printing is left to us, science can never be retrograde; what is once acquired of real knowledge can never be lost. To preserve the freedom of the human mind then & freedom of the press, every spirit should be ready to devote itself to martyrdom; for as long as we may think as we will, & speak as we think, the condition of man will proceed in improvement.*

In his excitement over the subject, he sometimes got carried away and mixed up his metaphors, calling freedom *the first-born daughter of science* one day and the *great parent of science* the next, but the idea was clear in his mind: Science begets freedom, and freedom begets science. Writing to Joseph Willard, president of Harvard College, about the prospects for the development of science in the United States:

> *What a field have we at our doors to signalise ourselves in! The Botany of America is far from being exhausted, its Mineralogy is untouched, and its Natural History or Zoology, totally mistaken and misrepresented. As far as I have seen, there is not one single species of terrestrial birds common to Europe and America, and question if there be a single species of quadrupeds. (Domestic animals are to be excepted.) It is for such institutions as that over which you preside so worthily, Sir, to do justice to our country, its productions and its genius. It is the work to which the young men, whom you are forming, should lay their hands. We have spent the prime of our lives in procuring them the precious blessing of liberty. Let them spend theirs in shewing that it is the great parent of science and of virtue; and that a nation will be great in both, always in proportion as it is free.*

Internet Connectivity

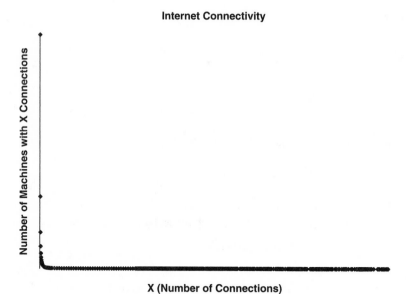

FIGURE 6.1 Internet Connectivity.

It's unexpected, and startling—as startling, I think, as those seashells in the mountains. We might have expected the distribution to be random (see fig. 6.2), or perhaps to follow the familiar "bell curve" of the Normal (or "Gaussian") Distribution (see fig. 6.3).

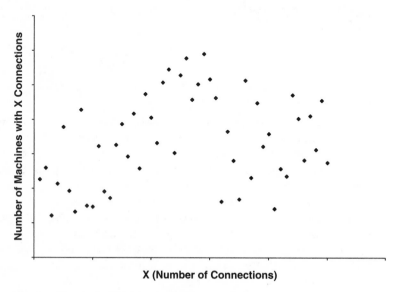

FIGURE 6.2 Hypothetical Random Distribution.

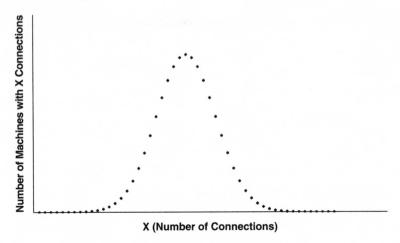

FIGURE 6.3   Hypothetical Normal Distribution.

Instead, we see that the distribution in figure 6.1 has a very different, lop-sided (or "skewed," the statisticians would say) shape: **Lots** of machines have a mere handful of connections (the left-hand portion of the curve), and, conversely, a handful of machines have lots of connections (the right-hand portion of the curve). The most-connected 1 percent of all machines (the points way out there on the right-hand side of the curve) account for more than **one-third** of the total number of connections in the sample as a whole.[3]

The distribution of connections follows a mathematical function known as a "power law": the number of machines with X connections is inversely proportional to X raised to some power:

$$Y \sim 1/X^{[\text{constant}]}$$

---

3   As the authors of the study put it:

> The wide adoption of the Internet has fundamentally altered the ways in which we communicate, gather information, conduct businesses and make purchases. As the use of the World Wide Web and email skyrocketed, computer scientists and physicists rushed to characterize this new phenomenon. While initially they were surprised by the tremendous variety the Internet demonstrated in the size of its features, they soon discovered a widespread pattern in their measurements: there are many small elements contained within the Web, but few large ones. A few sites consist of millions of pages, but millions of sites only contain a handful of pages. Few sites contain millions of links, but many sites have one or two. Millions of users flock to a few select sites, giving little attention to millions of others. (Lada Adamic and Bernardo Huberman, "Zipf's Law and the Internet," 3 *Glottometrics* 143 [2002].)

or, equivalently,

$$Y \sim X^{-[\text{constant}]}$$

We can see how closely it follows a power law function by plotting the data along **logarithmic** X- and Y-axes, where each step along the axis represents a ten-fold increase in the number of connections (X-axis) and the number of machines (Y-axis). Power law distributions plot as a straight line against logarithmic axes,[4] and the Internet connection data fall almost perfectly along a straight line:

Internet Connectivity–Logarithmic Scales

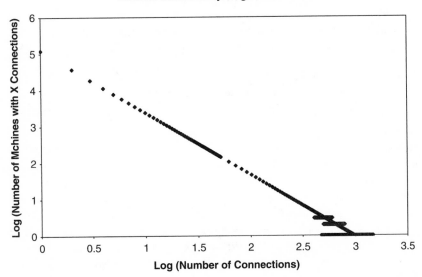

FIGURE 6.4 Internet Connectivity—Logarithmic Scales.

Many other measures of Internet connectivity—the number of in-links from, and out-links to, different websites, for example, the distribution of message volume over time, the number of visitors to different websites—are similarly distributed according to a power law distribution.

---

4 A little simple mathematics will show why plotting log(Y) against log(X) yields a straight line when Y is a power law function of X. Suppose

$$Y = 75 \times X^{-2}$$

Taking logarithms of both sides of this equation:

$$\log (Y) = \log (75) + (-2) \times \log (X)$$

which, you may recall from high school geometry, is the equation of a straight line with a Y-intercept at 75 and a slope of –2.

How does it happen? Nobody plans for it to be that way, for there is nobody (at least, on a TCP/IP network) in a position to do so even if they wanted to; there's no central monitor, no Director, no Control Board, that is in a position to make sure that the number of connections or links follows this (or any other) particular distribution, nobody who orders more connections for machine #429 to "match" an increase in #5123's connections (and thereby maintain the shape of the overall distribution), or more links to the website at **www.xyz.com** when the number of links to **www.123.com** changes. It's as though the machines were coordinating their activities in some way, and quite precisely at that—but how?

And why **this** particular distribution—the power law? Power law distributions have some extremely unusual characteristics, mathematically speaking—highly asymmetric,[5] "long-tailed,"[6] and "scale-free."[7] Notwithstanding those rather odd features, they appear to be ubiquitous in the physical, social, and biological worlds:

> Power law distributions occur in an extraordinarily diverse range of phenomena: the sizes of cities, earthquakes, moon craters, solar flares, computer files, and wars, the frequency of use of words in any human language, the frequency of occurrence

---

5   Unlike the bell curve of the Normal Distribution, where most observations cluster around the average, or mean, value, the vast majority of observations in a power law distribution will be far **below** the mean ((lots of machines with very few connections), and a small number of observations will be far above the mean (a few machines with many).

6   Power law distributions are "long-tailed" distributions in the sense that observations 10, or 100, or 1,000 times greater than the average have a low, but nonetheless appreciable, likelihood of appearing. Human height obeys a Normal Distribution (with a mean of around 5.5 feet); if it were distributed according to a power law, walking about town would be a very strange experience indeed; every so often you'd come across someone 20 feet tall, and, on occasion, there'd be the odd 100-, or 1,000-footer.

7   Power law distributions are "scale-free" in the sense that they have no natural, or correct, scale; they have the same shape and mathematical characteristics at **all** scales, no matter how much you "zoom in" or "zoom out." Normal distributions only look like normal distributions—bell-shaped, symmetrical around the mean value—when viewed at the correct scale; if you change the scale by "zooming in," say, on the people between 5.2 and 5.3 feet tall, or between 6.8 and 6.9 feet tall, the distribution won't be look bell-shaped any more. (See fig. 6.5 in the appendix.)

But power law distributions always look the same, no matter where on the curve you look, and no matter what magnification scale you use; the distribution of the number of machines with between 1 and 10,000 connections will look like a power law, as will the distribution of the number of machines with between 1,000 and 2,000 connections, or between 1,500 and 1,600. It's a bit dizzying—no matter how you zoom in or out, the distribution stays the same. It's as if power law curves were made up of lots and lots of little tiny power law curves; no matter how much we magnify it, it always looks the same. (See fig. 6.6 in the appendix.)

of personal names, the numbers of papers scientists write, the number of citations received by papers, the number of hits on web pages, the sales of books, music recordings and almost every other branded commodity, the numbers of species in biological taxa, people's annual incomes and a host of other variables all follow power-law distributions.[8]

As far as I can tell, nobody is certain precisely how to account for this—how to explain why the number of visitors to websites, the population of Brazilian cities, the intensity of earthquakes in the Pacific Basin, the frequency of word usage in Romanian, and the number of enzyme catalysts in the flatworm cell all show the same pattern. There is, at present, an enormous amount of energy and research being devoted to resolving that question, attempting to determine whether there is some unifying mechanism that accounts for the appearance of this distribution across these very different phenomena (and what that mechanism might be). I'm reasonably certain that if you happen to be reading this book fifty or one hundred years from now, you are probably finding all of this groping around for an explanation pretty funny—as funny as we find Jefferson's groping around for an explanation of those seashells, or why nobody had yet brought back a live mammoth from Ohio—a nice illustration of just how little we understood, back then, about how the world works.

But whatever the explanation might turn out to be—and even whether there *is* any one, unified explanation for these diverse phenomena—the fact that machines on the Internet connect together in this power law manner was of crucial importance

---

8 Mark Newman, "Power Laws, Pareto distributions, and Zipf's Law," available at http://arxiv. org/abs/cond-mat/0412004. Newman's list could be expanded almost ad infinitum—the life spans of organisms, the size of firms, the distribution of wealth and income, the frequency of words in spoken and written text, the number of links between enzymes in cellular metabolic networks, the intensity of earthquakes, the population size and biomass of different species within a patch of forest, the size of meteor impact craters, the variations in stock prices, the relative frequencies of particular sequences in DNA fragments, the rate at which species go extinct, the number of in- and out-links within protein networks, the distribution of organism life spans and metabolic rates), to name just those I happen to know something about—all are distributed according to power laws. Specialists in many different disciplines have different names for this common phenomenon—seismologists call it the "Gutenberg-Richter Law," economists "Pareto's Law," linguists "Zipf's Law," information scientists "Lotka's Law," geographers "the City-Size Rule," comparative anatomists and zoologists "Laws of Allometric Scaling," but they're all describing the same pattern. Pick any university at random, and you will easily find people in a dozen different departments–economics, political science, linguistics, planetary physics, evolutionary biology, cellular and molecular biology, systems engineering–working on some version of it.

for allowing this inter-network to scale as well as it did. It meant that the "distance" between any two machines on the inter-network (measured as the number of intermediate "hops" between them) is **much** smaller, and increases **much** more slowly as the network grows, than expected.

Networks in which connectivity follows a power law are what network scientists call "small worlds," because they can grow to immense size while remaining astonishingly compact with respect to getting from one point on the network to the other. In power law networks, the average distance between any two members increases, roughly, only as fast as the **logarithm** of network size—so a **tenfold** increase in the size of the network adds, on average, only a one additional hop between all members. [9]

---

9   For instance, the connectivity between social acquaintances follows a power law distribution quite precisely (lots of people with small numbers of acquaintances, a small number of people with many); if you take a random sample of a hundred thousand, or a hundred million, people, and ask each of them to count the people with whom they are on a first-name basis, the resulting distribution would look just like the distribution of Internet connectivity shown in figure 6.1. As a result, if we were to choose any two people at random from among the 200 million or so U.S. adults, for example—you and I, say—there will be, on average, somewhere between six and twenty (researchers disagree on the precise number) "hops" from one to the other through the network (i.e., a friend of mine has a friend who has a friend who has a friend who is a friend of yours—six hops).

It really is remarkable, when you think about it—200 million people is a lot of people, but each is connected to everyone else, on average, in no more than a handful of hops.

This is the basis for the well-known (and quite startling) "six degrees of separation" (or "six degrees of Kevin Bacon") phenomenon, which has become so deeply engrained in popular culture in such a remarkably short period of time. The original experiment from which the meme derives, conducted by Stanley Milgram in the 1960s, involved a kind of distributed routing in realspace. Milgram gave a bunch of letters, addressed to actual people in Massachusetts, to a group of randomly selected people in Kansas and Nebraska; he asked them to try to get the letters to the designated recipients using the "routing rule" that you could give a letter only to someone you knew on a first-name basis (who could, in turn, give it only to someone he/she knew on a first-name basis, and so on). Much to Milgram's astonishment, over half of the letters actually arrived at their destinations—and the median number of "hops" they took to get there was between five and six—hence the quasi-folkloric meme that we're all only "six degrees of separation" from everyone else in the country. The "Kevin Bacon" reference is to the popular "six degrees of Kevin Bacon" game, in which players try to connect any randomly chosen actor or actress to Kevin Bacon via the movies in which they have appeared together—Bela Lugosi was in *Abbott and Costello Meet Frankenstein* with Vincent Price, Vincent Price was in *The Raven* with Jack Nicholson, and Jack Nicholson was in *A Few Good Men* with Kevin Bacon (giving Bela Lugosi a "Kevin Bacon number" of three). See The Oracle of Bacon at Virginia, http://oracleofbacon.org/.

It doesn't sound like a big deal. But it is. To put it in perspective: In the late 1990s, there were around 800 million documents on the power law/small world network known as the World Wide Web, and you could, on average, get from any one page to any other page, following the hyperlinks from one page to another, in around nineteen steps. Pretty amazing. But even more amazing: if you were to increase the size of this network **100-fold**—adding an additional **80 billion new pages**—the average distance from any one page to any other page would increase **only by two** (to around twenty-one).

Now **that's** scaling! 80 billion new pages is a lot of pages—but in a network configured as a "small world," they're not going to have much of an impact on the length of the pathways between any two points. Amazing! Let the network machines connect themselves together "any which way" and it turns out that you get a network that can grow and grow and grow and grow with hardly any increase in the amount of "bouncing around" necessary to get from one end to the other.

It's yet another reason **this** inter-network could become "the Internet." Distributed routing—bouncing messages from machine to machine—can scale on a small world network, because you can add orders of magnitude more machines, and more information, without proportionally increasing the length of the journey from one point on the network to any other point. It doesn't take hundreds of thousands, or millions, of hops to get a message from any one of the 500-million machines to any other; if it did, the Internet would long ago have bogged down under the accumulated weight.[10]

---

10 There's an important caveat here: knowing that there exists a path, of no more than twenty "hops" or so on average, between any two machines on the inter-network is not the same as finding that path, a task that can be, in large, complicated networks, a very difficult challenge. As I mentioned earlier, distributed routing on the TCP/IP network does not, in fact, bounce messages from machine to machine at random; the routing protocols have, over the past several decades, been refined to incorporate a variety of algorithms designed to find the shortest path between network machines (or a reasonable approximation) with a minimum amount of computing effort, and to route messages accordingly.

CHAPTER SEVEN

LANGUAGE I

A language cannot be too rich. The more copious [it is], *the more susceptible of embellishment it will become... The variety of dialects constitutes* [its] *riches.*

TJ TO J. EVELYN DENISON, NOVEMBER 9, 1825/TJ TO JOHN WALDO, AUGUST 16, 1813

Remember agar, from high school biology class? Agar is the name given to the class of disgusting nutrient-rich gelatinous slops (consisting mostly of simple sugars) used in laboratories throughout the world as a medium for growing bacteria and other microbial organisms. Put some agar into a dish and leave it out on the windowsill overnight, and in the morning you'll have a dazzling stew of dozens of different kinds of microbes that have fallen out of the air and into the soup and started multiplying.

The TCP/IP network is like that—it's an agar, not for growing the little bits of code we call microbes but for growing the little bits of code we call computer applications and computer languages.

Take the World Wide Web, for example. In the late 1980s, Tim Berners-Lee and Robert Cailliau, two physicists working at CERN (the "Conseil Européen pour la Recherche Nucleaire," or European Center for Nuclear Research) in the Jura Mountains in western Switzerland, and some colleagues came up with an idea for a new protocol to run in the Application Layer, a new set of rules for generating and interpreting the strings of bits that the TCP/IP Network Layer would carry from place to place. Their new protocol would let you do two things:

(a) embed information into a file regarding the existence and the location of **other** files ("hypertext links"); and

(b) request copies of those other files.

To make this work, they needed, first, some standardized format for these hypertext documents, i.e., rules about how these "hypertext links," containing the information about the existence of other files, were to be embedded into documents. They called this set of rules "HTML," the Hyper Text Markup Language. Second, they needed to standardize a protocol for communication between "web servers" (i.e., machines with files that had been formatted in accordance with the HTML rules) and "web browsers" (machines capable of decoding and displaying those files), a kind of grammar that would enable "browsers" to request files from "servers" and for "servers" to send those files (the hypertext transfer protocol, "HTTP"). Finally, they needed some standard addressing format that would be used to identify the location of these remote files (the uniform resource locator ["URL"] system).

Those are large tasks, to be sure. But it's what they **didn't** need that is more interesting; they didn't need to tell anyone or get anyone's permission to start using their new language over the existing TCP/IP network. The Network Layer will do its job—moving bits from one place to another—regardless of what's happening up there in the Application Layer. There's nobody from whom they needed to obtain authorization or permission to use their new application protocols, nobody at Internet Central who first had to certify that the new language was OK—that it wouldn't interfere with other protocols, for example, or that it worked as Berners-Lee and Cailliau said it did, or that it was consistent with some larger policy goal for the Internet. There is no Internet Central, of course—that's the point: a stupid network doesn't need a brain, a central information-processing and information-storage "command center," and this is, as I said earlier, a very, very stupid network. It just moves bits from one place to another; the Network Layer protocols don't have to "understand" (i.e., to process, or decode, or otherwise act upon) anything that's going in the higher levels of the protocol stack to do what they are supposed to do, which is just to get messages where they're supposed to go.

So once Berners-Lee and Cailliau had developed what they believed to be working versions of their new protocols, they could simply try them out for themselves. They could just start using them to communicate with each another (and with anyone else they could persuade to "speak" in the new language), using the existing TCP/IP network to transport their requests and their files as directed. **End-to-end**. It didn't matter, to the network or to any of the other machines on the network, that the messages traveling between Berners-Lee and Cailliau were completely unintelligible to all but a handful of machines. It's all just ones and zeroes; the network layer would treat these strings of ones and zeroes the way it treats all the others, shuffling them along as directed, from sender to recipient.

It's a funny way to run a network, perhaps[1]—but it seems to have worked, at least as an agar, a medium for growing things. When Berners-Lee and Cailliau launched

---

[1] Again, the contrast is with the POTS telephone network (see note 3, chap. 5). The telephone network is so smart, concentrating so much complicated processing in the network layer,

their new protocol, they hadn't really created the "World Wide Web" at all, of course; they had created the "Just-a-Few-Folks-at-CERN-Wide Web," linking together a handful of machines capable of communicating in the new language. Useful and interesting, perhaps, for the (very small) community of researchers at CERN, but not particularly noteworthy (let alone earth-shattering).

Things get a lot more interesting when the protocol spreads—when the CWW (the CERN Wide Web) becomes the World Wide Web, when large numbers of machines across the entire TCP/IP network speak the new language to one another, linking and cross-linking and cross-cross-linking to each other's documents using the new protocols. Language communities are themselves a kind of network, sub-ject to the same bigger-is-better scaling principle as other networks: the more speakers of a language there are, the more useful and powerful the language is to **each** of them. So a place where languages are being born is a much more interesting place if it allows them—some of them, at least—to grow in size.

The TCP/IP network turns out to be such a place. It was not at all obvious that it would be so; indeed, one might have thought that the absence of a central con-trol mechanism would make it impossibly difficult for languages to grow in size. Because there's nobody "in charge" of the inter-network, there's nobody to "adopt" the new HTTP protocol, no switch that can be thrown to convert everyone on the inter-network into HTTP compliance, nobody with the authority (or the ability) to mandate the use of the new language, to declare that from now HTTP-compliant code can travel over the network. End-to-end. Users have to decide for themselves which protocol(s) to use—which languages their machines will speak. The CWW can become the WWW only when the several hundred thousand machines (and networks) on the Internet in 1990 (not to mention the hundreds of millions more to come) are configured to speak the new language, i.e. capable of comprehending and creating messages using the new protocol.

We'd surely say it couldn't possibly happen—what odds would you have given Berners-Lee and Cailliau in 1990 that it **would** happen?—except, of course, for the fact that it did happen. And virtually overnight, at that.

Innovation on this inter-network doesn't come from the center spreading out-ward; it comes from the periphery, spreading in and around. (And on this inter-network, remember, the "periphery" is growing in size, geometrically, all the time.) It has happened again and again on the Internet. Napster is the poster child here; a nineteen-year-old college dropout right out of Central Casting develops a string of code and throws it onto the inter-network, and twelve months later it has spread

---

that the applications have to be very, very simple. It took decades before something as simple as Caller ID was added to the applications available on the POTS network, because adding Caller ID functionality meant, literally, reprogramming **the whole network**.

to more than 70 **million** users. Now that's scaling! The Web, email, peer-to-peer file-sharing, instant messaging, VOIP (Voice over Internet Protocol) applications (like Skype), applications that let you collaborate on a manuscript, place bets on football games in real time, or play chess or Dungeons and Dragons with thousands of other people simultaneously... it's a lot of new languages, and a lot of innovation, in a couple of decades. And these are just the ones that got big, the ones that took root in the medium and grew to prodigious size. For every Napster or Skype or Bit-Torrent or World of Warcraft, there are dozens, or hundreds, or thousands—nobody knows, or can know, for sure (which is also part of the point)—of new languages whose bloom is much smaller and much briefer.

It was the seemingly unending supply of new applications, new languages that could make those bits do useful and interesting things, running "over the Internet"—"on top" of the Network Layer protocols—that made **this** inter-network so interesting, and that attracted users to it (which then, of course, made it even **more** attractive to others—Metcalfe's Law!). All that the Network Layer protocols had to do was to move the bits around as directed from one place to another—and to be able to handle the extraordinary surge in the number of messages (and the number of network members) that would accompany each successful new application.

Perhaps it was a coincidence that the network that became "the Internet" was the one that operated this way: end-to-end, innovations coming from the edges via this strange kind of creeping consensus among users, no centralized control. I doubt it, though.

There is a lot that we do not understand about how this phenomenon works—about **how** languages grow on the Net, about how consensus among users about the use of any particular language does (or does not) develop, about the different forms that language growth can take, about the determinants of growth rates, about the "shape" of different language networks, or about the thousands of other questions that would form part of a complete natural history of the Internet. I'd settle for just a picture, a way to visualize—in living color, as it were—this throbbing mass of linguistic organisms being born and growing and dying in the giant petri dish of the TCP/IP network; it would be an impressive sight, and we might better appreciate how spectacular—even beautiful—it is.

Though beauty, I suppose, is always in the eye of the beholder. Beautiful or not, though, it does (speaking of Napster) raise a question: Who controls these languages of cyberspace? Who decides what languages we may use, and what we may say? Who "governs" here?

INTERLUDE

TWO KINDS OF PEOPLE

Men by their constitution are naturally divided into two parties.... The division is founded in the nature of man; it has existed from the first establishment of governments to the present day [and] will continue through all future time.... In every country these two parties exist; and in every one where they are free to think, speak, and write, they will declare themselves. Call them Whigs and Tories; Republicans and Federalists; Jacobins and Ultras; Liberals and Serviles; Aristocrats and Democrats, or by whatever name you please, they are the same parties still, and pursue the same objects.

TJ TO HENRY LEE, AUGUST 10, 1824/TJ TO JOEL BARLOW, MAY 3, 1802

There is an old joke: There are two kinds of people in the world—those who think there are two kinds of people in the world, and those who don't.[1]

But I'm with Jefferson on this one; I think there really **are** two kinds of people in the world (though I am not as certain as he was that the division is *founded in the nature of man*—part of *natural, as well as civil, history*, as he put it elsewhere). He usually called them, using language that is now decidedly out of style, "whigs" and "tories." I prefer "Jeffersonians" and "Hamiltonians."

They are the two great pole stars in American politics, Thomas Jefferson and Alexander Hamilton—each thoughtful, brilliant, often profound, always unafraid of new ideas and new intellectual challenges. You couldn't have made up a more extraordinary pair of combatants for the soul of the new nation—as Jonathan Spence put it, one of history's uses being to remind us how unlikely things can be. Their feud is the longest-running in American political history, for they stood on opposite shores of a great intellectual divide, a divide that encapsulates something fundamental in the way we think about society and government. In the "balance between liberty and authority," Merrill Peterson wrote, "Jefferson tipped the former scale, Hamilton the latter:

> One despised, the other idolized, rulership. One located the strength of the republic in the diffuse energies of a free society, the other in the consolidation of authority.... Hamilton feared most the ignorance and tumult of the people, Jefferson

---

1 Or, a variant I heard recently: There are 10 kinds of people in the world—those who understand binary notation and those who don't.

feared the irresponsibility of rulers independent of them. Hamilton labeled his rival a visionary and a demagogue, while Jefferson named his a corrupter, a monarchist, and an Angloman.

Jefferson and Jeffersonians think centrifugally, outwards from the center. End to end, as it were: Liberty, Chaos, The Many, Diffusion. Hamilton and Hamiltonians think centripetally, towards the center: Authority, Order, The Few, Concentration. Jeffersonians love turbulence—*I like a little rebellion now and then; it is like a storm in the atmosphere*—while Hamiltonians prize stability: when the "zeal for liberty becomes predominant and excessive," Hamilton wrote, "only the principle of strength and stability in the organization of our government," and the "vigor in its operations," could put things right. Jeffersonians mistrust concentrated power: *It is not by the consolidation or concentration of powers, but by their **distribution**, that good government is effected... Were we directed from Washington when to sow, and when to reap, we should soon want bread.* Hamiltonians counter that "too little power is as dangerous as too much; as too much power leads to despotism, too little leads to anarchy, and both eventually to the ruin of the people." Jeffersonians look forward, drawing inspiration from unpredictability and possibility; *I like the dreams of the future better than the history of the past.* Hamiltonians look back, drawing inspiration from the certainty of the past and from the ideas that have proven themselves over time.

Jeffersonians think that governments can be saved by their people: *The will of the people... is the only legitimate foundation of any government, [and] the people of every country are the only safe guardian of their own rights... No other depositories of power have ever yet been found, which did not end in converting to their own profit the earnings of those committed to their charge....* To Hamiltonians, it is the other way around: "The people are turbulent and changing; they seldom judge or determine right... Mankind in general [are] vicious... Our prevailing passions are ambition and interest; and it will ever be the duty of government to avail itself of those passions, in order to make them subservient to the public good."

It was an extraordinary conversation about (among other things) the shape of the network they were helping to build, with Hamiltonians in the center and Jeffersonians at the edge. Much of the history of the early days of the American republic can be (and has been) described in terms of the opposition between these two great competing visions. On virtually every issue, large and small, facing the new nation—states' rights versus a strong national government, the need for a central bank, free trade versus mercantilism, the location of the national capital, the value of naval versus land-based armed forces, agriculture versus manufacturing, legislative versus executive power, a foreign policy tilting toward France versus a foreign policy tilting toward England—the two men staked out opposing positions, and two parties, Republican and Federalist, coalesced around their views.

Jeffersonian energy and Hamiltonian power. Jeffersonian chaos and Hamiltonian order. Jeffersonian liberty and Hamiltonian authority. The challenge for the

BOX I.1

JEFFERSON	HAMILTON

Government wherein the will of every one has a just influence...has its evils, the principal one of which is the turbulence to which it is subject. But weigh this against the oppressions of monarchy, and it becomes nothing. **Malo periculosam libertatem quam quietam servitutem.** [*I prefer the tumult of liberty to the quiet of servitude.*]

TJ TO JAMES MADISON,

JANUARY 30, 1787

The people of every country are the only safe guardian of their own rights, [and] the will of the people...is the only legitimate foundation of any government. Whenever the people are well-informed, they can be trusted with their own government; whenever things get so far wrong as to attract their notice, they may be relied on to set them to rights.... The cherishment of the people was our [party's] principle, the fear and distrust of them that of the other party.

TJ TO JOHN WYCHE, MAY 19, 1809

TJ TO DR. PRICE, JANUARY 8, 1789, AND

TJ TO JUSTICE WILLIAM JOHNSON,

JUNE 12, 1823

The voice of the people has been said to be the voice of God; however generally this maxim has been quoted and believed, it is not true in fact. The people are turbulent and changing; they seldom judge or determine right.

The rights of government are as essential to be defended as the rights of individuals. The security of the one is inseparable from that of the other.... History is full of examples where...a jealousy of power has...subverted liberty by clogging government with too great precautions for its security, or by leaving too wide a door for sedition and popular licentiousness. In a government framed for durable liberty, no less regard must be paid to giving the magistrate a proper degree of authority, to make and execute the laws with vigour, than to guarding against encroachments upon the rights of the community. As too much power leads to despotism, too little leads to anarchy, and both eventually to the ruin of the people.

HAMILTON, LETTER TO JOHN

DICKINSON (1783)

HAMILTON, *THE CONTINENTALIST* NO.

1 (1781)

new republic was to link them together, to find the sweet spot, the point of optimum tension, between the two. Determining who was right and who was wrong, who "won" and who "lost," is akin to determining whether the glass is actually half-full or half-empty.

Each had his triumphs (usually at the other's expense): Jefferson got Louisiana, Hamilton got a national bank; Jefferson got the Bill of Rights, Hamilton got his preferred interpretation of the powers "implied" by the Constitution; Jefferson got a national capital located far away from the dens of financial speculation in New York, Hamilton got debt financing.

It's as though the new country were oscillating between two great magnetic attractors, kept aloft by the powerful tug of two contrary forces.

Everyone takes his side, according to his constitution and the circumstances in which he is placed. Opinions, which are equally honest on both sides, should not affect personal esteem or social intercourse.... Difference of opinion leads to inquiry, and inquiry to truth....A truth that has never been opposed cannot acquire that firm and unwavering assent, which is given to that which has stood the test of a rigorous examination.

LOOKING WEST

Kentucky, the great wilderness beyond the western edge of the world,... seemed to the colonists along the eastern North-American seaboard as far away, nearly, and as difficult of approach, as had the problematical world beyond the western ocean to the times prior to Columbus. "A country there was, of this none could doubt who thought at all; but whether land or water, mountain or plain, fertility or barrenness, preponderated; whether it was inhabited by men or beasts, or both, or neither, they knew not."...Clinging narrowly to their new foothold, dependent still on sailing vessels for a contact none too swift or certain with "home," the colonists looked with fear to the west...Opposed to this lay the forbidden wealth of the Unknown.

WILLIAM CARLOS WILLIAMS, "THE DISCOVERY OF KENTUCKY"

That the United States came to span the entire expanse of territory from the Atlantic to the Pacific Ocean is, when you stop to think about it, really quite remarkable. The sheer immensity of it is so audacious; against the background of eighteenth-century Europe, it looks like the fourth grader whose hormones have kicked in too early, and who towers over his or her peers in the class photograph.

Some philosophers of history say that it was all quite inevitable, that, in the grand sweep of things, unstoppable forces—economic, demographic, and political—were at work, driving people west and, simultaneously, driving the settlements they occupied into the arms of the United States. Others say that history has no "inevitability" to it, that small, quasi-random events can have large consequences, that it all could have played out quite differently had certain things not transpired as they did—had, say, Aaron Burr gotten that one extra vote in the House of Representatives that would have made **him** president in 1800 (instead of Jefferson), or had the railroad locomotive been invented a few years later than it was, or had Lewis and Clark drowned on the banks of the Missouri, or...

I don't have a good enough theory of history to take a position one way or another. But I do know one thing: it sure didn't **seem** inevitable to many people—many very smart people—in 1787. In fact, not only did it not seem inevitable, it seemed, to many, hardly possible at all.

The central problem was one of scale: the Problem of the Extended Republic. How could a government remain true to "republican" principles—that the governed rule their governors, and that ultimate power is lodged in the people themselves[2]— when spread over large territories and large numbers of people?

The best and most advanced thinking of the time had it that it couldn't be done— certainly not on a continental scale. To begin with, it had never **been** done. Republics had always been small-scale affairs—the Roman Republic, Carthage, Athens, Iceland, the Florentine and Venetian Republics, the Swiss cantons—far smaller than even the state of Virginia in 1787, let alone the thirteen United States taken together, and positively microscopic when measured against the vast expanse of the entire American continent from ocean to ocean.[3] Larger states had always been despotic affairs, empires, not republics, ruled by the whim of one man—Caesar, Alexander the Great, the Tsar, the Emperor of China, Genghis Khan, Montezuma—and his

2   *The term "republic,"* as Jefferson put it, *is of very vague application in every language.* Including our own. As Akhil R. Amar has noted, there has been a fundamental shift in our use and understanding of the term over the past two hundred years or so. These days, as we learn in junior high school social studies class, "republics" are distinguished from "democracies": the former has representative institutions, while the latter involves direct action by all citizens acting en masse (in the manner of a New England town meeting or the Athenian assembly). Viewed from this perspective, the Founders' frequent references to "republican government" and "republicanism"—for instance, in the guarantee of Article IV of the Constitution that every state shall have "a Republican Form of Government"—is seen by some as reflecting an antidemocratic impulse, a desire to take control of the government out of the hands of the people and into a more select band of rulers.

Nothing could be more misguided. In eighteenth-century usage, the two terms were largely indistinguishable and interchangeable; the critical distinction was not between "republican" and "democratic" governance, but between "republican" and "democratic" governance on the one hand and monarchical or aristocratic governance on the other, between sovereignty lodged in the people and sovereignty lodged in a select ruling class. The *mother principle of republicanism,* Jefferson called it: *that all power is inherent in the people [and] that they may exercise it by themselves in all cases to which they think themselves competent.*

Government by its own citizens in mass, acting directly and personally, according to rules established by the majority.... Governments are republican only in proportion as every member composing it has his equal voice in the direction of its concerns, and only in proportion as they embody the will of their people, and execute it. The true foundation of republican government is the equal right of every citizen in his person and property, and in their management.

3   "World history...furnished no model of a genuinely democratic regime stretching across a continental expanse.... No democracy in world history had ever spanned so vast a range encompassing such diverse weather zones, dominant sects, labor systems, and local temperaments. The widely admired French writer Montesquieu was commonly read as suggesting it could not be done" (Akhil R. Amar, *America's Constitution: A Biography* (2005), 41).

chosen confederates, held together only by the projection of powerful military force under their command.

"Montesquieu's Law," it was called, in honor of the great French political philosopher who explained most cogently and comprehensively why republican government could survive **only** in small communities. In Gordon Wood's words:

> The best political science of the century, as expressed most pointedly but hardly exclusively by Montesquieu, had told them "that so extensive a territory as that of the United States, including such a variety of climates, productions, interests; and so great differences of manners, habits, and customs" could never be a single republican state. "No government formed on the principles of freedom can pervade all North America." An extended republic ... could never be "so competent to attend to the various local concerns and wants, of every particular district, as well as the peculiar [local] governments who are nearer the scene and possessed of superior means of information" ... The idea of a single republic ... one thousand miles in length, and eight hundred in breadth, and containing six millions of white inhabitants ... [is] "in itself an absurdity, and contrary to the whole experience of mankind." "Nothing would support government, in such a case as that, but military coercion."

From this perspective—the "European perspective," we might call it—the size of the new American republic that had declared itself into existence in 1776 was **already** its most serious liability.[4] Surely, were it to get bigger and attempt to project its authority across the continent, republican institutions would, as Peter Onuf puts it, "have to be jettisoned in favor of the despotic forms that enabled the great European kingdoms to rule far-flung subject populations."

———

Writing to a friend in 1790 about the prospects for the newly formed United States, Hamilton referred to Florida "on our right" and Canada "on our left." It was a revealing turn of phrase, for Hamilton was always more comfortable facing east, toward Europe and the Old World; when he turned around, he didn't always like what he saw.

Hamilton had personal experience with Montesquieu's Law and the difficulties of governing the extended republic. In 1794, while he was serving as George Washington's secretary of treasury, the new nation faced its first great domestic crisis: the so-called Whiskey Rebellion, armed attacks by settlers in the hills of western Pennsylvania against federal agents attempting to collect the new federal tax on distilled spirits.

---

4   Even Jefferson's close colleague James Madison was apprehensive about expanding the Union westward. It is "fraught with danger," he wrote to Jefferson in 1784:

> As settlements become extended the members of the Confederacy must be multiplied, and along with them the wills which are to direct the machine. And as the wills multiply, so will the chances against a dangerous union of them. We experience every day the difficulty of drawing thirteen States into the same plans. Let the number be doubled and so will the difficulty." (James Madison to TJ, Aug. 20, 1784.)

The tax was very much Hamilton's tax—enacted at his urging by the first Congress in 1791, enforced by agents of his Treasury Department, and a critical piece of his great plan to have the federal government pay off the states' accumulated debts—and the Whiskey Rebellion became Hamilton's war. He wrote a confidential memorandum to President Washington warning of the "persevering and violent opposition to the law" and calling for "vigorous and decisive measures": "It is indispensable," he wrote, "to exert the full force of the law against the offenders, [and] to employ those means which in the last resort are put in the power of the executive." He drafted the stern words of the Presidential Proclamation issued by Washington, warning against interference with the tax collectors and declaring that "the laws will be strictly enforced against the offenders." At the emergency cabinet meeting called by the president in August 1794 as the crisis deepened, he argued forcefully (and ultimately persuasively) for swift military action against the rebels: "Moderation enough has been shown; 'tis time to assume a different tone."

He took, as he often did, to the newspapers in an attempt to marshal public opinion to his side, calling on all to reject the "apostles of anarchy" who were spreading "sedition and popular licentiousness" through the Pennsylvania hills.[5]

> Government is frequently and aptly classed under two descriptions, a government of FORCE and a government of LAWS; the first is the definition of despotism—the last, of liberty. But how can a government of laws exist where the laws are disrespected and disobeyed? **Government supposes control.** It is the POWER by which individuals in society are kept from doing injury to each other and are brought to co-operate to a common end. The instruments by which it must act are either the AUTHORITY of the Laws or FORCE. If the first be destroyed, the last must be substituted; and where this becomes the ordinary instrument of government there is an end to liberty.[6]

5 "Fresh symptoms every moment appear of a dark conspiracy, hostile to your government, to your peace abroad, to your tranquility at home.... Were it not that it might require too lengthy a discussion, it would not be difficult to demonstrate, that a large and well organized Republic can scarcely lose its liberty from any other cause than that of anarchy, to which a contempt of the laws is the high road.... [If] force is not to be used against the seditious combinations of parts of the community to resist the laws ... this would be to give a carte blanche to ambition—to licentiousness ... The goodly fabric you have established would be rent assunder [sic!], and precipitated into the dust. You knew how to encounter civil war, rather than surrender your liberty to foreign domination—you will not hesitate now to brave it rather than surrender your sovereignty to the tyranny of a faction—you will be as deaf to the apostles of anarchy now as you were to the emissaries of despotism then. Your love of liberty will guide you now as it did then—you know that the POWER of the majority and LIBERTY are inseparable—destroy that, and this perishes.... (Hamilton, *Letters to the American Daily Advertiser* [the "Tully Letters" nos. 3 and 4], Aug. 28, 1794, and Sept. 2, 1794.)

6 Ibid.

And last, but hardly least, when President Washington called for 15,000 federal troops to march on Pittsburgh—the first time in the country's history that the military was called into action against U.S. citizens—who rode into battle as commander of the troops but Hamilton himself!

There wasn't, as it turned, to be much of a battle—the rebellious settlers fled into the hills before the advancing troops, no shots were fired, and the rebellion quickly quieted down (enough so, at least, to allow Hamilton's tax collectors to operate more-or-less freely in the area).

To Hamilton, the Whiskey Rebellion episode was proof (if proof were needed) of the truth of Montesquieu's Law; the new United States was going to have its hands full keeping the peace and maintaining control over its already-enormous territory.[7] After the dust had settled, Hamilton wrote to Washington and called for **permanent** military occupation of the western Pennsylvania hills, a force of 500 infantry and 100 cavalrymen "to be stationed in the disaffected country."

---

7   Jefferson, predictably, saw things differently. To his eye, it was all much ado about nothing, an attempt *to slander the friends of popular rights,* an "excessive and unnecessary military response," as Joseph Ellis put it, "to a healthy and essentially harmless expression of popular discontent by American farmers, [and] his first instinct was to blame Hamilton for the whole sorry mess." *The excise tax,* he wrote to James Madison, *is an infernal one:*

> You are all swept away in the torrent of governmental opinions. The first error was to admit it by the Constitution; the 2d., to act on that admission; the 3d & last will be to make it the instrument of dismembering the Union, & setting us all afloat to choose which part of it we will adhere to.

The so-called "rebellion" had been *nothing more than riotous:*

> There was indeed a meeting to consult about a separation [from the Union]. But to consult on a question does not amount to a determination of that question in the affirmative, still less to the acting on such a determination. But we shall see, I suppose, what the court lawyers, & courtly judges, & would-be ambassadors will make of it.
>
> [Hamilton's army is] the object of laughter, not of fear; 1000 men could have cut off their whole force in a thousand places of the Alleganey.
>
> But the settlers' detestation of the excise law is universal, and has now associated to it a detestation of the government; & that separation which perhaps was a very distant & problematical event, is now near, & certain, & determined in the mind of every man.

Hamilton, it is probably fair to say in retrospect, won that round; although historians still debate the question, the military operation was largely a success: no shots were actually fired, there was a lot of noise but no real action, two "rebels" were convicted of treason (and later pardoned), federal tax collectors were able subsequently to go about their lawful business without too much interference, and Jefferson's fear—that the use of military force made separation from the Union *near, & certain, & determined in the mind of every man*—appears to have been unfounded.

Without this, the expense incurred will have been essentially fruitless... The political putrefaction of Pennsylvania is greater than I had any idea of. [!] Without rigor everywhere, our tranquility is likely to be of very short duration, and the next storm will be infinitely worse than the present one.

You can imagine, then, his reaction when, less than a decade later, his old nemesis Jefferson, now president, acquired on behalf of the United States the entire Louisiana Territory—a chunk of territory so big nobody really had the faintest idea how big it was. (Around 827,000 square miles, as it turned out.)

"At best, extremely problematical," Hamilton wrote.

The western region [is] not valuable to the United States for settlement....Should our own citizens, more enterprising than wise, become desirous of settling this country and emigrat[ing] thither, it must not only be attended with all the injuries of a too widely dispersed population, but, by adding to the great weight of the western part of our territory, must hasten [either] the **dismemberment** of a large portion of our country or a **dissolution** of the Government. (Emphasis Hamilton's]

The new nation, Hamilton wrote, had no need of more territory: "When we consider the **present** extent of the United States, and that not even one-sixteenth part of [our] territory is yet under occupation,"—a curious turn of phrase, that "under occupation"!—"the advantage of the acquisition [of the Louisiana Territory], as it relates to actual settlement, appears too distant and remote to strike the mind of a sober politician with force." The most that could be said for it was that it might allow the United States "at some distant period" to trade the whole territory to Spain in exchange for Florida, a territory "obviously of far greater value to us than all the immense, undefined region west of the [Mississippi] river."

Expansion of the Union, Hamilton believed, could only proceed hand-in-hand with federal power, the new government's ability to project force and to maintain order from its base of operations on the eastern seaboard. Overextend the union beyond that limit, and the result would be, as Hamilton put it, "despotism or anarchy...dismemberment or dissolution."

————

Jefferson, of course, had other ideas. Unlike Hamilton, he liked looking west; although he would never actually set foot on the other side of the Alleghenies, he lived, in John Logan Allen's wonderful phrase, "farther west in his mind" than any other major political figure of the time. And when he looked west—with Canada on his right and the Floridas on his left—he saw a very different landscape there than Hamilton did. To Jefferson, the West wasn't a problem to be solved, it was an opportunity to be seized; not a bug, but a feature. He had a vision for the new American nation—remember those "New States" on his map?—and he had a plan to bring it into being.

He was convinced that Montesquieu had been wrong, Montesquieu's "Law" no law at all. Republican government **could** scale; in fact, it could get **stronger** as it got bigger.

> I have much confidence that we shall proceed successfully for ages to come, and that, contrary to the principle of Montesquieu, it will be seen that **the larger the extent of country, the more firm its republican structure,** if founded, not on conquest, but in principles of compact and equality.

Its size could be its strength, and its strength could be its size; Montesquieu, turned upside down. The New World, he was convinced, would *furnish proof of the falsehood of Montesquieu's doctrine that a republic can be preserved only in a small territory. The reverse is the truth.*

How would **that** work? How do you build a democratic system that would scale, that would get stronger as it got bigger, and bigger as it got stronger?

It was without historical precedent, and it was going to take some hard thinking, hard work, and new ideas to make it happen. Luckily, Jefferson was never afraid of hard thinking, hard work, or new ideas:

> Our Revolution...presented us an album on which we were free to write what we pleased. We had no occasion to search into musty records, to hunt up royal parchments, or to investigate the laws and institutions of a semi-barbarous ancestry. We appealed to those of nature, and found them engraved on our hearts....
>
> [This] chapter of our history furnishes a lesson to man perfectly new. We can no longer say there is nothing new under the sun, for this whole chapter in the history of man is new... The great extent of our Republic is new. Its sparse habitation is new. The mighty wave of public opinion which has rolled over it is new.... Before the establishment of the American States, nothing was known to history but the man of the Old World, crowded within limits either small or overcharged...A government adapted to such men would be one thing; but a very different one, that for the man of these States....
>
> My hope of its duration is built much on the enlargement of the resources of life going hand in hand with the enlargement of territory, and the belief that men are disposed to live honestly, if the means of doing so are open to them....I have [the consolation] of other prophets who foretell distant events, that I shall not live to see it falsified. My theory has always been that if we are to dream, the flatteries of hope are as cheap, and pleasanter, than the gloom of despair.

LOOKING FORWARD

Cyberspace is not the American West of 1787, of course. But like the American West of 1787, cyberspace is (or at least it has been) a Jeffersonian kind of place. Jeffersonians always predominate in new places, because new places attract people who find new places attractive and repel people who do not. Jefferson biographer Joseph Ellis called cyberspace the "perfect Jeffersonian environment," all decentralization and disorder, growth and expansion, a frontier that is constantly expanding and seemingly illimitable. Hamiltonians, though, inevitably make their way to Jeffersonian places (certainly once gold is discovered there!), claims of order and authority and power assert themselves, and struggles over the shape of the place begin in earnest.

BOX I.2   JEFFERSON ON CYBERSPACE

Were it left to me to decide whether we should have a government without newspapers or newspapers without government, I should not hesitate a moment to prefer the latter.

TJ TO EDWARD CARRINGON, JANUARY 16, 1787

And like the West of 1787, cyberspace poses some hard questions, and could use some new ideas, about governance, and law, and order, and scale. The engineers have bequeathed to us a remarkable instrument, one that has managed to solve prodigious technical problems associated with communication on a **global** scale. The problem is the one that Jefferson and his contemporaries faced: How do you build "republican" institutions—institutions that respect the equal worth of all individuals and their right to participate in the formation of the rules under which they live—that scale?

NOTES ON THE STATE OF CYBERSPACE
PART II: ORDER

When? Where? and How? is the present Chaos to be arranged into Order.

JOHN ADAMS TO JEFFERSON, JULY 15, 1813

In the beginning, all the world was America, and more so than that is now.

JOHN LOCKE, SECOND TREATISE ON CIVIL GOVERNMENT

CHAPTER EIGHT

LANGUAGE II

Behold, the people is one, and they have all one language; and this they begin to do:
and now nothing will be restrained from them, which they have imagined to do.
GENESIS 11:6 (KING JAMES VERSION)

One of the Enlightenment's Big Ideas was that languages evolve, changing over time
in systematic ways. Though the idea was not original to him, Jefferson probably
understood and appreciated it as well, or better, than anyone then alive.[1] It was pretty

1 It is no surprise that Jefferson—the man who, in Robert Dawidoff's words, "gave us our
   national words, and translated into sentences the sentiments we have chosen to be guided
   by"—had an abiding passion for the study of language. It was, Jefferson wrote, a *pursuit to
   which I felt great attraction, a hobby which too often runs away with me where I meant not
   to give up the rein*; though he complained late in life that *my life has been too busy in pursuits of another character to have made much proficiency in it,* he managed to do enough
   to become America's first serious comparative linguist (again, before there were words like
   "linguist," or "linguistics," to describe what he was doing).
       He had a lifelong fascination with Anglo-Saxon, the language spoken by the inhabitants
   of what was to become England prior to the eleventh-century Norman Conquest. While still
   a student at the College of William and Mary in the 1760s, he translated the Lord's Prayer
   into Anglo-Saxon:—
       Faeder ure thu the eart in heofenum, si thin nama gehalgod. to becume thin rice...
   and he began compiling a list of the Anglo-Saxon roots of English words, a project that bore
   fruit in 1798 when he produced—while serving as vice president of the United States—both
   a rudimentary Anglo-Saxon–English dictionary (the first of its kind), and his remarkable
   "Essay on the Anglo-Saxon Language."
       And his interest in Native American languages was, if anything, even more intense. He
   compiled, over a thirty-year period, what was without question the most comprehensive
   collection of American Indian vocabularies then in existence. *Very early in life*, he wrote to
   his friend John Sibley, he compiled a list of 250 objects *which being present everywhere,
   would probably have a name in every language*—"tree," "star," "bird," "moon," "arm," etc.

radical stuff, for the late eighteenth century; it meant that the biblical story of the Tower of Babel, with its simultaneous creation of all human languages in a single cataclysmic moment, was not to be taken literally. It meant that Anglo-Saxon, and Chaucerian English, and the English of Shakespeare, Samuel Johnson, and Thomas Jefferson were all connected to one another through an unbroken chain of intermediates, *the many shades of mutation by which the language has tapered down to its modern form.*

It meant that you could use the present to reconstruct the past, that by comparing similarities and differences among existing languages you could "roll back" the tree of evolutionary descent to common linguistic ancestors farther and farther back in time to determine *how many ages have elapsed since the English, the Dutch, the Germans, the Swiss, the Norwegians, Danes and Swedes have separated from their common stock,* much as today's evolutionary biologists use comparative anatomy or comparative DNA sequences among living species to reconstruct lines of evolutionary descent.

And, if languages have a past—a rich evolutionary history, full of change and modification—it meant that they must also have a future; if they are not today what they were yesterday, then presumably they will not be tomorrow what they are today.

He spent much of the rest of his life attempting to obtain the words for each of those objects in each of the Native American tribal languages. He amassed a truly staggering collection; by 1809, he could write:

> *I have now spent thirty years availing myself of every possible opportunity of procuring Indian vocabularies to the same set of words. My opportunities were probably better than will ever occur again to any person having the same desire. I collected about fifty, and digested most of them in collateral columns.*

It was not only the most comprehensive collection of information on Native American languages then in existence, it was probably the most comprehensive collection of information on **any** set of related languages in the world.

He had long intended to have the entire collection of vocabularies printed up, *lest by some accident it might be lost.* He kept putting that off, for one reason or another—in 1800, he was awaiting vocabularies for *the great southern languages: Cherokee, Creeks, Choctaw, Chickasaw;* in 1809, he had not *yet digested Captain Lewis's collection* (i.e., Meriwether Lewis's collection of vocabularies and grammars from the tribes west of the Mississippi), *nor having leisure then to do it* [during his term as president], *I put it off till I should return home.*

A bad idea, as it turned out. Returning to Monticello from Washington, D.C., at the end of his second term as president, he packed up the vocabularies . . . *in a trunk of stationery, and sent round by water with about thirty other packages of my effects. [W]hile ascending the James River, this package, on account of its weight and presumed precious contents, was singled out and stolen. The thief being disappointed on opening it, threw into the river all its contents, of which he thought he could make no use. Among these were the whole of the vocabularies. Some leaves floated ashore and were found in the mud; but these were very few, and so defaced by the mud and water that no general use can ever be made of them.*

Which raises a (new) question, one that had not been asked before: Who controls that future, and how?

In 1780 John Adams dispatched "A Letter to the President of Congress," proposing that Congress establish "the American Academy for refining, improving, and ascertaining the English Language."

> It is not to be disputed that the form of government has an influence upon language, and language in its turn influences not only the form of government, but the temper, the sentiments, and manners of the people....
>
> Most of the nations of Europe have thought it necessary to establish by public authority institutions for fixing and improving their proper languages. I need not mention the academies in France, Spain, and Italy, their learned labors, nor their great success. But it is very remarkable, that although many learned and ingenious men in England have from age to age projected similar institutions for correcting and improving the English tongue, yet the government have never found time to interpose in any manner; so that to this day **there is no grammar nor dictionary extant of the English language which has the least public authority**...
>
> The honor of forming the first public institution for refining, correcting, improving, and ascertaining the English language, I hope is reserved for Congress... It will have a happy effect upon the Union of the States to have a public standard for all persons in every part of the continent to appeal to, both for the signification and pronunciation of the language.... The authority of Congress is necessary to give such a society reputation, influence, and authority through all the States and with other nations.

Jefferson, as you might have guessed, wanted none of this. He was no fan of the European language academies,[2] whose sole purpose, as he saw it, was *to arrest the progress of language by fixing it to a Dictionary, outside of which no word can be sought, used, or tolerated.*

> *I am no friend to what is called Purism, but a zealous friend to the Neology which has introduced these two words* [i.e., "purism" and "neology"] ***without*** *the authority of any*

An irreparable misfortune, he called it; perhaps, he wrote mournfully, I may make another attempt to collect, although I am too old to expect to make much progress in it.

2 Foremost among the great language academies of Europe to which Adams was referring was the renowned Académie Française, which began life as an informal literary circle in Paris in the early 1630s but was taken over, first by the Church and then by the State; by the 1670s, King Louis XIV had declared himself "protecteur" of the Académie and given the Académie's linguistic decrees on correct usage and grammar and rhetoric the force of State-backed law. Jefferson came to know it well during his years in France, and he was not impressed. Its goal, as he put it, was to *arrest the progress of* [the French] *language by fixing it to a Dictionary, outside of which no word was ever to be sought, used, or tolerated.*

dictionary. *I consider the* [former] *as destroying the nerve and beauty of language, while the* [latter] *improves both, and adds to its copiousness.*

"Without the authority of any dictionary." *If dictionaries are to be the arbiters of language,* he asked slyly, *in which of them shall we find "neologism"?*

Dictionaries are but the depositories of words already legitimated by usage. **Society** *is the workshop in which new ones are elaborated. When an individual uses a new word, if ill formed, it is rejected in society; if well formed, adopted, and after due time, laid up in the depository of dictionaries.*

The horrors of Neologism, which startle the purist, have given me no alarm.

Uncouth words will sometimes be offered. But the public will judge them, and receive or reject, as sense or sound shall suggest, and authors will be approved or condemned according to the use they make of this license.... Where brevity, perspicuity, and even euphony can be promoted by the introduction of a new word, it is an improvement to the language. It is thus [that] *the English language has been brought to what it is; one-half of it having been innovations, made at different times, from the Greek, Latin, French, and other languages. And is it the worse for these?*

He practiced what he preached; this *zealous friend to neology* was one of the great neologists of all time.[3]

He noted with pleasure, late in life, that the French had seen the error of their ways and had revoked the Académie's public charter, removing it from State control as part of the Revolutionary reforms of 1793. All to good effect, he thought:

> *What a language has the French become since the date of their revolution, by the free introduction of new words! The most copious and eloquent in the living world... at this time it is the language in which every shade of idea, distinctly perceived by the mind, may be more exactly expressed, than in any language at this day spoken by man.*

3 The Oxford English Dictionary credits Jefferson with the first recorded use of more than sixty words, including such beauties as:

Anglophobia	*authentication*	*belittle*	*bibliograph*
catenary	*countervailing*	*discountable*	*doll-baby*
indecipherable	*inheritability*	*post-note*	*public relations*
reticulate	*sanction*		

and my personal favorites, "*vomit-grass*" and "*tolerablish.*"

See *Authors in the OED: Jefferson,* http://etext.virginia.edu/jefferson/oed/

Other notable Jeffersonian neologisms include:

amovability	*bountied*	*enregistry*	*Angloman*
Anglomania	*bread-stuff*	*retard*	*circumanbulator*

A language cannot be too rich. The more copious [it is], *the more susceptible of embellishment it will become.*

The greater the degree [of enlargement] *the more precious will it become as the organ of the development of the human mind. . . . Not by holding fast to Johnson's Dictionary; not by raising a hue and cry against every word he has not licensed; but by encouraging and welcoming new compositions of its elements.*

Positive feedback: the more language is embellished, the more susceptible it becomes to embellishment; the more it grows, the more it can grow, and so on.

New and unanticipated circumstances, new knowledge, and new forms of social organization would require new words, new dialects, and new languages.

Had the preposterous idea of fixing the language been adopted by our Saxon ancestors, the progress of ideas must have stopped with that of the language. . . . Nothing is more evident than that as we advance in the knowledge of new things, and of new combinations of old ones, we must have new words to express them. Without [neologism] *we should still be held to the vocabulary of* [the ancients], *and held to their state of science also, for I am sure they had no words which could have conveyed the ideas of oxigen* [sic], *cotyledons, zoophytes, magnetism, electricity, hyaline, and thousands of others expressing ideas not then existing.*

And nowhere would this be more true than in the New World:

Necessity obliges **us** *to neologize. . . . Certainly so great growing a population* [as ours], *spread over such an extent of country, with such a variety of climates, of productions, of arts, must enlarge their language, to make it answer its purpose of expressing all ideas, the new as well as the old. The new circumstances under which we are placed, call for new words, new phrases, and for the transfer of old words to new objects.*

---

intercolonnation	*non-intercourse*	*snowberry*	*belittle*
palinodial	*plexi-chronometer*	*unconciliatory*	*Bonapartism*
drayage			

Interestingly, the OED lists Jefferson as the first **and last** user of four of the words listed above: Angloman, enregistry, intercolonnation, and plexi-chronometer. He would have been particularly disappointed, one suspects, that "Angloman" didn't catch on; he used it—incessantly—to describe those who, like archfiend Alexander Hamilton, were in the iron grip, as he saw it, of English customs and English ways of thinking.

CHAPTER NINE

GOVERNING CYBERSPACE I
CODE

What has destroyed liberty and the rights of man in every government which has ever existed under the sun? The generalizing and concentrating all cares and powers into one body

TJ TO JOHN CABELL, FEBRUARY 2, 1816

*It is not by the consolidation or concentration of powers, but by their **distribution**, that good government is effected. In government, as well as in every other business of life, it is by **division and subdivision of duties alone** that all matters, great and small, can be managed to perfection. . . . Follow principle, and the knot unties itself.*

TJ, *AUTOBIOGRAPHY*

Who controls the Internet? Who makes its law, and what does that law look like? Who governs there, and how?

As the fledgling TCP/IP inter-network grew to become "the Internet," it was inevitable that more and more people would start asking these questions; they're a lot more interesting, and a lot more important, in 2008 than they were in 1988, because the TCP/IP inter-network's a lot bigger in 2008 than it was in 1988, and there has indeed been an accelerating stream of conferences, governmental white papers, scholarly books and articles, and the like focusing on them over the past decade or so.[1]

---

1 Looking for evidence in support of the proposition that there has been an upsurge in the debate about "Internet governance" over the past several years (for the benefit of those of you who, for any number of reasons, might not have been paying much attention to it), I searched through the Lexis-Nexis News database for news stories using the words "govern" (or variants: governed, governs, governing, etc.) and the words "Internet" or "cyberspace" in the same sentence. I received an error message; the search had turned up more than the allowable maximum number of stories (3,000). So I restricted the search to documents from the previous five years, but I got the same result: "More than 3,000 Documents Retrieved." Same for the previous three years, the previous year, and even the previous month; only when I restricted the search to documents published just in the preceding **week** did I finally fall under the 3,000-story limit. And that, of course, are just the ones written in English.

They're important questions; I wouldn't think there'd be much disagreement, today, about that. Not that long ago—fifteen years or so—a very large number of intelligent and well-informed people had never heard of the Internet, and many others regarded it as some kind of bastard offspring of CB radio, the pet rock, and Pong, an interesting but ultimately rather silly and ignorable fad that would have its day and fade ingloriously away.

But hardly anybody thinks that way any more; whatever you think about the Internet, it is clear to pretty much everyone, by now, that something important is going on "out there." If nothing else—and there is a great deal else—there is serious money being made there. If one were to try to attach a number to the aggregate monetary value of the Internet—the "fair price" you'd pay to own it all, the entire Internet—it would surely run to the many trillions of dollars, and the prospect of trillions of dollars, as Samuel Johnson said about the prospect of a hanging, does help concentrate the mind.

So "Who makes its laws?" and "Who governs?" can't help but be important questions.

At the same time, though, it's difficult to wrap one's mind around them and to think coherently about them—and I say this as someone who's been trying to do just that for more than a decade. It is difficult enough to bring the place, or the thing, itself—the Internet, cyberspace, the global network—into focus, let alone to think of it as "having law," or as "being governed." It just moves bits from one place to another; what kind of law or governance does it have, what kind of law or governance **can** it have, and what kind of law or governance does it need? What would it mean, to "govern the Internet," or to "make law" there?

And it's also difficult to wrap one's mind around these questions because so much of the language we use to talk about law and governance is tied to law and governance in realspace, in Virginia—but we're not, to paraphrase Dorothy, in Virginia anymore.

Consider, for instance, the following: the United Nations has declared that "Internet governance" is a "core issue for the Information Society agenda," and it defined it as:

> The development and application by governments, the private sector, and civil society, in their respective roles, of shared principles, norms, rules, decision-making procedures, and programmes that shape the evolution and use of the Internet.

After holding several "World Summits" on the topic, it adopted a "Statement of Principles":

> International management of the Internet should be multilateral, transparent and democratic...Internet governance is an essential element for a people-centered, inclusive, development-oriented and non-discriminatory Information Society. [The

UN commits itself] to the stability and security of the Internet as a global facility, and to ensuring the requisite legitimacy of its governance.

What **are** they talking about? Even by UN standards, this is incomprehensible. Ensuring "the requisite legitimacy of its governance" sounds like a terrific idea—who's against ensuring the requisite legitimacy of governance? But what does that mean, applied to the Internet? What **could** it mean? What governance are they talking about, the legitimacy of which they hope to ensure? And these "shared principles, norms, rules, decision-making procedures, and programmes that shape the evolution and use of the Internet"—where do those come from, exactly? What kind of "management," international or otherwise, does the Internet have, and what kind of management does it need?

And hardest of all: **Who decides all of that?**

It's not just the UN that's had a hard time articulating precisely what it's talking about when talking about "Internet governance" (although the UN's pronouncements on "Internet governance" do sound particularly Orwellian to my ear—"designed," as Orwell put it, "to give an appearance of solidity to pure wind"[2]); pretty much everyone who writes about Internet governance (myself included) has been guilty of imprecision on this score.

But these questions really are important—too important to let them wallow around in some kind of linguistic slop. Whatever this Internet is, it has changed the way hundreds of millions of people live, work, find information, and communicate with each other, all within a couple of decades. Maybe it has peaked; maybe it will become less interesting, less valuable, and less transformative of the ways that people live, work, find information, and communicate with each other from here on out. If you believe that, you probably want to stop reading here, for I doubt that

---

2   The Orwell I'm referring to is not the Orwell who, famously, warned of the dangers of deceptive political language (*1984, Animal Farm*), but the Orwell who railed against the merely slovenly (in his essay on "Politics and the English Language"):

> In our time it is broadly true that political writing is bad writing . . . a mixture of vagueness and sheer incompetence is its most marked characteristic. . . . Where that is not true, it will generally be found that the writer is some kind of rebel, expressing his private opinions and not a "party line." Orthodoxy, of whatever color, seems to demand a lifeless, imitative style. . . . On ought to recognize that the present political chaos is connected with the decay of language, and that one can probably bring about some improvement by starting at the verbal end. . . . If you simplify your English, you are freed from the worst follies of orthodoxy, [and] when you make a stupid remark its stupidity will be obvious, even to yourself. Political language—and with variations this is true of all political parties, from Conservatives to Anarchists—is designed to make lies sound truthful and murder respectable, and to give an appearance of solidity to pure wind. One cannot change this all in a moment, but one can at least change one's own habits.

much of what follows will be of interest to you—if the Internet is going the way of CB radio, why bother trying to figure out what its governance is, and how it works?

But if I were wagering, I'd gladly take the Over on that bet; my guess is that the Internet gets more interesting, more valuable, and more transformative moving forward, making these questions of law and governance themselves more interesting, and more important, over time.

So: who governs the Internet?

CODE AS LAW

[S]omething fundamental has changed...Cyberspace presents something new for those who think about regulation and freedom. It demands a new understanding of how regulation works and of what regulates life there. It compels us to look beyond the traditional lawyer's scope—beyond laws, regulations, and norms....In cyberspace we must understand how code regulates—how the software and hardware that make cyberspace what it is regulate cyberspace as it is. As William Mitchell puts it, this code is cyberspace's "law." **Code is law.**

LAWRENCE LESSIG, *CODE AND OTHER LAWS OF CYBERSPACE*
(EMPHASIS IN ORIGINAL)

Lessig's (and Mitchell's) insight—"code is law"—has quickly become conventional wisdom among those who study and write about Internet law and regulation, and with very good reason: it captures (in only three words!) something of fundamental importance about the place. The network, in a sense, **is** its code—the "instructions imbedded in the software and hardware that make cyberspace work," as Lessig puts it, the languages and protocols that collectively determine how messages are moved from place to place and what happens to them when they arrive. The code—or, more properly, the codes, the many languages that flourish up and down the Internet's protocol stack—is law on the network in the sense that, like law, it constrains what you may or may not do there. Code doesn't necessarily **replace** what we ordinarily think of as "law" on the network—the law of statutes and regulations and court decisions and the rest—so much as it functions alongside, and interacts with, that law to govern what you can or cannot do there.[3]

To illustrate, consider the following:

HTTP Referrer. The HTTP Protocols specify that part of every message sent by a web browser is set aside for what is called "Referrer" information—the IP Address of the machine that "referred" (through a hyperlink) a visitor to a website. It works like this: My homepage consists of a file that, when displayed in your browser, has a

---

3 "East Coast code" and "West Coast code," Lessig calls them, the formal law of statutes and regulations, and the software protocols and programs.

box in the corner that says: "**Click here** to buy my book about Thomas Jefferson and the Internet." If you do click, your machine sends a message to whatever address I have placed in the underlying code—say, "www.amazon.com/12345abcde.html"—requesting transmission of the file stored at that address. The HTTP Protocols specify not only the location in your message where your "return address" appears (which enables the machine at www.amazon.com to send the file that you requested to you), but also the location in your message where the address of the "referrer" site—in this case, my webpage, from which you obtained the www.amazon.com address—appears.

It doesn't sound like a very big deal, and in some ways it isn't. But Internet commerce would look **very** different if the HTTP Protocol did not provide a place—a "field"—for this Referrer information. Google, for instance—at the moment, the largest and most successful online commercial entity of all—makes most of its money from the Referrer field; the Referrer field enables those who advertise with Google to distinguish between messages arriving at the advertiser's website that were "referred" by Google and those that were not; it therefore allows Google to charge advertisers for messages in the first category. Without the Referrer field in the HTTP Protocol, Google's business model (and Yahoo's, and MSN's, and Amazon's, and many, many others) would of necessity have been dramatically different, for it could not have relied upon the information currently provided in the Referrer field to organize its revenue-generating activities.

Lessig's point is not that the HTTP Referrer field is "law" in the ordinary sense but rather that, **like** law, it constrains or regulates what you can and cannot do, enabling certain kinds of activities while disadvantaging or disabling others. And in a place like cyberspace constructed entirely out of such "West Coast code," sometimes it is **that** code, and not the "East Coast code" in the statute books and judicial opinions, that has the greatest impact on what can and cannot be done there. I have on my shelf a book titled *Proposed Laws Governing the Internet, 1997*, filled with more than 350 pages of East Coast code—the Uniform Computer Information Transactions Act, the Prohibition of Internet Sales of Ammunition Act, the Electronic Disclosures Delivery Act, the Electronic Commerce Crime Prevention and Protection Act, the Inbox Privacy Act, the Millennium Digital Commerce Act, the Promote Reliable On-Line Transactions to Encourage Commerce and Trade (PROTECT) Act, and the like. But if you had asked, back in 1997, "what rule will have the greatest impact on Internet commercial activity over the next decade?" the correct answer would probably have been: the HTTP Referrer code.

Who decides? Who decided to put a Referrer field into the HTTP Protocol?

This is what governance questions look like here, in cyberspace. If governance is about the process of lawmaking, in a place constructed entirely out of code, where code is law (or at least some kind of law) and where the shape of the code(s) deeply affects the kind of place it is and the kinds of things one can and cannot do there, **code-making is governance**.

The Numbers Crunch. Here's another example, from farther down the protocol stack. Over the past decade or so, a pretty serious problem—possibly even a crisis—has arisen on the Internet: it may be running out of numbers. (More scaling!)

Every machine on a TCP/IP network has to have a unique identifier—its own "IP Address"—if it is to be "on the network," able to send and receive messages to others using the network. Internet Protocol Addresses are defined to be 32 bits long (i.e., they consist of a string of 32 0s or 1s). That means that there are "only" 2^{32} = 4,294,967,295 possible IP addresses, starting with IP Address

00000000000000000000000000000000 (= 0)

and going up to IP Address

11111111111111111111111111111111 (= 4,294,967,294)

It's a big number, 4,294,967,295, and it's a lot of IP Addresses. You'd be forgiven for thinking that it would be enough; the engineers who developed the first versions of the IP in the late 1970s and early '80s certainly thought that it would be enough. This inter-network is going to need more than **4 billion** IP Addresses? You've got to be kidding.

But, for various reasons—the staggering growth in Internet use, obviously among them, but also various inefficiencies in the way that IP allocates IP Addresses—it may **not** be enough, and we may run out of IP Addresses, soon.[4]

What is to be done? Should the Internet Protocol be changed in order to fix this problem? If so, in what way?

I haven't the faintest idea, needless to say. I'm a law professor, not a network engineer, and these are, first and foremost, technical questions of network engineering. I don't know the first thing about how to construct network protocols, and I couldn't begin to evaluate—or even to make any sense out of—the various proposals that have been put forward to deal with this problem.

---

4   If you were to gather together a group of network engineers, you'll get a good argument going about how to fix this numbers crisis—in fact, you'll get a good argument going about whether it really **is** a true crisis that requires some sort of major overhaul. Starting in the early 1990s, as pressure on the numbering system mounted, the engineers developed several "kludges"—solutions that, while inelegant and perhaps overly complicated, are nonetheless operationally effective. These techniques—known as "dynamic allocation," and "Network Address Translator" boxes, and "Classless Inter-Domain Routing," and a number of others—allowed machines on the Internet, in effect, to share IP Addresses with one another while retaining the ability to route messages correctly. I don't understand too much about the engineering behind these techniques, but I do know that there is disagreement in the engineering community about whether they are a workable, scaleable long-term solution to the numbers crunch.

They're technical questions, but they're not **just** technical questions; the rules, even this far down in the protocol stack—especially this far down in the protocol stack—will have far-reaching consequences for everyone who uses the network, constraining what they can and cannot do, enabling certain kinds of activities while disadvantaging or disabling others. Take those IP Addressing rules, for example. China's Information Ministry understands that they matter; it is, at present, one of the strongest supporters of a specific proposal to revise the IP protocols, a proposal known originally as "IPng" (for "Internet Protocol, next generation"), now as IPv6 ("Internet Protocol, version 6"). IPv6 enlarges the space allocated to IP Addresses from 32 bits to 128 bits. So instead of having a lot of IP Addresses (2^{32} = 4,294,967,295, the current limit), we'd have an incomprehensibly immense number of IP Addresses: 2^{128}—a number many times larger than the number of atoms in the human body, and large enough so that there would be many **trillions** of IP Addresses for every person on earth.

IP Addresses would (again! Back to the Future!) be in seemingly inexhaustible supply. With 2^{128} IP Addresses available, surely we would not run out of numbers again, at least for a very, very long time. It really is awfully difficult to imagine a world in which everyone needs more than a trillion IP Addresses.

The consequences of this change for what we can and cannot do on the Internet would be far reaching. To begin with, with so many numbers at our disposal, every single device that might conceivably be used to exchange information over the Internet—every cell phone, every toaster oven, every automobile engine monitor, every compass, every video recorder, every computer, every satellite radio receiver, every billboard, every television—could have its very own IP Address (or even multiple IP Addresses) permanently built in, hardwired into its circuitry as it leaves the factory. Pretty much everything—everything man-made, at least—could now be, as the engineers put it, "addressable."

I'm not exactly sure what kind of an Internet it is in which, as my friend and colleague David Johnson once put it, my refrigerator is in constant communication with my microwave oven—but I'm pretty certain it's a very different Internet than the one we have now. There will be hordes of new applications emerging to take advantage of this new capability, applications that, if you are reading this in 2058, might seem quite unremarkable but which are, to us in 2008, unimaginable—as unimaginable as Wikipedia or the blogosphere would have seemed to us in 1958.

And the Internet service provider's role, on that Internet, will probably change dramatically, changing the very shape of the inter-network itself. On today's Internet, ISPs provide users with both a connection to the Internet and an IP Address; because IP Addresses have to be shared between machines (see footnote 4), the latter function involves some pretty complicated engineering, engineering that becomes unnecessary when every device comes with its own hardwired IP Address(es). When we're carrying our IP Addresses around with us, we no longer need ISPs to provide them to us, and we no longer need all the complicated engineering of dynamic allocation and NAT boxes and CIDR protocols and all the rest. All we will need, to access the Internet, is the pipe—the connection to a router.

That's a big change in the relationship between the user and the network provider on whom the user relies for access to the Internet. Nothing's harder to predict than the future, as the old saying goes, but my guess is that when we are able to open up our computers anywhere on the globe and find that we already have a valid IP Address, without having to go find someone who will give one to us, the entire relationship between the user and the entities that provide inter-network access—the phone companies, cable companies, satellite companies, universities, private employers, Internet cafe operators, etc.—changes rather significantly. Our old friend the Peacock Map—which depicts those network operators and their relationships with one another—could look very different in an IPv6 world.

And a switch to IPv6 might also make Internet communications **much** easier to trace than on today's Internet. Because of all those complicated kludges that enable users to share IP Addresses so that the current system doesn't run out of numbers, messages on today's Internet can be difficult to trace.[5] Under IPv6, because every machine has its own permanent (static) IP Address built in, whenever there's a message from IP Address X to IP Address Y, we will know precisely which machines were involved.

I don't know whether all of this makes for a better Internet under IPv6 or not, but I'm damn sure it's a **different** Internet than the one we have now—that the decision about whether to adopt IPv6 matters, and not just to the engineers.

So **who decides what is to be done**? Who decides whether we need a new version of the Internet Protocol, and what that new version should look like?

These are just two examples among many. As we saw in chapter 4, there are lots of things the TCP/IP inter-network **could** do, but doesn't (at present)—more aggressive checking for hostile code, message tracing, identity authentication, message verification, discrimination between messages, and the rest. Who decides whether (and how) to incorporate any, some, or all, of these functions in the inter-network?

If code is law, then, as William Mitchell writes, "control of code is power": "For citizens of cyberspace . . . code . . . is becoming a crucial focus of political contest. Who shall write that software that increasingly structures our daily lives?" As the world is now, code writers are increasingly lawmakers. They determine what the defaults of the Internet will be; whether privacy will be protected; the degree to which anonymity will be allowed; the extent to which access will be guaranteed . . . Their decisions, now made in the interstices of how the Net is coded, define what the Net is."

---

5   So even if you can determine, for example, that at precisely 12:26:29 GMT on May 13, 2008, a message went from machine 155.155.242.1 to machine 128.001.11.144, it can be difficult—at times, literally impossible—to determine which machines had been assigned those particular IP Addresses at that particular instant in time.

Nothing about the Internet is more remarkable than the process by which new protocols become (or don't become) part of the TCP/IP protocols (and by which existing TCP/IP protocols are modified). These basic rules for the Internet—this multi-trillion dollar, globally transformative thing, or place, or medium, or whatever you want to call it—are set by anyone who wants to participate in the process of setting them, through an organization that has no formal legal existence or fixed place of operation or salaried employees, that is open to anyone who wishes to join, that has no dues or other membership requirements, and that takes action only when there is a consensus among everybody involved that it should do so.

The organization is known as the Internet Engineering Task Force (IETF). The IETF publishes and maintains the set of documents that, collectively, make up the "Internet Standards"—the "official" protocol set for the global TCP/IP network.[6] The IETF's composition and structure are impenetrably complex—perhaps by design, perhaps not—and it is almost impossible to describe them succinctly, but I give it my best shot in footnote 7 (and fig. 9.1 in the appendix).[7] Its closest analogues are, I think, professional associations—organizations like the International Crystallographic Union, or the National Association of Automotive Engineers, or the International Society for the Study of Classical Literature—though it is not quite identical to any of them. It is, in its own words, less an organization in the ordinary sense and more "a collection of happenings"—a large, and fairly chaotic, series of overlapping ongoing discussions about standards and protocols for the Internet.

---

6   The IETF's "Internet Standards" are publicly available at www.ietf.org. They are "official" only in a rather particular sense—more on this below.

7   The IETF has no formal legal structure. It is what is known in the law as an "unincorporated association" or "a bunch of folks who get together from time to time and do things." A compete analysis of the relationships between these organizations would undoubtedly make for an interesting study in organizational design. Anyone may join the IETF—though by the very nature of the work it does, there are few non-engineers in its ranks. There are no dues; having no formal legal structure, the IETF doesn't have a bank account. There is a chairman, and eight "area directors," each of whom is responsible for one of the eight general areas of interest (e.g., "Internet Applications," "Routing," "Security," and the like) and the supervision of "Working Groups" within those areas where most of the IETF's protocol-setting work gets done.

The IETF chair and the eight area directors together form what is known as the Internet Engineering Steering Group (IESG). Each is each selected from among candidates put forward by the IETF Nominating Committee (see fig. 9.1 in the appendix) by the members of a different organization, the Internet Architecture Board (IAB) (which is also responsible for reviewing and approving the charters of all new IETF Working Groups). The IAB, in turn, is a creature of yet a third organization, the Internet Society (ISOC), whose Trustees appoint the ten members of the IAB (again, from a list of candidates put forward by the IETF Nominating Committee).

The IETF protocol-setting process works something like this. The overall process is governed by what the IETF calls its "RFC"—Request for Comment—procedures. Proposals for new Internet Standards, or changes to existing Internet Standards, have to come from a "Working Group." A Working Group is simply a public discussion group with a designated leader, focused on some specific Internet-related problem and possible solutions, conducted primarily (but not exclusively) online, and open to anyone who wishes to join—a "mailing list with adult supervision," as one of the IETF documents nicely puts it. Anyone may set up a Working Group—all it takes is persuading one of the IETF "Area Directors" that there is a specific problem on which the Working Group will focus that can be described precisely enough to constitute a charter for the Working Group's efforts, and that there are a sufficient number of people interested in the problem to participate in a meaningful discussion about it. At any given time, there are usually a hundred or more active Working Groups (115 as I write this).

A proposal for a new protocol has to complete three full circuits up and down the IETF before it becomes an "Internet Standard." Completing a circuit means obtaining approval of the proposal by (a) the Working Group itself, (b) the Area Director, and (c) the group consisting of all eight Area Directors and the IETF chair (a group known as the Internet Engineering Steering Committee, or IESG).

The process is one of distillation and refinement: each time through, the proposal has to meet more stringent criteria for approval. In the first round of review, the proposal circulates as a Proposed Standard—a "good idea with no known technical flaws [that] appears to enjoy enough community interest to be considered valuable." If approved by the Working Group, the Area Director, and the IESG under this criterion, it becomes a Draft Standard. A Draft Standard has to be more than just a good idea with no known flaws; it has to actually **work**. Approval of a Draft Standard requires that there has been "successful operational experience" with the new protocol, including "at least two genetically independent, interoperable implementations of the proposal." If the Draft Standard is approved (again, by the Working Group, the Area Director, and the IESG), it returns for a final

---

ISOC is an international nonprofit membership organization concerned, in its words, "with the growth and evolution of the worldwide Internet and with the social, political, and technical issues that arise from its use." It has a fairly traditional governance structure, organized (in 1992) as a District of Columbia nonprofit corporation. Members join by paying the annual dues (at this writing $75 USD). It has trustees, elected annually by those members, and a president, selected by the trustees.

The IETF Nominating Committee, in turn, consists of voting members who are chosen **at random** from among any and all volunteers with the IETF, and a (nonvoting) Chair (chosen by ISOC).

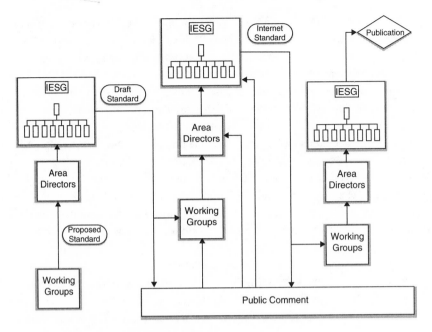

FIGURE 9.2 The IETF Protocol-Setting Process.

circuit as an "Internet Standard"; here the yardstick is whether there has been "significant implementation and successful operational experience... characterized by a high degree of technical maturity and by a generally held belief that the specified protocol or service provides significant benefit to the Internet community." (See fig. 9.2.)

The process is completely transparent; each step is documented and publicly available on the network, and anyone who wishes may join in the discussion at any point.

At each step, the decision whether to approve the proposal and to keep it moving forward is based on the two fundamental IETF criteria: **rough consensus** and **running code**.

BOX 9.1

We reject: kings, presidents, and voting. We believe in: rough consensus and running code.

DAVE CLARK'S VERSION OF THE IETF MOTTO

"Rough consensus" is both undefined and, probably, undefinable. It means—roughly—that pretty much everybody agrees that the proposal has met the required criteria for approval. Not necessarily everybody; true unanimity is not required. But a "very large majority of those who care must agree," with no "substantial" or "significant" disagreement; a proposal that cannot demonstrate that "most of the working group members think that it is the right thing to do" will not be approved.

BOX 9.2

The exact method of determining rough consensus varies from Working Group to Working Group. Sometimes consensus is determined by "humming"; if you agree with a proposal, you hum when prompted by the chair; if you disagree, you keep your silence. Newcomers find it quite peculiar, but it works.

RFC 3160, "THE TAO OF THE IETF"

No votes are ever taken, and there's no fixed percentage of support that a proposal must achieve in order to be approved, no attempt to impart mathematical precision to the meaning of a "very large majority," or "pretty much everybody," or "significant," or "substantial." As the proposal moves through the process, each decision-maker has to satisfy him or herself that "rough consensus," whatever it may mean to the individual concerned, has been achieved; the chair of the Working Group has to persuade the Area Director, and the Area Director has to persuade the other Area Directors in the IESG, that the interested community has reached a rough consensus on the proposal, and, finally, the IESG itself has to reach the same sort of rough consensus that the proposal is a good one.

"Running code" means that the protocol works—not in theory or on the blackboard but in actual practice, **on the network**. "Quit jawing; throw it out on the Net and see if it works," in Pauline Borsook's nice paraphrase. The proposal must actually have been implemented (in at least two "independent implementations") in actual code built in accordance with the proposed protocol's specifications, and the code has to have been used operationally on the actual Internet without screwing things up—without interfering or somehow conflicting with the other functions the Internet is performing or with any of the **other** code out there built in accordance with **other** Internet Standards (the requirement of "interoperability").

At the end of all this, if (pretty much) everybody involved agrees that the protocol is a good one—that it **works** ("significant implementation and successful operational experience"), and that it "provides significant benefit to the Internet community"—it is published as a final Internet Standard on the official IETF website.

It's a hell of a way to run one of the most complex, and arguably the most successful, international engineering projects of all time. If code is law, then this is lawmaking, and if this is lawmaking, it's a pretty remarkable form of lawmaking—an ongoing series of little town meetings, with dozens, or perhaps hundreds, of documents making their way up, or down, the review chain at any point in time, everyone looking to see whether there's a rough consensus that whatever is described in the document is a good thing to do (or at least that there are no good reasons to believe that it's **not** a good thing to do).

Who gave the IETF the authority to do this? Who put them in charge?

The answer, of course, is that nobody did. The IETF doesn't exercise the kind of power that requires it to **be** authorized to do what it does; it just documents consensus.

It promulgates rules that have a curious property: people—hundreds of millions of them—adhere to them even though they are not compelled to do so. As the IETF itself describes it, designation of a protocol as an Internet Standard means only that:

> the IETF has agreed that "if you want to do this thing, this is the description of how to do it." It does not imply any attempt by the IETF to mandate its use, or any attempt to police its usage—only that "if you say that you are doing something according to this standard, do it this way." The benefit of a standard to the Internet is in interoperability—that multiple products implementing a standard are able to work together in order to deliver valuable functions to the Internet's users.

"Internet Standards," in other words, are just documents labeled "Internet Standards" by the IETF. They say nothing more than this: "If you want to do X on this inter-network"—display a video image in a document or transfer an audio file as part of an Instant Messaging application, or the like—"and if you do it the way we specify here, it will 'work'; we've given it a pretty thorough going-over, and we have determined that it will inter-operate with other products built in accordance with the other 'Internet Standards,' and it will not conflict with other inter-network applications." Internet Standards are "authoritative" and "official" not because they are promulgated by the authorized, official body, but because, and only because, and only to the extent that, everyone—the hundreds of thousands of hardware manufacturers, and software developers, and Internet Service Providers who build and implement the codes built in accordance with those standards—treats them as "authoritative" and "official."

The IETF's in charge only because, and only to the extent, everyone treats it as being in charge. No force stands behind the IETF rules, and there's no mechanism to "enforce" them. The IETF issues no mandates; it takes no steps whatsoever to see that people comply with its Internet Standards. It can't (and doesn't try to) force anyone to implement any of its Internet Standards, it can't (and doesn't try to) stop anyone from using a **different** protocol to do X than the one that the IETF has designated an Internet Standard, and it can't (and doesn't try to) stop anyone from doing something ("Y") for which there is no published Internet Standard at all.

It is nothing short of astonishing that it worked, that **this** process—this nobody-in-charge, nobody-can-enforce, consensus-based, anyone-who-wants-to-participate-may-do-so process—produced the technical underpinnings for what became the global Internet, and we should, at least for a moment, stand back and admire the achievement. It is, as far as I'm aware, entirely without precedent; I can't think of any other international organization responsible for managing something of this magnitude that operates remotely like it. **The rules for a common global language were developed by consensus.** You would have gotten **very** long odds, back in 1980 or 1985, against that happening. If someone had said, back then, that they were hoping to build a global inter-network, one that would have hundreds of millions of users, connecting pretty much everyone on the planet to everyone else, and that they were going to use **this** process to provide its underlying technical standards, I doubt you could have found a hundred people on earth who would have said that it could work.

Consensus governance can scale. I'm no political scientist, but I don't think we knew that before. The very existence of "the Internet" is proof that it can—not in theory but in actual practice.[8] Remember Montesquieu's "Law"? Wrong again! Democratic governance, not just on a continental, but on a global, scale.[9]

Perhaps it is a coincidence that this decentralized "there-is-no-there-there" process produced this decentralized "there-is-no-there-there" network. I doubt it, but I can't demonstrate, even to my own satisfaction let alone a critical reader's, exactly where the cause-and-effect lines are.

---

8 In an old joke, the French philosopher says "Yes, yes, it works in practice—but does it work in theory?" The Internet, obviously, was not built by French philosophers.

9 Paulina Borsook, in a provocative 1995 article in *Wired* magazine, described IETF rule-making as "a kind of direct, populist democracy ... a true grass-roots political process that few of us have ever had the privilege to participate in." Law professor Michael Froomkin went even farther; drawing on the work of the influential legal philosopher Jürgen Habermas, Froomkin argued that the IETF rule-making process—in its openness, and the manner in which any and all interested voices get a respectful hearing in the course of developing a "reasoned consensus" on possibly controversial matters—has a kind of moral legitimacy that few rule-making processes of the more traditional sort can claim. There is, Froomkin argues, "striking similarity" between the IETF's procedures and the fundamental criteria Habermas set forth to determine whether a rule-making system is "capable of legitimating the rules it produces": (1) it is open to all who want to participate, (2) any participant can introduce any proposition into the discussion, or challenge any proposition previously introduced, (3) no speaker is prevented from exercising the rights in (1) and (2) by any kind of coercion internal or external to the discourse, and (4) only the "unforced force of the better argument" determines the responses of the participants to any proposal.

But one thing is clear: the UN this ain't.

As I said at the beginning of this chapter, I am not entirely sure **what** the UN has in mind with its talk about the "international management of the Internet," and "ensuring the requisite legitimacy of Internet governance." It might seem far-fetched to suggest that it has these protocol-design and protocol-development processes in mind, that it is talking about "governance" at **this** level of technical detail, this low down in the protocol stack. Surely that pushes the "code is law, therefore codemaking is lawmaking" metaphor too hard, envisioning the United Nations involving itself in the design of router algorithms and packet-verification procedures and the like.

But it's actually not so far-fetched. Few people recall it or talk much about it these days, but the UN **was**, once, engaged quite intensively in developing inter-networking protocols—a project known as the Open Systems Interconnection ("OSI") protocols. The OSI protocols were developed in the late 1970s and early 1980s by the International Telecommunications Union, a UN affiliate institution composed of representatives from each UN member-state and charged with oversight over international telecommunications policy.

OSI was the anti-TCP/IP, consciously designed to implement an alternative, and very different, network architecture. OSI networks were designed to look a lot like the then-existing, centralized, circuit-switched telephone networks—not surprisingly, given that the ITU was composed primarily of state-owned telephone companies. OSI didn't have the capability to accommodate hundreds of millions of networks because it didn't need that capability; there'd be one network for Romania, one for Egypt, one for Canada, and so on, and the OSI designers were only trying to figure out how to link **them**, not 100 million or so private networks, together. And the process by which the OSI protocols were designed, needless to say, could not have been more different than TCP/IP's: to participate in it, you—literally—had to have a seat at the UN, a credential not many people possess.

For a considerable period of time during the late 1980s and even into the early 1990s—before anyone really noticed, or cared much about, inter-networks or inter-networking protocols—**the OSI inter-network was "the Internet,"** the "authorized" set of inter-networking protocols, the "official" version of the future. Many governments mandated its use for all inter-networking projects; difficult though it is to believe today, it was actually illegal, for many years, to use TCP/IP over German telephone lines, and even in the United States, from 1989 to 1994, the U.S. government—which, of course, helped fund most of the early development of TCP/IP—required use of OSI on all government networks (other than those in the Department of Defense, which were already well along in their use of TCP/IP).

Of course, the OSI network didn't remain "the Internet" for long. The OSI protocols went, for all intents and purposes, extinct; you can still find a few OSI networks out there, and I'm told that they can serve as very useful teaching devices for students learning basic principles of systems engineering, but that's about it. Notwithstanding the extensive government support it received around the world and the substantial resources devoted to building OSI networks in many countries, OSI was a failure (and a rather spectacular one at that). Not a failure in the abstract; many networking experts seem to agree that OSI contained some useful ideas that have been incorporated into and built upon in many subsequent networking projects. But a failure in fact. It didn't become the Internet, and it didn't become the Internet because the UN couldn't build a network that could become the Internet. I can't prove that, though I'm quite certain it's true. The UN couldn't build a network that could grow as fast as the TCP/IP network could grow, not because it didn't have access to some very smart and talented systems engineers, but because it couldn't build a network that would grow uncontrollably, and uncontrollable growth—if you can handle it—will beat controlled growth every time.

There are plenty of signs that the UN and the ITU, having tried once to nip TCP/IP in the bud and failed, as it were, are at it again, seeking a much more expanded role in—or even possibly control over—various parts of the Internet protocol-setting process.[10] How one feels about that depends, I suppose, on whether you're a Hamiltonian or a Jeffersonian. Maybe it's just the Jeffersonian in me, but it doesn't strike me as an encouraging development. *It is not by the consolidation or concentration of powers, but by their distribution, that good government is effected.* The IETF processes split the governance power up into a million little pieces and distribute a piece to anyone who wants one, rather than concentrating it all in one place. It has worked, astonishingly well, up to now. And in a place where the governance questions going forward—at least, the governance questions at **this** level of the protocol stack—seem so difficult, and where I'm not at all sure which answers are the "right" ones, that strikes me as a reasonable way to proceed. Now that the Internet has become what it has become, the power to set the TCP/IP rules, at the very bottom of the stack, is immense, and I like the idea that it can be exercised only when there is a broad global consensus, among anyone interested in participating in the discussion, that it should be exercised.

---

10 For example, discussion at the UN's World Summits has focused on a greater role for the UN in the Internet's numbering and naming systems, which we'll look at in more detail in chapter 10. In addition, the ITU has recently been involved in efforts to wrest control of protocol-definition out of the hands of the IETF in two important areas (the definition of the Session Initiation Protocol [SIP] for Internet telephony, and the IP-TV protocols for streaming television broadcasts over the Internet).

There is considerable irony in these developments, given that in 1985, at a meeting in Geneva, a number of the key members of the IETF inner circle actually offered to give the ITU a central coordinating role in the continued development of the TCP/IP protocols and were turned down cold.

CHAPTER TEN

GOVERNING CYBERSPACE II
NAMES

Nothing better illustrates the new and complex nature of the relationship between code-making and lawmaking and Internet governance at the bottom of the protocol stack than the story of ICANN—the Internet Corporation for Assigned Names and Numbers.

ICANN was born in October 1998, its birth the culmination of the first (but probably not the last) crisis in "Internet governance." To understand the crisis, and ICANN's role in it, we need to take a closer look at the way that the Internet Protocols manage the assignment of **names** on the inter-network—the so-called Domain Name System, or DNS.

WHAT IS THE DOMAIN NAME SYSTEM, AND HOW DOES IT WORK?

TCP/IP networks rely, as we saw earlier, entirely upon **numerical** IP addresses to move messages from one place to another on the network. It is the one irreducible requirement for communication over the Internet: every communication must contain the recipient's IP address in order for the network to do its job—its **only** job—of routing it properly to its destination.

But as everyone who uses the Internet is well aware, the network manages to route messages based on machine **names** rather than numbers; you can address a message to "temple.edu," or "eff.org," or "google.com," rather than to 155.155.002.14 or 44.127.001.44 or 128.111.55.1, and the message will, in fact, be routed to the right machine. How does that work? How does the network determine which of its more than 500 million machines bears the name "temple.edu," or "eff.org," or "google.com"? How does it ensure that there's only one machine bearing each of those names? How does it find the correct IP Address for that machine, so that a message addressed to it by name alone can be properly delivered?

The ability to use names instead of numbers makes the network much easier to use, of course, given how much easier it is to remember names than to remember numbers. The designers of the early versions of the TCP/IP protocols recognized this simple and obvious fact, and, after a relatively short period during which network users actually had to enter numerical addresses for all messages, by the mid-1970s they had devised a naming system that was as simple and straightforward as you can imagine. A single database file—known as "hosts.txt,"—would list the name, and corresponding numerical IP Address, for each machine on the network:

TABLE 10.1

NAME	IP ADDRESS
...	...
ISI	49
UCLA	11
UniversityofUtah	121
DoD-009	232
...	...
Elmer	63
...	....

It was exactly like a simple telephone book—names associated with numbers. In the network's early days, of course, it was only a couple of dozen, then a couple of hundred, lines long.

Every machine on the inter-network would have its own copy of the "hosts.txt" file. Then, when a message was sent from anywhere to "UCLA," the address field could read "UCLA"; the sender's machine would then perform what engineers call a "lookup"—it would search through its copy of the hosts.txt file to find the matching string ("UCLA"), insert the correct numerical address for that machine into the message ("11"), and off the message would go.

To make this system work, someone had to maintain a master copy of the hosts.txt file—the Keeper of the Names and Numbers. That job fell to Jon Postel, then a graduate student in computer science at UCLA (and subsequently a member of the faculty at the Information Sciences Institute at the University of Southern California). If you wanted to hook your machine up to this network, you had to sign up with Postel; he'd give you a name and a number and insert your entry into the hosts.txt file. Every so often, Postel would send out a fresh copy of the file to everybody on the network, so that they each had an up-to-date listing.

It was as simple as could be, and it worked perfectly well—but only for a short while. As the network started growing, the engineers quickly realized that this system wouldn't scale. It couldn't handle 500 million machines—not (literally) in a million years. A 500-million-line hosts.txt file is a very big file—just imagine if **every** message sent out from every machine on today's Internet required a lookup in a database 500 million entries long. Computers are fast—but they're not fast enough for that; even at 1 million operations a second, that's 500 seconds—more than eight minutes—of processing for every single message going out over the network. I connect to the Internet over a Temple University host computer that probably processes 10 million messages a day—that's 4 billion seconds (about 125 years) worth of processing for one day's worth of messages. Exponential growth of a network designed like this would mean exponential growth of the size the hosts.txt file, and that exponentially growing file would have to be sent out more and more frequently (to keep it up-to-date on all machines), and to an exponentially increasing number of machines, and every message sent by any of those (exponentially growing) number of machines would require a lookup through this exponentially growing hosts.txt file to find the proper IP Address for the recipient.

It wouldn't work. In 1983 Postel and several colleagues proposed a series of Internet Standards defining a new naming scheme—the Domain Name System, which, with some modifications, persists today. The new system had two significant new features: (1) names would be **hierarchically nested** within "domains," and (2) the databases associating names and IP Addresses would be **distributed** around the network.

Hierarchical nesting works as follows. The space of all usable names is divided up into "domains." At the top are the **top-level** domains (or TLDs). Postel's initial specification called for seven so-called "generic" TLDs—"EDU," "ORG," "COM," "MIL," "NET," "GOV," and "INT"—as well as top-level domains representing individual countries (the "country-code TLDs," or ccTLDs) that would have names in accordance with the list prepared by the International Standards Organization—"JP" for Japan, "DE" for Germany, "US" for the United States, etc.).

Each top-level domain can contain any number of 2d-level (second-level) domains. So, for instance, the EDU top-level domain contains a 2d-level domain named "temple"—conventionally represented as "temple.edu," the convention being that domain names are read from right to left, the top-level ORG domain contains a 2d-level domain named "EFF" (EFF.org)—the top-level COM domain contains a 2d-level domain named "google" (google.com), etc. (see fig. 10.1). Each 2d-level domain can contain any number of named 3d-level (third-level) domains; so, for instance, "www" is the name of a third-level domain within the "temple" 2d-level domain within the "EDU" top-level domain (www.temple.edu), "download" is a 3d-level name within the "google" 2d-level domain within the "COM" top-level domain (download.google .com), "about" is a third-level domain within the "EFF" 2d-level domain within the "ORG" top-level domain (about.eff.org). And so on (up to 127 levels deep).

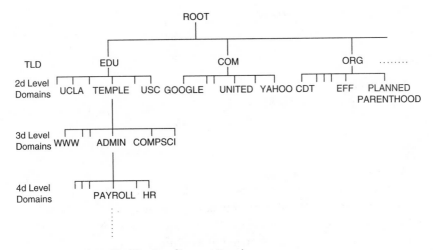

FIGURE 10.1 Hierarchical Nesting of Internet Domains.

The DNS is **distributed** in the sense that there is no longer a single source of information associating names with their addresses—no more telephone-book-type listing all of the names on the entire inter-network, no more "hosts.txt" file. Instead, the information associating any specific name with an IP Address is scattered in bits and pieces around the network. Each domain maintains a database of names and associated IP addresses for **all domains beneath it in the hierarchy**. So there is a database for EDU listing the names and IP Addresses for all 2d-level domains within EDU (and the same for COM, and UK, and SA, and all other TLDs). That database looks something like this:

TABLE 10.2 THE EDU DATABASE

NAME	IP ADDRESS
...	...
Temple	155.247.19.2
Stanford	36.56.0.152
UCLA	128.97.128.1
...	....

Each 2d-level domain (temple.edu, eff.org, google.com) maintains a database of names and IP Addresses for all domains beneath **it** in the hierarchy—i.e., for all **3d-level domains** within each respective 2d-level domain. Thus, "temple" in the "EDU" domain (whose IP Address, as shown above, is 155.247.19.2) must maintain the list of names and IP Addresses of all 3d-level domains beneath "temple.edu"—www.temple.edu, compsci.temple.edu, admin.temple.edu, etc.

TABLE 10.3 THE TEMPLE DATABASE

NAME	IP ADDRESS
...	...
www	155.24.24.100
compsci	155.24.24.110
admin	155.24.24. 211
...	....

And so on.

At the very top of the whole system is what is known as the ROOT database—the Ur-domain, as it were. The ROOT continues this hierarchical pattern "upwards"; the ROOT database lists the names and IP Addresses for all domains immediately beneath it in the hierarchy, i.e., all of the **top-level domains:**

TABLE 10.4 THE ROOT DATABASE

NAME	IP ADDRESS
...	
COM	192.5.6.30
EDU	192.41.162.32
ORG	204.74.112.1
...	...
JP	202.12.30.33
DE	193.141.40.1
UK	128.16.5.32
...	....

Here's how it all works in practice—the "magical mystery tour," as Anthony Rutkowski, one of the early DNS engineers, called it, of name-to-number resolution. Suppose you are sending a simple message to the machine named "www.temple.edu"—a standard "http" request for the "home page" stored at that address, say. Here's how the network protocols find the IP Address for that machine.

Step 1: You send your message, addressed to "www.temple.edu," to your Internet service provider—i.e., to whoever provides you with your connection to the inter-network. Your ISP then sends the following query to the ROOT:

"Dear ROOT: I need an IP address in the EDU top-level domain; where can I find the database for the EDU domain?"

The ROOT performs a lookup in its database, finds the IP Address for the EDU domain nameserver, and sends back the appropriate response ("The EDU database is at IP Address 192.41.162.32.").

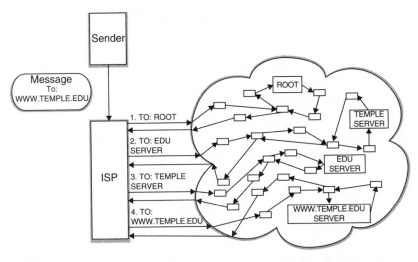

FIGURE 10.2 The "Magical Mystery Tour" of Name-to-Number Resolution on the Internet.

Step 2: Your ISP then sends a query to the machine identified in Step 1 (192.41.162.32—the EDU domain nameserver):

"Dear EDU domain nameserver: I'm looking for an address in the 'Temple' 2d-level domain; where can I find the database for the Temple domain?"

The EDU nameserver looks in **its** database and sends back the appropriate IP Address in response ("The Temple domain nameserver is at IP Address 155.247.19.2").

Step 3: Your ISP then sends a query to **that** machine (155.247.19.2, the Temple domain nameserver):

"Dear Temple nameserver: I'm looking for the machine named "www" within your domain; what is its IP Address?"

The Temple server looks in **its** database and sends back the appropriate IP Address in response (" 'www' is at IP Address 155.247.128.4").

Step 4: Your ISP inserts this IP Address—155.247.128.4—into the appropriate space in your original message, and off it goes to the routers and, ultimately, to machine 155.247.128.4.

It was (another) brilliant bit of engineering. The answer to the question "Who is going to keep track of all of the names and IP Addresses as the network gets bigger?" would be: Nobody! Instead, "pointers" would be distributed around the network to resolve address queries—the ROOT pointing to the source of information for the domains beneath it in the hierarchy, each top-level domain pointing to the source of address information for "its" 2d-level domains, each 2d-level domain pointing to the address information for "its" 3d-level domains, and on and on. Nobody searches through a 500-million-entry database to find www.temple.edu's IP Address from among the 500-million machines on the Internet; there is no such database anymore. The task of finding the IP Address for www.temple.edu has been broken into small pieces, and while there's still a lot of searching and lookup to do, considerably less work is involved in the aggregate than dragging out the hosts.txt file and searching through it to find every address for every message. Like its close cousin, distributed routing (see chap. 3), it was truly innovative; no other inter-networking protocols in 1983 solved the addressing problem in this manner. And, like distributed routing, it scales—the Internet itself is proof of that, proof that the system can handle hundreds of millions of names (and associated IP Addresses), and that it could resolve addresses for billions of messages each day, all more or less flawlessly.[1]

THE DNS CRISIS

It all purred along quite smoothly through the late 1980s and into the 1990s. Jon Postel, along with a few colleagues at ISI and in the relevant IETF committees and working groups, stayed at the helm, maintaining and updating the various interlocking pointer databases that kept the whole system operating, funded by grants from the U.S. Defense Department and the National Science Foundation (NSF).[2]

---

1 As with distributed routing, the DNS scaling story is more complicated than this. Two other engineering tricks—"replication" and "caching"—have been developed and deployed across the Internet to help the DNS to scale as well as it has. **Replication** refers to the simple process whereby copies of the various name/number databases are placed on multiple machines—there are, for example, thirteen separate machines across the Internet holding identical copies of the ROOT database, dozens of COM nameservers with identical copies of the COM database, etc.—as a way of reducing traffic to, and processing load on, any single machine. **Caching** refers to the process whereby ISPs store IP Addresses in a memory "cache" after going through the "Magical Mystery Tour" of multiple queries described in the text (and in fig. 10.2) to find the correct IP Address. So, for instance, when I logged onto the Internet this morning through my ISP (Temple University) and sent a message to "www.google.com" (requesting the display of the Google "home page"), the Temple host machine didn't actually have to send queries to the ROOT, the COM nameserver, and the Google nameserver to find the correct address; because it had surely received many requests for this IP Address previously, even within the last minute or so, it probably stored a copy of that IP Address in its memory "cache" and retrieved it from there, rather than from the distributed databases, thereby speeding up the process significantly.

2 In the late 1980s, Postel and his IETF colleagues began referring to this database management and coordination work as the "IANA" function—the Internet Assigned Numbers Authority. IANA took on the responsibility for all of the tasks related to the naming and numbering system: (a) handing out IP Addresses (to entities that would distribute them to end-users, and that were now becoming known as Internet Service Providers); (b) maintaining the ROOT database (so that it pointed to the "correct" top-level domain databases), (c) maintaining the top-level domain databases (or delegating the responsibility for

In late 1992—with the number of machines on the TCP/IP network numbering just under 1 million—the National Science Foundation decided to "farm out" some of Postel's DNS database maintenance work. It awarded a five-year contract to a small start-up firm, Network Solutions, Inc. (NSI), under which the National Science Foundation (i.e., the U.S. taxpayers) would pay NSI to maintain the DNS (up to a maximum of around $5 million). Specifically, NSI, in cooperation with the IETF and IANA, would have the responsibility for (a) maintaining the ROOT file and (b) maintaining the .COM, .NET, and .ORG domains—that is, keeping and updating the IP Address databases for these three domains, and processing incoming applications for new 2d-level domains within each of them.

Who noticed, at the time? Who would have cared, even if they **had** noticed? The answer: virtually nobody. Outside of a few technical publications, there was not a single reference in a newspaper or magazine article (or, needless to say, on television or radio), as far as I can determine, to the NSF-NSI Agreement in 1992. It's perfectly understandable; in 1992, this network wasn't "the Internet" quite yet; it was still just a quasi-experimental inter-networking scheme that mostly connected a bunch of scientists and engineers at U.S. universities together. Nor was it at all clear that this inter-network would or could become the Internet; you may recall from the discussion in the previous chapter that the NSF itself wasn't even permitted, in 1992, to use TCP/IP for its own networking projects, because the U.S. government was still requiring all nonmilitary federal agencies to use of the International Telecommunications Union's "OSI" protocols.

But then the wave hit. Just as the NSF-NSI contract takes effect, in January 1993, the exponential growth of the TCP/IP network starts to pick up steam. Not coincidentally, it was around this time, in early 1993, that the National Center for Supercomputer Applications at the University of Illinois releases the first "web browser," Mosaic; by January of the following year (1994), there were already 20 million web users, and the World Wide Web—which, as we all know, uses domain names as part of its "Uniform Resource Locator" (URL) system to locate specific files—was on its way to becoming the most popular application on a now-exploding (and increasingly global) Internet.

The "dot-com" boom had begun—the name nicely capturing the significance, at the time, of the top-level domain in which everyone, suddenly, was very interested.

---

maintaining those databases (COM, DE, RU, EDU) to entities that would, in turn, delegate responsibility for maintaining the second-level domain databases (microsoft, deutsche-bank. de, temple), and so on down the line, and (d) coordinating the whole interlocking scheme.

IANA activities were all performed in accordance with the procedures set forth in several dozen IETF Internet Standards dealing with naming and numbering. It was never entirely clear whether IANA referred, as its name seemed to imply, to a separate **organization**,

The mainstream press, during this period, discovered the Internet—indeed, we might say that during this period the TCP/IP network **became** "the Internet"—and with it, its curious "domain names."[3] Not everybody knew what they were, exactly, but everybody—well, almost everybody, individuals and businesses by the thousands, and then the hundreds of thousands, and then the millions—wanted one. Applications for new names, especially within the .COM domain, soared, from around 200 per month at the start of the NSF-NSI contract in January 1993 to over 30,000 per month by late 1995, to more than 200,000 per month when the NSF-NSI contract expired in January 1998—a 100,000 percent increase! After two years (January 1995), there were already 1.3 million machines in the .COM domain, and by January 1998 there were over 8 million.

The technical demands that this extraordinary growth in the numbers placed on the DNS were prodigious. But the engineers had (more or less) solved those scaling problems. It wasn't the numbers that precipitated the DNS crisis but what the numbers brought along with them—a new set of constraints and pressures that we might call, for want of a better term, "interest," a combustible mixture of attention, power, money, and politics.

---

or just to the collection of **activities** being performed; like the IETF itself, IANA had no formal existence, no documents that even described what, exactly, "it" was. But whatever it was, it ran the DNS.

The emergence of IANA was, as Milton Mueller describes it, something of a turning point in what he calls the "technical community's growing conception of itself as an autonomous, self-governing, social complex."

> Explicit claims on the right to manage name and address assignment were being made by an authority structure that existed solely in Internet RFCs and lacked any basis in formal law or state action. The authority claims nevertheless had significant legitimacy within the technical community [because] Postel was known, respected, and trusted within the IETF and the supporting government agencies....One former NSF official described the situation as an "enlightened monarchy in which the federal government funded the best brains." Their output was RFCs, which were approved through a collegial, though sometimes brutal, process of someone advancing an idea and everyone beating on it until the group consensus was that it would work. These RFCs became the "law" of the internet—"law" in the sense of operational practice, not legal jurisdiction. (Milton Mueller, *Ruling the Root*, 94–95)

3   The Lexis-Nexis "All News" database contains seventy citations to stories in 1993 containing the phrase "domain names"—all from publications with names like "UNIX World," or "LAN Technology," or "InfoWorld." That jumped to around 1,700 by 1996 and more than 4,000 by 1998—an increase of over 5,000 percent in five years—by which time it included many stories in the *Boston Globe*, the *New York Times*, the Cleveland *Plain Dealer*, and similar mainstream publications.

Domain names had become—literally, almost overnight—a VERY BIG DEAL. There was now **lots** of money at stake; individual 2d-level domains, especially in the .COM top-level domain, were turning out to be very valuable things. An active secondary market in .COM domain names sprang up, in which names registered with NSI were bought and sold, and some names were commanding prices in the thousands, some even in the tens of thousands, of dollars. Estimates of the **aggregate** value of the .COM domain were, suddenly, astronomically large. At the start of the NSI-NSF contract, NSI was giving names away for free, on a simple first-come first-served basis; that's how it had always been done up to that point, with all associated costs of database management and administration subsidized by the U.S. taxpayer. That wouldn't last too long; it was politically insupportable—downright absurd, even—for taxpayers to continue to subsidize the infrastructure for a system that was clearly capable of paying its own way. In March 1995 the NSF-NSI Cooperative Agreement was amended to permit NSI to sell 2d-level domain names (at the fixed price of $100 for a two-year registration).

NSI was sitting on a gold mine. At $100 each, 200,000 registrations a month, and exponential growth in demand with no limit in sight, you're talking real money. You could take that to the bank—which NSI promptly did, in 1997, when it raised about $60 million dollars in a public stock offering in which the company was valued at just over a quarter of a billion dollars—entirely on the strength of its role in the DNS registration system.

It wasn't **just** the money, of course—but with that kind of money in play, people will start to pay attention, and to ask questions, questions of a kind nobody had asked before: What do I get for my $100, exactly—a line in a database? Do I "own" that domain, once I register it? What happens if "my" name is already taken? How do I "oust" someone who is "squatting" on a domain that rightfully should be mine? And questions like:

- Why had the U.S. government given a private company a monopoly franchise over the most valuable portion of name space? It smelled a bit like King George and the Hudson Bay Company—here, you take Canada and the Northwest Territory and extract all the value you can from it, while we keep potential competitors at bay. That's not how we like to think the U.S. government does business these days—but somehow it appeared to have given NSI something like that, control over the entire .COM domain. (And NSI, as you might expect, was making noises indicating that it would vigorously resist, using all means at its disposal, any attempt to wrest that control away from it.)
- Why weren't there more top-level domains? Scarcity creates value; NSI's monopoly over the .COM domain was so valuable in part because there were only seven global top-level domains in Postel's original scheme—"EDU," "ORG," "COM," "MIL," "NET," "GOV," and "INT"—and only one designated for "commercial" uses. But there was nothing sacrosanct about Postel's scheme for the top level; the DNS could, as a

technical matter, accommodate hundreds, even thousands, of domains at **any** level of the hierarchy, including the top. There was a great deal of interest from people and organizations willing to set up .BIZ, .MUSIC, .EUR, .MUSEUM, .INFO, .NEWS, .LAW, .MALL, .AEROSPACE, .XXX, and many others—why had nothing come of that?

- Who gets to be in charge of the country code TLDs? Who decides whether Palestine, or Kosovo, or Tibet, or Taiwan should have their own country code TLDs? Nothing better illustrates the ambiguities and informalities under which the DNS had operated during the first decade or so of its existence than the process by which the entities responsible for the country code domains were chosen. It couldn't have been simpler: Jon Postel decided. If he thought you were the right person for the job, he gave you responsibility for the domain—that is, he put **your** machine's IP Address into the ROOT file as the authoritative source of addresses for the domain. If you were interested in running a ccTLD, you sent Postel a message, and if he felt you were the right person for the job, he gave it to you.

- And finally, what's up with the ROOT? The whole system—the whole Internet, really—seemed to hinge on one little text file, less than 200 lines long, listing all of the top-level domains and the IP Addresses where addresses for 2d-level domains can be found. If the ROOT file stopped working correctly—if it points to the wrong machines, or to nonexistent machines, for each TLD—the whole inter-network, for all intents and purposes, goes dark. Jon Weinberg put it well:

By virtue of the structure of the DNS, the ability to modify (or to refuse to modify) the root zone files in the root servers carries with it considerable power. If a user types in a domain name incorporating a top-level domain that is unknown to the root servers, then the DNS will be unable to find the corresponding computer. The power to control the root servers is the power to decide (1) which top-level domains are visible in the name space and (2) which name servers are authoritative for those top-level domains—that is, which entities get to say who controls the various second-level domains in that top-level domain.

The top-level domains—.COM, .ORG, .JP, .DE and all the rest—exist only because the ROOT says they exist—because there is a listing in the ROOT file for each of them. The "authoritative" source for names and addresses within each TLD is whatever machine the ROOT says it is; if the ROOT points to NSI's machine as the source for .COM addresses, then NSI's database is the authoritative source for .COM addresses. Delete an entry from the ROOT and the corresponding domain disappears in its entirety (along with all lower-level domains beneath it in the hierarchy). They don't really disappear, of course; the physical machines continue to exist, and those machines remain connected, physically, to other machines on the inter-network; but there's no way for those other machines on the network to find them, or to get messages to them—so for all intents and purposes they have ceased to exist on the Internet.

The ROOT controls the very existence of all of the TLDs (and all of their subordinate domains). Inevitably, people started to wonder: **Who controlled the ROOT?** Who had the right or authority to modify, or to refuse to modify, the ROOT file?

Amazingly enough, **nobody knew for certain!** It had never been spelled out clearly, because the question had simply not come up in this way before; there hadn't been any conflicts about what should appear in the ROOT (a tribute, at least in part, surely, to Postel's able stewardship), so nobody had given much thought to questions of "rights" and "authority" and "control." The U.S. government owned the machine—the "A" root server—on which the ROOT file had always been stored, so it, presumably, had the right to do what it wished with the ROOT file. That was clear enough. What was not clear was whether the government "owned" the ROOT, in the sense of having the **exclusive** right to make changes in the ROOT. Could NSI, for instance, make changes in the ROOT? NSI had operational control over the "A" root server under the 1992 Agreement; did that carry with it the right to change the contents of the ROOT file? And what about Postel and his IANA/IETF colleagues? The Cooperative Agreement obligated them to "cooperate," in some unspecified fashion, with NSI in maintaining the ROOT. Were they authorized to act unilaterally, if they thought some change needed to be made and NSI disagreed?

These questions started to take on real urgency as 1998 approached—the date on which the U.S. government's contracts with NSI (and with Postel and IANA) were set to expire. It was as though a spotlight had suddenly been turned on a corner of the world that had previously been operating in almost total darkness, and the DNS turned out to be like one of those little mites or beetles that thrive in darkness, under rocks, and which go scurrying for cover when the rock is pried loose and the sunlight beams in. All of a sudden, the DNS had "stakeholders"—individuals and companies and governments and nongovernmental organizations of all sizes and stripes, with differing views about, and differing interest in, how the DNS should grow and how it should be organized and managed.

Beginning in mid-1996 or so, there's a flurry, which then becomes a frenzy, of public and private attention focused on the DNS: Congress holds hearings, the White House appoints an "Interagency Task Force," the European Union convenes its own series of Conferences and publishes several white papers on the subject, the UN's World Intellectual Property Organization, after a number of public and private meetings, issues a "Report on the Management of Internet Names and Addresses," the IETF, and IANA, and ISOC, and the International Telecommunications Union, and the Association for Computing Machinery, the American Bar Association, and for all I know dozens or hundreds of similar groups hold their own meetings, debate proposals and counterproposals, issue discussion papers, policy positions, and the rest.

On January 28, 1998, Postel conducted what he would later call a "test" (and which others labeled a "hijacking") of the entire DNS system. He copied the ROOT file over to a machine at ISI, and he redirected all queries going to the ROOT to that machine. The White House—by 1998 the Clinton White House was heavily involved in the DNS affair, through that Interagency Task Force chaired by one of Clinton's "inner circle" of advisors, Ira Magaziner—was not amused; Magaziner threatened Postel with criminal prosecution (though it was by no means clear what law, if any, Postel had broken by his actions).

And finally, just to add to the confusion, it was during this period that a number of "alternate ROOTs" began to appear—and there didn't seem to be anything anyone could do to stop them from appearing.[4] Several enterprising entrepreneurs, starting around 1996, began offering up their alternate versions of the ROOT file. If the ability to put 2d-level domains into the .COM database is worth $60 billion or so, surely, they figured, we can pick up a few million here or there by setting up .MED, or .XXX, or .BIZ, or .WEB or . . . and selling 2d-level names in those new domains. Their pitch to the ISPs of the world was this: You should use our ROOT; it will be **identical** to the NSI/USGovernment/IANA ROOT, because we'll copy theirs every day; ours, though, will have **more** top-level domains than theirs.

Some ISPs had signed on. It looks like a pretty good deal, actually—it's just like the old Internet, but bigger. What could be wrong with that? Why would an ISP turn that deal down?

Imagine trying to explain all of this, in 1996, to a Congressional Committee, or the Commissioners of the European Union, or the Board of Directors of McDonalds, Inc. "Let me get this straight: There's this ROOT file. Without it, the whole thing—this all-of-a-sudden, billion-dollar, exponentially growing

---

4 The idea of an "alternate ROOT" is pretty simple—alarmingly simple, to some. Anyone—you or I or anyone else—can download the ROOT file and post it on his or her machine; it's just a little 2 K text file, a couple of hundred lines long, and it is publicly accessible because it **has** to be publicly accessible, given its role in the system. You can easily modify this file in your text processor, if you want—you could, for instance, add a new line to the database, establishing .JEFFERSON as a new top-level domain, inserting an IP Address (your own, perhaps) as the location of the authoritative domain name server for the JEFFERSON top-level domain. Presto! You can then announce to the world: "The ROOT is now located **here**, on my machine, IP Address 151.11.222.1. From now on, you may send all queries about all TLDs there."

You could do all of that easily enough; lots of twelve-year-old kids can do that these days. You wouldn't really be in possession of "the ROOT," of course; it's not the content of that little 2 K file (which is so easy to copy) that makes it "the ROOT," but the fact that all the other machines on the inter-network direct their queries to it that makes it the ROOT; the consensus of ISPs around the globe that one particular copy of the file is the ROOT makes it the ROOT. Unless and until you can somehow get those ISPs to direct queries your way, you don't have the ROOT, you just have a 2 K text file sitting on your server that looks like the ROOT.

inter-network, all of those "web sites," all of that "email," all of it—goes dark, disappears, fails to function. But we don't know who owns it, or who has the right to change it. Organizations that don't even exist as legal entities—the IETF, IANA—seem to be in charge. And anyone who wants to can set up his or own competing system? That's how this Internet works?"

THE BIRTH OF ICANN

These "DNS Wars," as they've been called, constituted a crisis of "governance" because the hard questions were all, ultimately, of the form: Who decides? Who decides what's in the ROOT? Who decides whether Palestine gets a top-level domain, or where COM addresses are to be found, or how many TLDs there will be and what they will be, or which organization should run the country code domains for Iran, or for Korea, or for Armenia, or whether trademark owners deserve a special entitlement to domains containing their trademarked names?

BOX 10.1

I am reminded of an insightful comment that computer scientist Scott Bradner once made about "Internet governance": the hard Internet governance question is not "who decides?" but "who decides who decides?"

The answers to these questions—sometimes "Jon Postel," sometimes "IANA," or "NSI," or "a rough consensus of the participants in the relevant IETF Working Groups"—were all perfectly reasonable in 1983 or even 1992, when the questions arose (if they arose at all) in the context of an inter-networking experiment within a small and relatively insular academic community. They seemed much less reasonable, though, to many people, in 1998, when they arose in the context of a critical part—in some ways, **the** critical part—of the infrastructure for the global institution that the Internet had become.[5]

---

5   Jon Postel's role in the shape and future direction of the entire DNS system (and hence the entire Internet) was a particular source of confusion and conflict. On the one hand, he had enormous prestige within the technical community, widely viewed as having been personally responsible for getting the whole system to work as well as it had, and for having exercised his authority over naming and numbering fairly and wisely and in an even-handed manner. On the other hand, as his January "test" showed, his power over the operation of the whole system had reached, by 1998, gargantuan proportions—not because his job description had changed over the years, but because the thing over which he had power had become so large. It was hard to defend lodging that kind of power in one person, even one person as respected as Postel was—as even Postel himself recognized, as the DNS crisis hit its peak.

Against this background, the U.S. government's contracts with NSI and IANA were about to expire, and with them the government's formal relationship to, and its legal obligations regarding, the continued operation of the DNS. A decision had to be made: What to do next?

Jeffersonians and Hamiltonians had very different ideas about that. The conversation went something like this:

J: The government doesn't have to **do** anything. Let the contracts expire, break out the champagne, give congratulations all around on a job well done, and that's the end of that. This is what the government ordinarily does when contracts like these come to an end (except perhaps for the part about the champagne). The purpose of the Agreements was to support the development of some new technology, and once the technology has been successfully deployed and "up-and-running"—as the DNS, obviously, is—the government steps aside and lets it run, having accomplished its task. Why is the DNS any different? Shut down the "A" root server, sever all ties to IANA and NSI and the other players, and let the various interested parties work things out on their own.

H: Bad idea. The DNS **is** different; it requires coordination to function effectively, and the government—or someone—needs to take responsibility for that. The Internet is a single, interconnected system because it has a single source of unique names—**one ROOT to which all machines point**, one source for COM and .JP and .RU addresses to which all machines point. Someone needs to be in charge of that, or the whole system will spin out of control and the Internet will fragment: alternate ROOTs will jockey for primacy, new TLDs will appear (and, probably, disappear), some users will be able to find .BIZ addresses and some won't.

J: Yes—that's called innovation. We've had this debate before—remember?—about formation of the American Academy. The DNS is, when all is said and done, just a linguistic device, a way to give names to things. Coordination is great, to be sure; but you can get coordination **without** control. Otherwise, you destroy its copiousness. The system will converge because it is consensus-based—and if there's no consensus about things, why should we impose one?

H: Easy for you to say, from up there on your perch in Monticello. The bottom line is that walking away will produce chaos and a kind of mob rule; maybe it will settle down into some equilibrium, and maybe it won't, and that's not good enough anymore—not with so much at stake. How long would that period of instability last? And what would the Internet look like when it was over?

When the dust settled, the Hamiltonians had (largely) carried the day. The government's final white paper (June, 1998) announced that **someone** would indeed take charge:

[C]oordination of the root server network is necessary if the whole system is to work smoothly. While day-to-day operational tasks, such as the actual operation and maintenance of the Internet root servers, can be dispersed, overall policy guidance and control of the TLDs and the Internet root server system should be vested in a single organization.

The government declared that it was prepared to "recognize" a new nonprofit corporation—it didn't exist yet, and was called, generically, "NewCo" in the white paper—that would "administer policy for the Internet name and address system [and] undertake various responsibilities for the administration of the domain name system now performed by or on behalf of the U.S. Government." It called upon "private sector Internet stakeholders" to form this new corporation, and it specified the broad outlines of how the new corporation should operate and the policies it should adopt: It would be based in the United States, and it would be run by a board of directors that was "balanced to equitably represent the interests of IP number registries, domain name registries, domain name registrars, the technical community, Internet service providers (ISPs), and Internet users (commercial, not-for-profit, and individuals)," and "broadly representative of the global Internet community."

It was Hamiltonian in spirit, and not only in its decision to centralize DNS management in a single organization. Despite a nod in the Jeffersonians' direction—the new organization "should, as far as possible, reflect the bottom-up governance that has characterized development of the Internet to date"—the white paper made it clear that the new organization's "first priority" would be the "stability of the Internet":

> The U.S. Government should end its role in the Internet number and name address system in a manner that ensures the stability of the Internet. The introduction of a new management system should not disrupt current operations or create competing root systems. During the transition and thereafter, the stability of the Internet should be the first priority of any DNS management system.

That was the one thing the Jeffersonians and their decentralized processes could **not** guarantee—stability, the absence of "disruption," the elimination of competing roots.

ICANN—the "Internet Corporation for Assigned Names and Numbers," a California nonprofit corporation—was formed in October 1998 in response to the white paper's call,[6] and on November 25, 1998, the U.S. Department of Commerce entered into an agreement with the new corporation to begin the "transition to private sector management of the DNS." Under the terms of the agreement, ICANN would be responsible to "design, develop, and test the mechanisms, methods, and procedures that should be in place and the steps necessary to transition management

---

6 Remarkably and tragically, just as the crisis was reaching its head, on October 18, 1998, Jon Postel, the one person who without question understood the DNS better than anyone else alive, passed away at his home in California.

responsibility for DNS functions now performed by, or on behalf of, the U.S. Government," including "oversight of the operation of the authoritative root server system," "oversight of the policy for determining the circumstances under which new top level domains would be added to the root system," and "coordination of the assignment of other Internet technical parameters as needed to maintain universal connectivity on the Internet." All those "who decides?" questions would now have a different answer: ICANN decides.

ICANN IN ACTION

In its first two-and-a-half years of operation, ICANN worked with the US Department of Commerce to transform administration of the DNS root into the platform for contract-based governance of the Internet. The new regime defined and distributed property rights in the domain name space, and imposed economic regulation on the domain name industry.

MILTON MUELLER, *RULING THE ROOT*

ICANN doesn't really "run the Internet," as press accounts occasionally have it. But it also does more than just "database management," or "technical coordination," as it sometimes claims. It is something in between, a new kind of hybrid regulatory institution—a "completely new institutional animal," the *Economist* magazine called it—that governs aspects of life in cyberspace by means of the control it asserts over technical resources and technical operations at the bottom of the protocol stack, using its control over the chain of databases extending downward from the ROOT to impose contractual obligations on anyone (and everyone) who wants to be in that chain.

"Contract-based governance," Milton Mueller aptly called it. Here's an illustration of how it works. One of the tasks with which ICANN was charged by the U.S. government was to deal with "cybersquatters"[7]—to come up with some process,

---

7   The term "cybersquatter" was widely used (even making its way into a federal statute, the "Anti-Cybersquatting Protection Act of 1998") to describe individuals registering 2d-level domains (almost always in the COM top-level domain—this was, after all, the "dot-com boom") with names similar or identical to well-known trademarks, for the sole purpose of reselling the domain to the trademark owner.

The practice can be traced, I think, to a 1994 story by Joshua Quittner in *Wired* and *Newsweek*. Quittner's story was to be about the ways in which corporations were using the World Wide Web. In the course of his research he contacted McDonalds, Inc., looking for whoever could explain the company's plans for the Mcdonalds.com domain. He discovered that, to his amazement, there was no such person, and that the company hadn't even bothered to register the Mcdonalds.com domain. Quittner promptly registered it in his name, and he asked readers for ideas about what he should do with the domain—put it up

as the government put it in the white paper, to "balance the needs of domain name holders with the legitimate concerns of trademark owners." ICANN's response was to promulgate, in 1999, new rules governing trademark use on the Internet, known as the Uniform Dispute Resolution Policy—or, in the acronym-crazed environment in which ICANN operates, the "UDRP."

The UDRP defines the offense:

- Registration of a domain name that is "identical or confusingly similar to a trademark" belonging to a third party,
- by someone with "no rights or legitimate interests" in that domain name, and who
- has registered, or is using, the domain name "in bad faith."[8]

It specifies a procedure for appointing an arbitrator, chosen from among ICANN-approved arbitration providers, to hear claims that the offense has been committed—to determine whether the offense has been committed—whether the name "goooooogle.COM," say, is "confusingly similar" to someone else's trademark, and whether it was registered "in bad faith" by someone with "no legitimate rights" to it.

And it has a mechanism for enforcing the arbitrators' judgments. The operators of the top-level domain databases are the enforcement agents. All ICANN-authorized TLD operators—known as "Registries," the Keepers of the Names for each top-level domain, the operators of the machines to which the ROOT points for resolving names in that domain—must agree, in their contracts with ICANN, to remove or modify the entries in their databases in accordance with the arbitrators' decisions. So if a UDRP arbitrator determines that your registration of "goooooogle. COM" violates the UDRP, the COM Registry operator will (because it is contractually obligated to) remove the entry associating the name "goooooogle" with **your**

---

for auction to the highest bidder, perhaps? (Quittner ended up selling the registration to McDonalds, Inc., and donating the sale price to charity.)

Cybersquatting became a thriving business; in the ensuing decade, hundreds, and then thousands, of registrations bearing trademarked names—Esquire.com, Zippo.com, Gateway. com, Plannedparenthood.com, Porsche.com, Academyaward.com, Prince.com, Millertime. com, Peterframpton.com, Panavision.com, Kaplan.com, MTV.com, Clue.com, Candyland.com, Panavision.com, Peta.com, Superman.com, and on and on it went—became the subject of disputes, and dozens of lawsuits complaining of the practice were instituted in the United States and, to a lesser extent, elsewhere around the globe.

8   The UDRP defines "bad faith" to mean registration of a domain for the purpose of (a) "selling, renting, or otherwise transferring the domain name registration to . . . the owner of the trademark or service mark," (b) preventing the owner of the trademark "from reflecting the mark in a corresponding domain name," (c) "disrupting the business" of a competitor, or (d) creating confusion in the minds of consumers "as to the source, sponsorship, affiliation, or endorsement" of one web site or product or service and the trademark owner's.

machine from its database of 2d-level COM names (and, if the arbitrator has so ordered, transfer that name to the another party—presumably, the trademark owner, Google, Inc.). ICANN imposes this condition on all ICANN-accredited top-level domain registries; ICANN won't accredit you unless you agree to enforce the UDRP in this way, and unless ICANN accredits you, it won't point the ROOT toward your database.[9]

It's a kind of global, Internet-only trademark law. Some of my law professor colleagues object to calling it "law" (and, therefore, to calling what ICANN is doing "lawmaking"). It is true that it is neither issued by a (realspace) sovereign state nor backed by any realspace enforcement powers. The UDRP operates entirely in "domain space"—inside the databases. UDRP proceedings don't (and can't) impose monetary penalties on anyone, they can't seize anyone's bank account, garnish anyone's salary, or take away anyone's house, or have anyone thrown into prison; they can only move entries around in the databases. So if you define law to mean only those rules that **are** backed by sovereign power and enforced by sovereign states, then—obviously—it's not law.

But whatever you call it, it looks a lot like law: it defines rights and obligations between parties who have conflicting claims to resources, it specifies a procedure for making judgments (hopefully, fair ones) in individual cases, and it has a mechanism for enforcing those judgments. It quacks like a duck, and walks like a duck, and looks like a duck; that doesn't necessarily mean that it **is** a duck, but it's a useful first approximation. The UDRP process has decided thousands of cases—more than 10,000, as of this writing. Without the enforcement powers of a realspace sovereign behind it, it can't mete out any realspace remedies. But to "govern" in namespace, on the inter-network, it doesn't really have to. The UDRP operates directly on the thing itself that the parties are fighting over—in this case, the database entry.[10]

9 The TLD Registries also agree to "flow-through" these provisions regarding compliance with the UDRP in their contracts with all "downstream" entities. That is, whoever wants to register the "goooooogle. com" domain name must consent, by contract, to submit any claims against the domain to the UDRP procedure, because the COM Registry operator won't put it in the COM database without that consent (and ICANN won't authorize it to be the COM Registry if it doesn't do that).

10 Lawyers call this an "in rem" proceeding—a proceeding whose judgments operate on the thing that the parties are fighting over—as opposed to a proceeding "in personam" (whose judgments operate on the person). To the engineers, it looks like "self-executing code": proceedings whose output (arbitrator's decisions) serves as input into the name databases, and where the system is configured so that those databases are automatically altered to conform with that output.

Strangely enough, Jefferson played a leading (though largely inadvertent) role in the development of the doctrines of in rem and in personam jurisdiction in the United States. In 1809 he was named as the defendant in a lawsuit filed by one Edward Livingston, a New

Its orders are enforced by changing that entry (or not, as the case may be), and all relevant parties have promised, through the web of ICANN-initiated contracts, to take the steps necessary to comply with the UDRP decisions.

Contract-based governance. It applies **only** on the inter-network—but **everywhere** on the inter-network, because it operates so far down in the protocol stack. It only covers a thin slice—a **very** thin slice—of the universe of inter-network legal disputes: only those disputes between trademark holders and domain name registrants over rights to their names. Thin, but wide; wherever you live, wherever, and from whomever, you obtained your domain name, the UDRP can be brought to bear on to determine whether you get to keep it.

It's a strange new kind of law, and a strange new kind of lawmaking process, and, frankly, I'm not quite sure what to make of it. Over and above the narrow (but important) questions about the substance of the rules ICANN has made—questions about whether the UDRP is "good" global trademark law or "bad," whether it is fair to the participants, and free from bias, whether it reasonably allocates rights and duties among the parties, whether it successfully distinguishes between those registrations that are in "bad faith" from those that are not—are the broader questions about the process of rule-making, the "governance" questions. ICANN has a kind of

---

Orleans land speculator, who sought $100,000 in damages for actions Jefferson had taken while president to oust Livingston and other "squatters" from land adjacent to the Mississippi River near New Orleans. John Marshall, then chief justice of the Supreme Court, assigned himself to preside over the case—a worrisome sign, Jefferson thought, for the animosity between the two men was deep and of long standing. Marshall was the last great Federalist holdout in Washington after the Jeffersonians swept into power in the election of 1800, having been nominated by Adams and confirmed by the Federalist Senate literally as they were packing up and preparing to move out of town, and the battles between the two men during the eight years they shared the national stage are legendary. Jefferson was understandably nervous that Marshall would be unsympathetic to the main argument that he was going to make in his defense, which was that personal liability for monetary damage could not attach to any actions taken by a sitting president in the performance of his official duties. *His* [Marshall's] *twistifications of the law show how dextrously he can reconcile law to his personal biases; and nobody seems to doubt that he is prepared to decide that Livingston's right to the batture is unquestionable, and that I am bound to pay for it with my private fortune.*

In fact, Marshall ruled in Jefferson's favor—though not for the reasons Jefferson had proffered. Instead, in a dense and highly technical opinion, he held that the court, sitting in Virginia, had no jurisdiction over Livingston's claim, which could be brought only where the alleged harm had occurred and where the land was located (i.e., in New Orleans). The framework Marshall constructed in *Livingston v. Jefferson* was to guide the development of much of the law of jurisdiction over the next one hundred years.

gatekeeper power, the power to decide who gets in and who doesn't, the power to make machines vanish from the inter-network—and that should make us all a little bit nervous. Gatekeeper power is the power to place conditions on participation in inter-network activities. Why stop at trademark-domain name conflicts? Why not couple the right to a name with compliance with other ICANN-promulgated rules of conduct—perhaps to enhance Internet security, or to eliminate spam, or to help track down copyright infringers, or to eliminate pornography?[11]

ICANN is already subject to pressure from all directions to do some or all of these things—from the UN, from the governments of the world acting unilaterally, from private intellectual property owners who want what the trademark owners got—and these pressures are likely to grow as the Internet grows. How ICANN responds will be one of the big "Internet governance" stories of the next decade. ICANN's power, like all power, can be abused, and like all power, it will likely expand until it is checked. I would reassure you, if I could, that ICANN will use its power wisely. It has, I think it fair to say, done so, by and large, up to now. But past performance, as the saying goes, is no guarantee of future success. I can't be more reassuring because I don't really understand the forces that keep ICANN in check—I don't think anyone really does.[12] So I don't really know what keeps it from expanding—all I know is that it has the power to do so.

Which is why perhaps it **does** matter whether we call what ICANN makes "law" or not. If we call it "law," more people will pay attention to it than if we call it "database management," and there will be more public discussion and debate and dialogue about what ICANN is and what it is doing. And, though this may again only be the Jeffersonian in me speaking, but more public discussion and debate and dialogue about lawmaking is, all other things being equal, a good thing.

11 Paul Twomey, the head of Australia's Office for the Information Economy, noted back in 1999 that control over the system of name databases could deliver Internet-wide regulation of "consumer protection," "resolution of intellectual property disputes," and "a capacity for indirect taxation of e-commerce." Twomey is currently the president and CEO of ICANN.

12 Although ICANN, unlike the IETF or IANA, **does** have a formal legal existence, it is no easier to penetrate its decision-making processes so as to understand precisely who, if anyone, is in control. The ICANN board of directors makes ICANN's decisions—that much is straightforward. But who decides who gets to be on the ICANN board of directors? That, it turns out, is almost impossibly difficult to describe; after several months of work, my research assistant and I could get it no clearer than the chart shown in figure 10.3, located in the appendix.

I recognize that figure 10.3 is hardly self-explanatory. But I also suspect that few of you would care to subject yourselves to a complete explanation of the board of directors selection process depicted there; if you are interested, you can find my attempt to summarize the process at www.jeffersonsmoose.org/ICANN.html.

CHAPTER 11

GOVERNING CYBERSPACE III
LAW

We hold these truths to be self-evident,...that governments are instituted among men, deriving their just powers from the consent of the governed...The present King of Great Britain...has combined with others to subject us to a jurisdiction foreign to our constitution, and unacknowledged by our laws.

TJ, *DECLARATION OF INDEPENDENCE* (1776)

The inhabitants of the several States of British America are subject to the laws which they adopted at their first settlement, and to such others as have since been made by their respective Legislatures, duly constituted and appointed with their own consent. No other Legislature whatever can rightly exercise authority over them; and these privileges they hold as the common rights of mankind.

TJ, *RESOLUTION OF ALBEMARLE COUNTY* (JULY 26, 1774)

Code may be law in cyberspace, but **law**—ordinary law, the rules contained in the statutes and ordinances and municipal regulations and constitutions and court decisions and all the rest—is also law in cyberspace. It, too, constrains—at the very top of the protocol stack, as it were—what you may or may not do on the inter-network.

The tricky part, though, is: Which law? Whose law? The international legal system is premised, at bottom, on the existence and mutual recognition of the physical boundaries that separate sovereign and independent lawmaking communities—nation-states—from one another. These boundaries **matter**, in that system, and they matter a great deal. But on the inter-network, information moves in ways that seem to pay scant regard to those boundaries, and mapping them onto network activity is a profoundly difficult challenge.

This problem is well-known to, and often debated by, anyone who spends time thinking about law and the Internet. Most discussions of the subject begin with something that looks like this:

A, in Austria, posts a file to the World Wide Web using a service provider in the Netherlands. The file is transported from the host machine in the Netherlands to C's service provider, located in Virginia, by way of intermediate machines located in Great Britain and Mexico. C retrieves the file and displays it on her screen in California. The file contains something that may be unlawful (either criminally or civilly) in California, Austria, the Netherlands, Great Britain, and Mexico, or in some of them but not others—a threat, perhaps, or an offer to sell securities, or a hard-core pornographic image, or the complete text of a poem that has fallen out of copyright in some countries but not others.

Whose law applies here? Which country can rightfully assert "jurisdiction" over this communication and these parties? Can California prosecute or punish A, under California law? Can Mexico, under **its** law? Austria? The Netherlands? If C has suffered harm as a result of this communication, where can she bring suit against A?

BOX 11.1

The realm of conflict of laws is a dismal swamp, filled with quaking quagmires, and inhabited by learned but eccentric professors who theorize about mysterious matters in a strange and incomprehensible jargon. The ordinary court, or lawyer, is quite lost when engulfed and entangled in it.

PROF. WILLIAM PROSSER

A generation of law students around the globe has been plagued by puzzles like these. And because life tends to imitate law school hypotheticals, as most law professors can attest, an actual case, involving a challenge to material available on Yahoo!'s website, teed up these issues so neatly that the whole bundle of questions is now known as the "Yahoo! Problem" among cyberlawyers and cyberlaw scholars.

THE YAHOO! PROBLEM

The facts of the actual Yahoo! case couldn't be much simpler—one of the reasons why it has been so useful as a focus for discussion and debate. Yahoo!, Inc., is the well-known provider of information and services over the World Wide Web. It operates—or used to operate—an auction website, at "auctions.yahoo.com," at which sellers could offer goods of all sorts for sale and buyers could bid on those goods. Yahoo! is a U.S. corporation, incorporated under the laws of one of the United States (Delaware), and with its principal place of business (and web servers) in another (California).

French law prohibits the display or sale of Nazi-related memorabilia; more precisely, it provides that anyone "exhibiting, in public, the uniforms, insignias, or emblems that were worn or exhibited by members of any organization declared criminal [by] the International Military Tribunal of 1945, or any such items worn by persons accused of crimes against humanity" can be punished by a fine and/or imprisonment. United States law does not similarly prohibit the display or sale of this material; indeed, it would almost certainly violate the First Amendment to the U.S. Constitution were the federal government, or any state government, to try to enact or enforce such a prohibition.

Nazi memorabilia of various kinds—medals, swords, printed publications— were available for purchase at auctions.yahoo.com. French Internet users could access the website at auctions.yahoo.com and display these items on their computers. A group of French plaintiffs—led by LICRA ("La Ligue Contre Racisme et Antisemitism"), an organization devoted to fighting racism and Nazism—brought an action in the civil court in Paris, seeking an injunction against Yahoo!'s continuing display of these items to French users.

Simple facts, but very hard questions arising out of them: Can Yahoo! be prosecuted or punished for having violated French law when it exhibits this material on its website? Does French law apply outside of French borders—"extraterritorially"— to reach Yahoo!'s actions? **Should** it apply? Is it reasonable for France to regulate Yahoo's conduct? Who decides **that** question?

Conflicts like these, involving differing judgments made by different lawmaking communities about how to order their respective legal worlds, are ubiquitous on the inter-network. They're not unheard of in realspace, of course; border-crossing transactions of all kinds have been steadily increasing in frequency over the past several centuries, hand in hand with improvements in information and transportation technologies that have combined to make the world a "smaller" place.

But on the Web, they are ubiquitous, because the Web is the application through which everyone can communicate, instantaneously and simultaneously, with everyone else on the inter-network.

Substitute "your daughter's junior high school newsletter website" for the Yahoo! auction site, and "material violating Saudi Arabian head-scarf law" for Nazi memorabilia, and multiply by 100 million, and you get the idea.

Given the ubiquity of the problem, it is perhaps surprising (or perhaps not) that legal scholars who spend their time thinking about these questions are in sharp disagreement about how they should be resolved. The rhetoric has gotten heated—perhaps overheated—at times, but that's understandable, because there's a lot at stake in this debate. Wars have been fought over seemingly arcane questions of "jurisdiction"—our own Revolutionary War among them—because seemingly arcane questions of jurisdiction are, at bottom, questions about who gets to make law for whom, and questions about who gets to make law for whom raise fundamental questions of power and order and right.

BOX 11.2

Self government today requires a politics that plays itself out in a multiplicity of settings, from neighborhoods to nations to the world as a whole.... The civic virtue distinctive to our time is the capacity to negotiate our way among the sometimes overlapping, sometimes conflicting obligations that claim us, and to live with the tension to which multiple loyalties give rise.

MICHAEL SANDEL, *DEMOCRACY'S DISCONTENT* **(1998)**

The Unexceptionalists. Cyberspace Unexceptionalists—a category in which a majority of my colleagues, I think it fair to say, would place themselves—see nothing illegitimate in France's exercise of legal authority over Yahoo!'s website. To Unexceptionalists, as their name suggests, there is nothing exceptional—nothing warranting an exception—in the fact that this interaction is taking place **on the Internet**. Here's how a leading Unexceptionalist, Professor Jack Goldsmith, put it:

Transactions in cyberspace involve real people in one territorial jurisdiction either (i) transacting with real people in other territorial jurisdictions or (ii) engaging in activity in one jurisdiction that causes real-world effects in another territorial jurisdiction. To this extent, activity in cyberspace is functionally identical to transnational activity mediated by other means, such as mail or telephone or smoke signal....

A government's responsibility for redressing local harms caused by a foreign source does not change because the harms are caused by an Internet communication. Cross-border harms that occur via the Internet are not any different than those outside the Net... [N]ations have a right and a duty to protect their citizens from harm, whatever the source and whatever the medium.

For all intents and purposes, the Unexceptionalists say, the Yahoo! Problem is just like the many old-fashioned border-crossing problems that have been around for centuries. Yahoo! might just as well have been conducting its auctions, and displaying the prohibited items, by sending catalogs or magazines or newspapers or television signals into France. There are well-settled principles of international law to deal with these problems, the Unexceptionalists point out, and it is perfectly reasonable to apply those principles here.

One of those well-settled principles permits nations to regulate conduct occurring outside their borders—"extraterritorial conduct"—if that conduct has "significant effects" **within** those borders:

It is settled, with respect to realspace activity, that a nation's right to control events within its territory and to protect its citizens permits it to regulate the local effects of extraterritorial acts.... [I]n modern times, a transaction can legitimately be regulated by the jurisdiction where the transaction occurs [and] the jurisdictions where significant effects of the transaction are felt.... When French citizens are on the receiving end of an offshore communication that their government deems harmful, France has every right to take steps [to] check and redress the harm ... regardless of the medium—World Wide Web, magazine, or video

In the Unexceptionalist view, then, the Yahoo! Problem isn't really all that difficult. Yahoo!'s conduct, though taking place outside of French borders, caused harm, as defined by French law, **in France**. French law provides a remedy for that harm. French citizens have a right, recognized under international law, to protect themselves against those who have caused them harm, even if they are standing outside of French territory when they did so. It is therefore reasonable and just to demand that Yahoo! take steps to comply with French law, and to punish it if it fails to do so.[1]

The Exceptionalists. To Exceptionalists, it **does** matter that Yahoo!'s actions took place on the Internet. Yahoo!'s website, Exceptionalists argue, is **not** the "functional equivalent of mail, or telephone, or smoke signals," (or television broadcasts, catalogs, magazines, newspapers, or other realspace analogues), and applying jurisdictional principles that were developed to deal with realspace border-crossing transactions to network transactions leads to troubling, and perhaps even absurd, results.

The problem is that website content appearing anywhere on the inter-network can have "significant effects" anywhere else on the inter-network, i.e., pretty much anywhere else on the planet.

It's not really a "problem," of course—it's one of the things that makes the Web so extraordinary a medium for human communication, not a bug but a feature.

But it **is** problematic for the Unexceptionalist view of things. A place where just about everybody can have significant effects on just about everyone else, everywhere, simultaneously, is a place where the "significant effects principle" cannot sensibly resolve jurisdictional questions. Unexceptionalist logic leads inexorably to the conclusion that (just about) everything you do on the Web may be subject to (just about) everybody's law. Simultaneously. If the **French** can legitimately assert that **their** law applies to the Yahoo! auction website (because it was accessible from within France), so, too, can the Brazilians, and (simultaneously) the Japanese, and (simultaneously) the Kenyans, and (simultaneously) the inhabitants of pretty

---

1   The French court that heard LICRA's case against Yahoo! adopted this Unexceptionalist position. It held that French law applied to Yahoo!'s auction website, that Yahoo! was violating that law in its display of the Nazi memorabilia, and it ordered Yahoo! to take all steps necessary to prevent the display of the offending items on French computers, whether that entailed removing the material from the website or filtering out incoming file requests that came from within France, or to face a fine of up to 10,000 euros per day.

much every other place on earth, because Yahoo!'s web page can be accessed just as easily from within those countries as from within France, and it is just as likely to be deemed to be causing "significant effects" in those countries as it was in France.

Unexceptionalists are well aware of this problem of multiple overlapping simultaneous jurisdictional claims, of course—they just don't think that it matters very much, as a practical matter. They acknowledge that courts in Brazil, and Japan, and Kenya might all (simultaneously) do what the French court did in the Yahoo! case: assert that their law applies to the Yahoo! website (or your daughter's newsletter), enter a judgment that the "wrongdoers" are violating that law, and order (on pain of some punishment) the offending conduct to cease immediately. But, Unexceptionalists contend, that's not really a problem, because Brazil, and Japan, and Kenya have no way to **enforce** those judgments and orders (unless the wrongdoer is located in, or has assets—property, or a bank account, or the like—located in, Brazil, or Japan, or Kenya). So for anyone who isn't located in, and doesn't have assets located in, Brazil, or Japan, or Kenya, the mere "theoretical possibility" that one of those countries might take action against you can, for all intents and purposes, be ignored. Professor Goldsmith again:

> A nation can purport to regulate activity that takes place anywhere. The Island of Tobago can enact a law that purports to bind the rights of the whole world. But the effective scope of this law depends on Tobago's ability to enforce it. And in general a nation can only enforce its laws against: (i) persons with a presence or assets in the nation's territory; (ii) persons over whom the nation can obtain personal jurisdiction and enforce a default judgment against abroad; or (iii) persons whom the nation can successfully extradite.
>
> A defendant's physical presence or assets within the territory remains the primary basis for a nation or state to enforce its laws. The large majority of persons who transact in cyberspace have no presence or assets in the jurisdictions that wish to regulate their information flows in cyberspace.... [F]or almost all users, there will be no threat of extraterritorial legal liability because of a lack of presence in the regulating jurisdictions.

So as long as you keep yourself, and your assets, out of Brazil, and Japan, and Kenya, you don't really have to worry about the ever-present, but entirely theoretical, problem of being hauled into a Brazilian, or Japanese, or Kenyan courtroom and forced to defend yourself against a charge arising out of something appearing on your website.

It's not, to my eyes, a satisfying resolution of the problem. It turns law, and the question of legal obligation, into something that looks more like a game—Three-Card Monte, or Jurisdictional Whack-a-Mole: If you (or your assets) pop up in Singapore,...**Wham**! Singaporean law can be—can **legitimately** be—applied to you. Once posted to the Web, your daughter's junior high school newsletter **is** indeed subject to Brazilian and Japanese and Kenyan (and Malaysian and Mexican and Latvian...) law simultaneously, because it may indeed be having "significant effects" in each country, and each country can therefore legitimately apply its coercive powers against the school or its officers or the newsletter editors (if it turns out to be in a position to do so). Yahoo!'s obligation, and your daughter's school's obligation, to comply with those laws is defined by the likelihood that it has assets in any one of them, or that any of its officers might travel to any of them.[2]

It's a strange kind of law being served up by the Unexceptionalists—law that only gets revealed to the interacting parties *ex post facto*, and which can therefore no longer guide the behavior of those subject to it in any meaningful way.[3]

BOX 11.3

Stripped of all technicalities, [the rule of law means] that governments are constrained by rules, fixed and announced beforehand, which make it possible to foresee with fair certainty how the authority will use its coercive powers in given circumstances and to plan one's individual affairs on the basis of this knowledge.

F. A. HAYEK

---

2   Jonathan Zittrain, with whose hypothetical ("A, in Austria, posts a file...retrieved by C, in California...") I began this discussion, puts it this way:

> The practical answer [is that] C can sue A (and A can be prosecuted) wherever a jurisdiction decides it cares to exercise its power—**and** can realistically make the defendant's life worse for failing to show up to contest the case, or for showing up and losing.

> That is, A is subject to any jurisdiction's laws where she, or her assets, can be found (and where, therefore, the court can "make [her] life worse for failing to show up...or for showing up and losing").

3   Suppose we turn the interaction around. Suppose Jane wants to know whether she is being "defrauded" by something posted on a website that she has just visited. (Oops! There I go again, with the spatial imagery. I should have said: "Suppose Jane wants to know whether she is being 'defrauded' by something contained within a file that was posted on a web server somewhere and that she has just downloaded to her machine.") Whose law of fraud does she look to? If she's in the United States, her best guess is that U.S. law applies, at least if the website owner/operator is located in, or has assets in, the United States. The website operator faces the same calculus. He's in _____, so his best guess is that _____'s law of fraud will apply (at least if Jane is located in, or has assets in, _____). Jane doesn't know where the website operator, or his assets, are located; the website operator doesn't know where Jane or her assets are located. Neither knows what the other's guess is; Jane doesn't know that the website operator might reasonably try to haul her into an _____-ish courtroom, and the website doesn't know that Jane might want to haul him into a courtroom in Ohio. There's no way for Jane or the website operator to conform their behavior to "the law" because there's really no way for them to know what the law might turn out to be.

What, though, is the alternative? What other answer might there be?

There is one obvious and straightforward "solution" to the Yahoo! Problem, but it is one that few people on **either** side of this debate think much of: international harmonization, a single global law for "hate speech," or copyright, or fraud, or libel, or pornography, or consumer protection, or data privacy, or what-have-you. If the nations of the world were to agree, by treaty or some other multilateral act, to such law, the Yahoo! Problem disappears; no more conflicts between the laws of different jurisdictions, no more concerns about the difficulties of complying with 175 different legal regimes. Global law for a global Internet.

There has been a good deal of movement in the international legal system in recent years in the direction of increasing global harmonization, and it is almost certain to pick up speed in the future.[4] But, most Unexceptionalists and Exceptionalists agree, this cure is worse than the disease. Countries have different laws because people have different histories, different cultures, different customs, and different views on important matters. Jack Goldsmith and Tim Wu themselves, in the leading Unexceptionalist manifesto, put it well:

> People with different values disagree about the type of information they want to receive and the type of information they deem harmful. Some societies tolerate Nazi goods; others don't. Some like privacy warning labels; others don't. Some accept online gambling; others don't. Some want strong protections for intellectual property; again, others differ. These differences are reflected in different national laws.... The advantage of decentralized governance is that it can better reflect differences among peoples.... Imagine a global law in the form of a world government or a world treaty. Set aside the insurmountable problem of creating a legitimate and reliable global executive to enforce such global norms. A more fundamental problem is that the global norms would often be unattractive, even if they could be enforced. When you choose a single rule for six billion people, odds are that several billion, or more, will be unhappy with it.

So at least there's a common project, uniting Unexceptionalists and Exceptionalists: how to bring law to the inter-network while preserving the diversity of values and viewpoints that characterize the global community. To Unexceptionalists like Goldsmith and Wu, Jurisdictional Whack-a-Mole—what they call the "bordered Internet," the Internet onto which the existing territorial boundaries between

---

4 Just in the areas of law with which I am familiar—intellectual property law and the law of commercial transactions and commercial contracts—there has been extensive movement in the last several decades to develop uniform international rules for patent, copyright, trademark, and contract law, through a variety of international treaties and conventions managed and coordinated by the World Intellectual Property Association (WIPO), the UN's Committee on International Trade Law (UNCITRAL), and the World Trade Organization (WTO).

sovereign nation-states are projected, and in which the laws of each of those nation-states are applied within those boundaries—while hardly perfect, remains the best, and perhaps the only, hope for accomplishing that goal:

> What we once called a global network is becoming a collection of nation-state networks ... [L]ike the international system itself, [the bordered Internet] lets many different peoples coexist on the same planet while maintaining very different values and ideas of the good life. In this diversity lies a happier world than one governed by a single global law for all matters. When dreaming of a better society centered on the Internet, the many virtues of a bordered system must not be overlooked.
>
> [T]he decentralized territorial system itself promotes diversity and self-determination, even with regard to Internet communication.... The question about the optimal form of Internet governance must always be 'compared to what?' While it is easy to criticize traditional territorial government and bemoan its many failures, there is no reasonable prospect of any better system of governmental organization.

"No reasonable prospect of any better system of governmental organization"? Perhaps—but I'm not quite so ready to give up on that yet.

BOX 11.4

We must avoid the two opposite social deaths of a global monoculture and a set of isolated cults, and the fractal patterns found in nature seem to present themselves as a good compromise. It seems that the compromise between stability and diversity is served by there being the same amount of structure at all scales.... It seems from experience that groups are stable when they have a set of peers, [and] when they have a substructure.... This seems to be a general rule which can guide our design, and against which we can measure actual patterns of use.

It is in fact another aspect of the tension between many languages and one global language. Locally defined languages are easy to create, needing local consensus about meaning: only a limited number of people have to share a mental pattern of relationships which define the meaning. However, global languages are so much more effective at communication.

TIM BERNERS-LEE, "THE FRACTAL NATURE OF THE WEB"

I know that the acquisition of Louisiana has been disapproved by some, from a candid apprehension that the enlargement of our territory would endanger its union. But who can limit the extent to which the federative principle may operate effectively? (TJ, Second Inaugural Address)

Jefferson's plan to bring republican government to the West, and to solve the Problem of the Extended Republic (see Interlude), was so out-of-the-box that it is difficult even to see the outlines of the box any more.

When Great Britain and the newly formed United States of America signed the Treaty of Paris in 1783, formally ending the hostilities between them, the new nation found itself sitting on a gigantic swath of new territory from the Alleghenies west to the Mississippi River, territory that the British had previously claimed. One of the first things the new Congress of the United States did, shortly after convening for the first time, was to establish a committee to "prepare a plan for temporary government of the western territory." It appointed Jefferson, then one of Virginia's congressional representatives, its chairman.

The Federalists and their allies, as we saw earlier, were deeply apprehensive about the prospects. George Washington himself, still the commander in chief of the Continental Army, summarized their concerns and fears in a remarkable letter he sent to Col. James Duane when he heard of Congress' plans to take up the question of the disposition of the western lands. As Washington saw it, the principal object of the plan should be to establish order and regulation in the new territories:

> To suffer a wide extended Country to be over run with Land Jobbers, Speculators, and Monopolisers, or even with scatter'd settlers, is, in my opinion, inconsistent with the wisdom and policy which our true interest dictates, [and] would be pregnant of disputes both with the Savages, and among ourselves.

Washington favored the idea of setting out a line of demarcation just west of the Alleghenies and making it a felony to settle, or to perform surveys, beyond the line; otherwise, he wrote, "the settling—or rather overspreading—the Western Country will take place by a parcel of Banditti, who will bid defiance to all Authority."

Jefferson's plan, embodied in the proposal the committee drafted and submitted to Congress (a proposal that was, historians agree, almost entirely Jefferson's handiwork) couldn't have been more different. At its core were three simple, but revolutionary, principles—none of which, standing alone, was uniquely Jefferson's, but which had never been put together in quite this way before.

The first principle was that the settlers in the western territories were *free and independent of all the world*, possessing, as a natural right common to all, the right to form self-governing communities and to live under law of their own choosing. They didn't need to be **ruled**, they could rule themselves; in Merrill Peterson's words, "while others distrusted westerners as banditti and wanted them ruled by military force, Jefferson wanted them to govern themselves."

> *The question "How may the [western] territory be disposed of so as to produce the greatest and most immediate benefit to the inhabitants of the **maritime** states of the union?" . . . is a question which good faith forbids us to receive into discussion. State the question in its*

just form: "*How may the territories of the Union be disposed of so as to produce the greatest degree of happiness to* **their** *inhabitants?*" . . .

The moment we sacrifice [*the settlers'*] *interests to our own, they will see it better to govern themselves; and the moment they resolve to do this, the point is settled.*

Jefferson's plan, incredibly—almost unthinkably, really, for the late eighteenth century—contained no provisions for colonial administration, no process for the appointment of colonial governors or administrative officials, no provision for the deployment of military force or other agents of the United States to maintain order. *Conquest is not in our principles; it is inconsistent with our government.* Instead, the committee's proposal contemplated that the (free, male) settlers themselves would "meet together for the purpose of establishing a temporary government," that such temporary government would "continue in force in any state until it shall have acquired 20,000 free inhabitants," at which point the settlers would "call a Convention of representatives to establish a permanent constitution and government for themselves."

BOX 11.5

I consider the people who constitute a society or nation as the source of all authority in that nation, free to transact their common concerns by any agents they think proper, to change these agents individually or the organization of them in form or function, whenever they please.

TJ, "OPINION ON THE NEUTRALITY PROCLAMATION OF 1793"

Principle #2 was that government would emerge in the new territories **from the bottom up**. Jefferson's plan called for dividing up the entire expanse of new territory, "when the same shall have been purchased of the Indian inhabitants," into lots one mile square; lots would be combined into "hundreds" or "townships" (consisting of 100 contiguous lots), townships would be combined into "districts," and districts combined into states.[5] Each smaller unit would participate in the governance of the larger units—*a gradation of authorities, standing each on the basis of law, holding every one its delegated share of powers, and constituting truly a system of fundamental balances and checks for the government.*

---

5   Jefferson's plan called for division of the western territory "by lines to be run and marked due North and South, and others crossing these at right angles" into lots one mile square— "each mile containing 6,086 feet and four-tenths of a foot," the so-called "geographical mile," which Jefferson preferred to the more familiar "statute mile" of 5,280 feet. (In a characteristically Jeffersonian touch, the report also decreed that "the Surveyors shall pay due

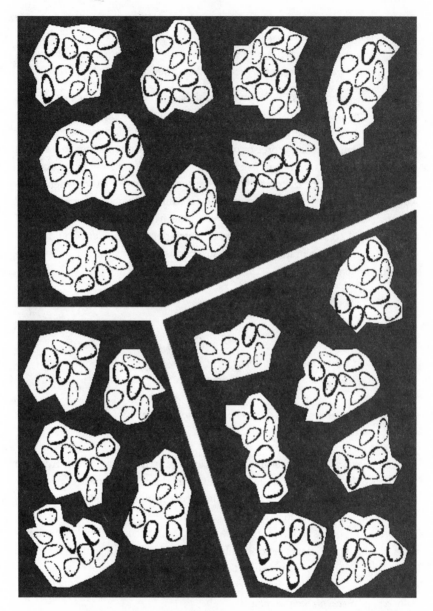

FIGURE 11.1 Ward Republics. A stylized view of Jefferson's idea of grouping of lots into townships (small dots), townships into districts (ovals), districts into counties (irregular white polygons), and counties into states (quadrilateral black polygons).

*The secret is in the making [each individual] himself the depository of the powers respect-
ing himself, so far as he is competent to them, and delegating only what is beyond his
competence, by a synthetical process, to higher and higher orders of functionaries, so
as to trust fewer and fewer powers in proportion as the trustees become more and more
oligarchical.*

Small pieces, loosely joined. He referred to it as a system of "ward republics." *As
Cato concluded every speech with the words "Carthago delenda est," so do I conclude every
opinion with the injunction "Divide the counties into wards."*

*What has destroyed liberty and the rights of man in every government which has ever
existed under the sun? The generalizing and concentrating all cares and powers into
one body, no matter whether of the autocrats of Russia or France, or of the aristocrats of
a Venetian Senate.*

*No, my friend, the way to have good and safe government, is not to trust it all to one, but to
divide it among the many, distributing to every one exactly the functions he is competent to.
Let the national government be entrusted with the defence of the nation, and its foreign and
federal relations; the State governments with the civil rights, laws, police, and administration of what concerns the State generally; the counties with the local concerns of the counties, and each ward direct the interests within itself. It is by dividing and subdividing these
republics from the great national one down through all its subordinations, until it ends in
the administration of every man's farm by himself, placing under every one what his own eye
may superintend, that all will be done for the best.*

*Where every man is a sharer in the direction of his ward-republic, or of some of the higher
ones, and feels that he is a participator in the government of affairs, not merely at an election
one day in the year, but every day; when there shall not be a man in the State who will not be*

---

and constant attention to the variation of the magnetic meridian"—the variation between
true North and magnetic North—when laying out these boundary lines.)

Each group of 100 lots (10 × 10 square) would be designated a "hundred" (or a "township")—with the lots in each township "numbered from 1 to 100, beginning at the Northwestern lot of the Hundred and applying the numbers from 1 to 10 to the lots of the first
row from West to East, those from 11 to 20 to the lots of the second row from West to East."
Each group of nine hundreds (3 × 3 square) would constitute a "district," and each district
would be placed within one of sixteen new states carved out of the territory. (Jefferson's
odd collection of names for the new states in his plan—among them Sylvania, Michigania,
Cherronesus, Assenisipia, Metropotamia, Illinoia, Saratoga, Washington, Polypotamia, Peli-
sipia—were greeted derisively by most of his colleagues in Congress.) "Beginning with the
hundreds most in demand," lots would be sold for a fixed price of not less than $1 per lot,
with the money raised by such sales "to be applied to the sinking of such part of the principal of the national debt as Congress shall from time to time direct, and to no other purpose
whatsoever."

*a member of some one of its councils, great or small, he will let the heart be torn out of his body
sooner than let his power be wrested from him by a Caesar or a Bonaparte.*[6]

And finally, Principle #3 was what Jefferson called the *federative principle*, the
principle under which these new self-governing units would be joined to the existing Union **as equals.** The proposal declared that whenever the population of one
of the new states reached a number equal to "the least numerous of the thirteen
original States," it could petition to be admitted into the United States "on an equal
footing with the original States... subject to the government of the United States,
and to the Articles of Confederation, in the same manner as the original States."

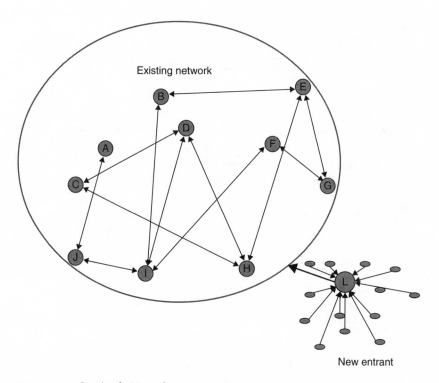

FIGURE 11.2 Growing the Network.

<hr>

6   Jefferson often referred to the New England townships as the closest approximation to his
vision of "ward republics." *These wards, called townships in New England, are the vital principle of their governments, and have proved themselves the wisest invention ever devised
by the wit of man for the perfect exercise of self-government, and for its preservation....* It
was no accident, Jefferson believed, that the New England states had been so well organized in their resistance to the British:

A good way, you'll recall from chapter 5 (see fig. 5.6), to grow big, fast.

Nothing like this had ever been seen before. It would create an "empire," but it would be *an empire built not on conquest, but on principles of compact and equality.* Westward expansion would proceed not by recapitulating the European model and establishing a despotic, colonial regime held together by military force, but by adding new branches—voluntarily and consensually—to the growing tree of the Union.[7] An *empire of liberty,* Jefferson called it, held together by consensual bonds and adherence to republican principles, not coercive power, an ever-expanding union of self-governing commonwealths joined together as peers. As Jefferson saw things, there was really no other choice:

> *Upon* [my] *plan we treat them as fellow citizens. They will have a just share in their own government, they will love us, and pride themselves in an union with us.* [Other plans] *treat them as subjects in which we govern them, and not they themselves; they will abhor us as masters, and break off from us in defiance.*
>
> *A forced connection is neither our interest nor within our power. If they declare themselves a separate people, we are incapable of a single effort to retain them. Our citizens can never be induced, either as militia or as soldiers, to go there to cut the throats of their own*

> We owe to them the vigor given to our revolution in its commencement in the Eastern States,... General orders are given out from a centre to the foreman of every hundred, as to the sergeants of an army, and the whole nation is thrown into energetic action, in the same direction in one instant and as one man, and becomes absolutely irresistible.

And he felt the brunt of that power himself, when, as president, he ordered the ill-advised embargo of 1807, which prohibited U.S. individuals and firms from engaging in commercial relations with the British and which was widely despised in New England:

> How powerfully did we feel the energy of this organization in the case of embargo? I felt the foundations of the government shaken under my feet by the New England townships. There was not an individual in their States whose body was not thrown with all its momentum into action; and although the whole of the other States were known to be in favor of the measure, yet the organization of this little selfish minority enabled it to overrule the Union. What would the unwieldy counties of the middle, the south, and the west do? Call a county meeting, and the drunken loungers at and about the court houses would have collected, the distances being too great for the good people and the industrious generally to attend.

7 Jefferson's plan was enacted into law as the Ordinance of 1784, and it was styled as an irrevocable promise, on the part of the existing states, to maintain equality among all states that might thereafter join the Union, a

Charter of Compact[,] duly executed by the President of the U.S. in Congress assembled, [which] shall stand as fundamental constitutions between the thirteen original

brothers and sons ... Nor would [the western] *country pay the cost of being retained against the will of its inhabitants, could it be done. But it cannot be done.*

An "epochal moment in the history of political civilization," historian Peter Onuf has called it:

The United States would be something new under the sun, a new political order that Europe, should it ever achieve sufficient enlightenment, might one day emulate. In sharp contrast to Old World regimes, the independence and prosperity of the new republican empire did not depend on the massive concentration of coercive force but rather on ties of affectionate union and harmonious interest.... An empire without a center, based on the paradoxical premise that the recognition of the equal rights of political communities, and therefore of their complete independence of each other and of all the world, was the necessary precondition for creating enduring, consensual bonds of union among them.... Dynamic and expansive, it would spread, diffuse, and equalize benefits through the vast system of inland waterways, improved and extended by the art of man, to its farthest reaches.

It was beyond audacious; we'd call it the work of some crazed Utopian madman, except for the fact that its principles would end up guiding U.S. territorial policy for the next several hundred years.

While writing this chapter in the autumn of 2007, I received the following email, which I reproduce here in its entirety:

BOX 11.6

Dear Luigi Paz:

Chiaretta Charron has invited you to join a group in Second Life.

There is no cost to join this group.

Gruppo:

ECONOMIA & INVESTIMENTI in SL: Studiamo e discutiamo dell'Economia di SL per investire al meglio e moltiplicare i vostri Linden Dollars (L$)

Deposita da noi i tuoi L$ e investili con sicurezza guadagnando ogni settimana interessi fino all'1,4% !!

Per informazioni contatta CHIARETTA CHARRON

Log in to accept or decline this invitation.

---

states, and those now newly described, unalterable but by the joint consent of the U.S. in Congress assembled and of the particular state within which such alteration is proposed to be made.

My rough translation from the Italian:

Group: Economics and Investing in Second Life: We will study and discuss the economics of Second Life by investing well and multiplying your Linden Dollars. Deposit your Linden Dollars securely with us, watching your money grow at up to 1.4% per week!! For information, contact Chiaretta Charron.

The email, as you can see, was addressed not to "David Post" but to "Luigi Paz"—the name of an "avatar" I control in the virtual world "Second Life."

Now, I have a number of things to say about this invitation. But first, for those of you who may be unfamiliar with Second Life or the concept of a "virtual world" (a category that will contain large numbers of readers only, I suspect, for the next year or two) a few words of description are in order.

The best way to understand the world of virtual worlds is to experience one or more for yourself, for which my description is an inadequate substitute. But here's the basic idea. Imagine, first, an ordinary video game, of the kind one can find on any Nintendo or Xbox player. The game lets you wander through some imaginary, programmed landscape projected onto the screen—a landscape that can be, in the best of the games, a vivid and seemingly three-dimensional space—looking for bad guys to shoot, cars to steal, aliens to do battle with, or what-have-you. You're not really "wandering" anywhere, of course; it's just electrons bouncing onto a two-dimensional screen. But the game simulates the experience by changing the visual display in response to your actions. It's like watching a movie—another form of entertainment consisting of electrons bouncing onto a two-dimensional screen—but a movie in which you're one of the characters, in (partial) control of the events taking place in the movie. Video games are great fun—I'm not a big fan, to be honest, but hundreds of millions of people think they're great fun—and they've spawned an immense worldwide industry that is already a good deal larger

---

In Jefferson's original draft, there were only five conditions placed on a new state's entry into the Union: (1) that its government must be *in republican form*; (2) that it would *admit no person to be a citizen who holds any hereditary title*; (3) that each new state would *for ever remain a part of the United States of America*; (4) that each new state would pay a portion of the federal debt *to be apportioned on them by Congress*, so long as Congress used the *same common rule and measure by which apportionments thereof shall be made on the* **other** States; and (5) that after 1800 *there shall be neither slavery nor involuntary servitude in* **any** *of the* [new] *States, otherwise than in punishment of crimes whereof the party shall have been convicted to have been personally guilty.*

The antislavery condition never made it into the final statute, defeated by a single vote. *Thus we see,* Jefferson later wrote, *the fate of millions unborn hanging on the tongue of one man, and heaven was silent in that awful moment.*

than the movie industry in terms of the dollar volume of sales, and growing a good deal faster to boot.

Now imagine that the actions of **all the other characters in the game**—those creatures you're chasing, or the ones who are shooting at you, or throwing obstacles in your way, or driving their cars into yours, etc.—are themselves controlled by other users just like you, people who are, at that very moment, playing the same game that you're playing. That dog, sitting in the window of the building across the street, is not just a little string of dog-simulating computer code programmed to respond when you call it, or throw a stone at it, or put a leash on it; it's a little string of dog-simulating code that is actually controlled by another user, a user who sees, on **her** screen, the same scene you see on yours, except from her perspective. You're a character in her game, on her screen, just as she's a character in yours. Same for that Viking you just walked by on the sidewalk, and the woman who just drove by in what looked a lot like a mint condition '57 Ford Thunderbird two-seater convertible. They're all playing the game at the same time, too.

These games—known as "massively multi-player online games," or MMOGs—are as different from ordinary video games as writing is from reading. Now, instead of being in someone else's movie, you, along with all the other participants, are creating the movie, on the fly, in real time. You're part of everyone else's game, and they're part of yours; what you see and experience and encounter on-screen at any moment is a function of what you are all, collectively, doing at that moment. Just like real life.

It's not too much of a stretch to call these, as people have taken to calling them, "virtual worlds." They certainly **feel** like true "worlds"; game designers call them "immersive environments," and most people, when they're playing, have the feeling that they're "in" a three-dimensional "place" (even though they know very well that they're not), a sense that they're moving around and acting and talking to and interacting with others who are in that place at that same moment. And they feel like true "worlds" because, unlike ordinary video games, they're **persistent**: they keep going, even when you're not there. The game landscape constantly changes via the actions of other players, whether or not you're logged on, just as your actions at any time change the landscape for the others who are not "there" at the moment. Should you accumulate enough points to become a Jedi knight while I'm offline, you will appear to me as a Jedi knight when I return. If you form a coalition with others while I'm away, I will have to face that coalition when I resume play. If you obtain a car, or build a house, in my absence, when I log back on I might see you drive the car into your driveway. I can unplug my machine, but the game goes on without me, and what I encounter tomorrow depends on what you and others did while I was elsewhere.

Again, just like real life.

Like the video games from which they are derived, MMOGs have proven to be wildly popular—the latest Next Big Thing. Though today's versions will undoubtedly seem as hilariously primitive in twenty years as Pac-Man or Pong seem to us today, tens of millions of people across the globe play one MMOG or another on a regular basis.[8] Not surprisingly, many people are working hard, and some are making prodigious amounts of money, serving that demand.

The numbers alone are enough to catch one's attention. But it's not just the numbers that make these multi-player games so interesting. In the past few years, a few of them have eliminated most, or in some cases all, of the things that made them "games" in the first place. There are no points to be accumulated, no levels of achievement to ascend, no "winning" and no "losing," no agreed-upon rules about what "moves" are allowed and what moves aren't. The only point to these games—and it's not at all clear that they're properly called "games" anymore—is to interact with other players, in whatever manner the game/world designers allow and with whatever tools the game/world designers provide.

You might not think that people would be much interested in these no-game games, but you'd be wrong. Second Life—at the moment, the most interesting, and the most popular, of these new no-game game worlds—is, as I write this, reportedly adding a million new subscribers each month.

What draws people there? What do they do there, if there's no "game" to play?

They gather together and communicate with one another. They make stuff—clothing and jewelry for their avatars, huge buildings, paintings to put on the walls of those buildings, automobiles or airships that can transport them from one "place" to another in the virtual world, videos...and they exchange what they make with others; if you like the virtual clothing or the virtual jewelry I'm wearing, or the virtual picture I've painted, or the virtual building or virtual airship that I've created, you can try to persuade me to give it to you.

Or sell it to you. For money. Not "real money," of course—play money, game money, Monopoly™ money, the fake currency known, in Second Life, as "Linden Dollars" (L$).

But here's the thing: It turns out that it **is** real money. Linden Dollars can be exchanged for things of value, including, if you visit the (very active) Second Life currency exchange, real, green, physical, tangible, U.S. dollars (or, if you prefer, euros or yen).

It is, according to Ted Castronova's groundbreaking economic analyses of virtual worlds, an online economy that's about the size of Bulgaria's, in dollar terms. And growing, at the moment at least, at a rate Bulgaria can only dream of.[9]

---

8   The names of the most popular MMOGs at the moment—Guild Wars, Ragnarok Online, Star Wars Galaxies, RuneScape, City of Heroes, Ultima Online, Final Fantasy XI, Dark Age of Camelot, The Lord of the Rings Online, World of Warcraft—give a pretty good idea of their subject matter.

9   In the popular Everquest MMOG, for example, there is an active real-dollar market in virtual goods that can be used in the game—gems, spells, swords, and the like—and in 2001

Many hundreds or thousands or hundreds of thousands of people (precise statistics are not easy to come by here) are, at the moment, earning some or all of their living in Second Life, buying and selling virtual "things,"—strings of code representing real estate, clothing, jewelry, buildings, furniture—to and from one another.

It does seem odd, at first glance, that people are paying real money for virtual objects. But it's not really so odd at all when you think about it. We do it all the time, in realspace. Whole industries, employing millions of people and turning over tens of billions of dollars every year, are built on the exchange of real money for strings of code—the television, movie, music, and videogame industries, just to take the most obvious examples.

As I said earlier, the prospect of being able to make "real money"—real money as in "significant amounts of money," and real money as in "money that is convertible into legal tender"—concentrates the collective mind. Predictably, as word gets around, lots of other people are thinking about how they might get in on that. Might I actually be able to earn my living—or even part of my living—teaching classes in the virtual world? Practicing law? Teaching Italian? Selling my CDs? Providing architectural advice? Doing accounting for others? Showing movies?

Which brings us back to Chiaretta Charron. It turns out that there are dozens of investment pools like hers (his? its?) now operating in Second Life, organized enterprises where individuals pool their money together in the hopes of seeing it grow by means of wise investment decisions. Some call themselves "banks," and, at least if they're doing what they **say** they're doing (a point to which I'll return below), they really **are** banks—pools of money collected from willing depositors and lent out to others at interest. Others call themselves "banks" but are actually little more than Ponzi schemes—paying off the initial suckers with the money from later-arriving suckers, and closing up shop and absconding with the dough when the supply of suckers runs out. (You could make a lot of money on Second Life, I suspect, if you could tell the one from the other.)

Castronova estimated the per capita productivity of the aggregate population of Everquest players to be approximately $2,000, somewhere between that of Bulgaria and Russia. With 60,000 or so players at the time, that gave "Norrath"—Everquest's imaginary world—an estimated total GDP of around $120 million dollars. There are now, in 2008, across all virtual world platforms, probably more than 20 million active participants—World of Warcraft alone has more than 10 million current paying subscribers, and Lineage, Second Life, and Everquest have numbers that are probably around that order of magnitude. If Castronova's per capita estimate is anywhere near correct, that would represent an economy generating around $40 billion annually—around the size of Bulgaria's, according to the World Bank's most recent figures.

Whose law governs? What happens when something goes wrong—to what law can the individuals concerned look for a possible remedy? What if I—or rather, what if "Luigi Paz"–deposits 500 L$ into this fund, and the money disappears? What if Luigi Paz promises to put money in later, and then reneges on the deal? What if the fund puts money into a Second Life storefront jewelry store that vanishes—literally!—the next day? Whose law determines whether Chiaretta Charron, or Luigi Paz, or the store owner did anything unlawful or not? By what standards will we decide whether Chiaretta Charron committed "fraud," or merely made "unwise investment decisions"? Whether Luigi Paz is, or is not, allowed to revoke promises that are not in writing? Whether the store owner was making a good faith effort to get business and simply ran out of customers, or was scamming us the whole time?

And what if, say, Korean banking or securities law prohibits any and all investment pools of this kind, while French banking or securities law allows them but only if they register with the relevant government authorities, and Russian law requires them to place a percentage of their funds into an insurance account, and U.S. law requires that once the fund reaches a certain dollar threshold the managers of the fund must make particular kinds of information available to the public about the compensation of the fund's managers, and ...? Does Chiaretta Charron have a legal obligation to comply with all of these laws?

Yes! the Unexceptionalists tell us, once again. This transaction, too, is unexceptional; smoke signals, the Web, telephones, virtual worlds, the telegraph, postal mail—they're all pretty much the same, "functionally equivalent" ways that people in one place communicate with people in another.

BOX 11.7

Faced with the choice between changing one's mind and proving that there is no need to do so, most people get busy on the proof.

JOHN KENNETH GALBRAITH (attr.)

The Unexceptionalists answer Chiaretta Charron's jurisdictional question ("Whose law governs here?") the same way they answered Yahoo!'s: If Korean law prohibits investing in schemes of this kind, and should you find yourself in Korea some day, or should you happen to invest in Korean real estate, or buy shares in a Korean corporation, then ... **Wham**! And if some of the Linden Dollars being placed in Chiaretta Charron's custody are, unbeknownst to any of the other participants in the transaction, coming from trust accounts in Malaysia or Russia or Brazil, then ... **Wham**!

That's the best we can do? I hope not. It has only irony to recommend it—the irony that law looks even **more** like a game—and a game of chance, at that—just as the "games" are themselves looking more and more like "real life." In the Unexceptionalist scheme, it is now no longer merely difficult for the participants in any transaction to know, in advance, what the law governing the transaction might turn out to be, it is completely impossible. The law can't possibly guide the participants in arranging their affairs, because the participants don't have the faintest idea in advance what that law might be. **Wham**! And any notion that governments derive, as Jefferson put it, their just power from the consent of the governed, or that the individuals to whom law is applied have the right to participate in formulating those laws, has been completely abandoned.

It won't work—by which I mean not just that some law professors (like me) think that it is theoretically unhinged, but that it won't do the things that law does when it **does** work, namely help people enter into complicated transactions involving lots of other people and with important things at stake, secure (to a degree) in their expectations of how others will behave and secure (to a degree) that they will be treated fairly in the event of a problem. The potential that these immersive virtual world environments hold for trade—for the exchange of goods and services and information and music and ideas and anything else that can be converted into digital form—on a global scale is enormous; nobody who spends a little time in one can fail to see that. There's real gold in those hills—but without a legal system that works, much of it will remain in the ground. How many people are going to give their hard-earned money—real money!—to Chiaretta Charron without some assurance that she (or he, or it) will behave reasonably with it? How many people will extend credit to anyone else without some way to enforce the obligation? How many people will invest large amounts of time or effort or money in any substantial undertaking—building a law school, say, or organizing a recording studio—without some assurance that it won't be destroyed by other participants in the "game," or by the operators of the virtual world themselves, for "no good reason" at all? (And what constitutes a "good reason" to take away someone's property in one of these virtual worlds, anyway?)

The answer, I think, is: not nearly as many people as would do so if there were a functioning legal system in place, one that could yield reasonable answers to these questions (and the thousands of other questions like them) without the need to consult the legal codes of every country in the world simultaneously. Are Ponzi schemes frauds, or are they instead just "part of the game"? Can merchants go bankrupt? How? Is gambling permitted here? Do I have to reveal property defects known to me when I offer that property for sale? Can I sell Nazi memorabilia? Display pictures of naked people? Pictures of famous people? Pictures of famous people naked? Can I copy the design of someone else's dress, or the features of someone else's building?

I'm reasonably certain that millions of people, perhaps hundreds of millions of people (*see* World Wide Web, growth of) are going to be entering virtual places of one kind or another, most for the first time, over the next few years. And some of them, at least, are going to be looking for—demanding, even—something that looks more like "law," something that more effectively helps them do the things they'd like to do there, than anything the Unexceptionalists, clinging to their "bordered Internet" and the law of geographically based sovereigns like a drowning man to a life raft, can provide.

It would be a shame, the waste of a global resource of potentially enormous value, if Jurisdictional Whack-a-Mole is the best we can come up with, and I don't think it is. There is an alternative, staring us right in the face; as complicated as the jurisdictional problem is on the Web, it is so much **more** complicated in virtual world space that, paradoxically, it is easier to solve. The Unexceptionalists are right about one thing: it's all just people in one place interacting and communicating with other people in other places. So why not begin by recognizing their right—perhaps even their **inalienable** right?—to govern themselves as they see fit? Why not let those who choose to enter, and to interact within, these online communities make their **own** law, deciding for themselves how they'd like to order their affairs?

What a crazy idea—self-governing communities!

Perhaps it is crazy—many of my colleagues seem to think so, and my colleagues are, generally speaking, sensible people.

But it doesn't seem so crazy to me. Indeed, asking those who spend their time in Second Life for the answer to those questions ("Are Ponzi schemes 'frauds' in Second Life?" "Is a seller obligated to reveal defects when selling something in Second Life?" etc.) seems a **lot** more reasonable to me than asking the people of Malaysia how Malaysian law answers those same questions.

It doesn't seem so crazy to me because there's a "place-ness" to these virtual places—not just in the way they look but in the way they persist through time, and in the way they present opportunities for an infinite variety of repeated interactions between individuals, for collective decision-making, and for common enterprise— that enables us to think about them and talk about them the way that the people who spend lots of time there often do: as true **communities**, with shared norms and customs and expectations characteristic of each and continually being created and re-created by the members within each. I don't see why they are somehow inherently less deserving of less respect than the other communities—Topeka, Kansas, say, or Leicester, U.K., or Sri Lanka—within the international legal order.

So it doesn't seem so crazy to me to begin the conversation about Chiaretta Charron's scheme **not** by asking "how can we apply the law of 175 or so sovereign states simultaneously to this transaction?" but by asking "what's the law of the place where the transaction is taking place?"

That is, to be sure, just the beginning of the conversation. At the moment, there **is** no law of the place—nothing that can fairly be called "Second Life law" or "There. com law" or "Lineage II law"—because no institutions or processes for making "law" have been developed in any of these virtual worlds. They are, at the moment, truly lawless places—or, more precisely, places where code, and only code, is law.

But I'd be very surprised if that were a permanent condition. Like I said, there's real gold in those hills, and much of it can be unlocked only with a functioning legal system in place. I'm hardly the only one who realizes this; so there will be plenty of "law entrepreneurs" who will seize on this problem and get to work; some have already begun.

I don't know, to be honest, what they'll come up with, what those lawmaking institutions and processes will look like, or should look like, in a virtual world—whether they'll have representative assemblies, whether they'll use juries, whether they'll separate executive and legislative powers, whether they'll have paid judges, or whether they'll have different tribunals for different kinds of actions.

What I do know is that people have the right to make those decisions and answer those questions for themselves.

And I just wish the Unexceptionalists would stop telling us that we don't, that we've somehow given up our right to create new communities and to live under law of our own devising, or that we've somehow finished designing legal institutions and are stuck, forevermore, with the ones we happen to have come up with by 1995.

I wish they'd stop telling people that because they're standing in the way of the hard work and experimentation and innovation that will be required to create fair, well-designed, and effective lawmaking institutions and processes that are appropriate for these places. Law, like many other important social phenomena—money, for instance—has a strange, self-fulfilling element to it: its existence depends on people believing that it exists. To become a lawmaking community, participants must believe that they're in a lawmaking community. If everyone believes that "real law" from "real sovereigns" is the **only** law that matters (or can ever matter)—that no matter what steps they take to set up a fair and reasonable system for resolving virtual world disputes in accordance with newly created virtual world law, their efforts will come to nothing because they can't create "real law"—then "real law" from "real sovereigns" will **be** the only law that matters, and we'll be stuck with the chaotic nonsense of Jurisdictional Whack-a-Mole. It's just play money until everyone believes it's real money, and it's just play-law until everyone believes it's real law, and who will undertake the hard work required to set up a legal system if it's just play-law?

Maybe the participants in these virtual communities don't want to create anything more than play-law. But I'm betting that they do—and it would help if the Unexceptionalists would stop telling them that they can't.

CHAPTER 12

NEWTON'S PLOW, AND THE CONDITION OF THE GENERAL MIND

No government ought to be without censors; and where the press is free, no one ever will. If virtuous, it need not fear the fair operation of attack and defence. Nature has given to man no other means of sifting out the truth, either in religion, law, or politics.

TJ TO GEORGE WASHINGTON, SEPTEMBER 9, 1792

Any system of laws applicable to Internet activities, wherever it comes from and whoever creates it and enforces it, must address two great and complex issues central to any legal order in cyberspace: first, where to draw the line between permissible and impermissible speech (a question of First Amendment law, in the United States) and, second, how much legal protection to provide for "intellectual property."

These two issues have been featured in virtually all of the Internet's Big Cases— the legal disputes generating lots of public debate and commentary, the ones that made it onto the docket of the Supreme Court or the front page of the *New York Times*—during the first couple of decades of its existence. It's just what we would have expected (and what many people did expect). For one thing, with hardly anything **but** "speech" out there in cyberspace, people in one place communicating with people in another place, it's no surprise that questions about the regulation of speech arose early on during the Internet's rise in the public's consciousness.[1]

---

1   The *Time* magazine July 3, 1995, cover story on "Cyberporn"—featuring a picture of a "horror-stricken, zombie-like child, mesmerized by a computer screen," in ACLU president Nadine Strossen's words, its headline blaring: "CYBERPORN: EXCLUSIVE: A New Study Shows How Pervasive and Wild It Really Is"—was as a milestone event in bringing the Internet into the main cultural stream in the United States, not least because the "new study" on which *Time* based its story turned out to be a complete hoax. The story, and the public attention that it helped to generate, led predictably to calls for congressional action, and to enactment of the first federal law dealing specifically with "the Internet"—the Communications Decency Act of 1996. And it was big news again, in 1997, when the Supreme Court struck

Similarly, the ability to copy and distribute information in digital form to vast numbers of people has, equally predictably, led to substantial and well-publicized disputes about the "ownership" of the bits whizzing around the network.[2]

Coincidentally or not, in no subjects in the law was Jefferson more interested, and about no subjects in the law did he have more interesting and important things to say, than these two.

His views regarding the line between permissible and impermissible speech were pretty simple—there shouldn't be any line, because there shouldn't be any impermissible speech. Jefferson was America's first, and probably its greatest, First Amendment absolutist[3]; he wasn't kidding when he said *were it left to me*

---

down the CDA on the grounds that it was an unconstitutional abridgment of the freedom of speech. A list of all of the headlines using the word "Internet" that appeared on the front page of the *New York Times* prior to 1998 makes for interesting reading:

> Doubts on Internet—August 10, 1994
> The '96 Race on the Internet: Surfer Beware—October 23, 1995
> China Issues Rules to Monitor Internet—February 5, 1996
> Judge Blocks a Law on Smut on Internet—February 16, 1996
> Judges Turn Back Law to Regulate Internet Decency—June 13, 1996
> Court Weighs Rules on Internet Decency—March 20, 1997
> U.S. Rebuffed in Global Proposal for Eavesdropping on the Internet—March 27, 1997
> A Seductive Drug Culture Flourishes on the Internet—June 20, 1997
> The Supreme Court, 9–0, Upholds State Laws Prohibiting Assisted Suicide; Protects
>   Speech on Internet—June 27, 1997
> Ignored Warning Leads to Chaos on the Internet—July 18, 1997
> U.S. to Go Back on Internet with Social Security Benefits—September 4, 1997
> Internet's Value in U.S. Schools Still in Question—October 25, 1997

Sex, drugs, and—with the Napster and other peer-to-peer file-sharing cases on the horizon—rock and roll to follow.

2   The well-known Napster story, told in *New York Times* front page headlines:

> Potent Software Escalates Music Industry's Jitters, (March 7, 2000);
> Unknown Musicians Find Payoffs Online (July 20, 2000);
> Cyberspace Programmers Confront Copyright Laws. (May 10, 2000).

Then:

> In Victory for Recording Industry, Judge Bars Online Music Sharing (July 27, 2000), but
> For Many Fans of Online Music, U.S. Court Ruling Is Call to Arms (July 28, 2000).

3   The other great First Amendment absolutist was Supreme Court Justice Hugo Black, famous (and, these days, often mocked) for his view that "no law means **no law**"—that what he called the First Amendment's "emphatic command" that "Congress shall make no law abridging the freedom of speech or of the press" was to be taken literally, and absolutely.

to decide whether we should have a government without newspapers or newspapers without government, I should not hesitate a moment to prefer the latter. Not even a moment!

> *To preserve the freedom of the human mind & freedom of the press, every spirit should be ready to devote itself to martyrdom; for as long as we may think as we will, & speak as we think, the condition of man will proceed in improvement.*

It was all an interconnected whole, for Jefferson—republican self-government, freedom of speech, freedom of conscience, and freedom of the press. You couldn't

---

Not coincidentally, in the words of one of his former law clerks, "among high-ranking public officials in the U.S. during the twentieth century, none was a more ardent admirer of Thomas Jefferson than Hugo Black."

Black was never more passionately, or eloquently, Jeffersonian than in his very last public utterance, his opinion in the "Pentagon Papers" case in which the Court struck down as unconstitutional the injunctions that had prohibited the *New York Times* and the *Washington Post* from publishing the so-called secret history of the Vietnam War, and it is worth quoting at length, for it remains one of the great defenses of free speech ever penned. "Every moment's continuance of the injunctions against these newspapers," Black wrote, "amounts to a flagrant, indefensible, and continuing violation of the First Amendment":

> The Framers of the First Amendment, able men that they were, wrote in language they earnestly believed could never be misunderstood: "Congress shall make no law ... abridging the freedom ... of the press ..." Both the history and language of the First Amendment support the view that the press must be left free to publish news, whatever the source, without censorship, injunctions, or prior restraints. In the First Amendment the Founding Fathers gave the free press the protection it must have to fulfill its essential role in our democracy. The press was to serve the governed, not the governors. The Government's power to censor the press was abolished so that the press would remain forever free to censure the Government. The press was protected so that it could bare the secrets of government and inform the people. Only a free and unrestrained press can effectively expose deception in government. And paramount among the responsibilities of a free press is the duty to prevent any part of the government from deceiving the people and sending them off to distant lands to die of foreign fevers and foreign shot and shell. In my view, far from deserving condemnation for their courageous reporting, the *New York Times* and other newspapers should be commended for serving the purpose that the Founding Fathers saw so clearly. In revealing the workings of government that led to the Vietnam war, the newspapers nobly did precisely that which the Founders hoped and trusted they would do.
>
> The Government's case here is based on premises entirely different from those that guided the Framers of the First Amendment. [W]e are asked to hold that despite the First Amendment's emphatic command, the Executive Branch, the

have any without the others; they were inextricably bound together into a single system, and they would stand, or fall, together. The principle of self-government—government not imposed on the governed but operating with the consent of the governed—meant that everyone had a stake, and an equal stake, in governing: *The true foundation of republican government is the equal right of every citizen in his person and his property, and in their management.* The *mother principle,* he called it: *Governments are "republican" only in proportion as they embody the will of their people and execute it.* Everyone, henceforth, gets to form his or her own opinions on all questions of public import, and regarding the administration of the laws: *No other sure foundation can be devised for the preservation of freedom and happiness* [than to] *enable every man to judge for himself what will secure, or endanger, his freedom.*

> *It is honorable for us to have produced the first legislature who had the courage to declare that the reason of man may be trusted with the formation of his own opinions* [and] *that man may be governed by reason and truth.* **Our first object should therefore be, to leave open to him all the avenues to truth.** *The most effectual way hitherto found is the freedom of the press. It is therefore, the first shut up by those who fear the investigation of their actions.*

Unrestricted public discourse, and an unfettered press, were the **only** "avenues to truth," because nobody ever knows, in advance, where the truth may lie. *Reason and free enquiry are the only effectual agents against error.* In a Jeffersonian world, the government simply has no role to play in telling us what we may think or what we may say. *Freedom of discussion,* **unaided by power**, *is sufficient for the propagation and protection of truth. It is error alone which needs the support of government. Truth can stand by itself.*

Governments may trample upon these rights of free speech and free thought and free inquiry by force, but they can never do legitimately, by right.

> *The error seems not sufficiently eradicated that the operations of the* **mind***, as well as the body, are subject to the coercion of the laws. But our rulers can have authority only over such natural rights as we have submitted to them. The rights of conscience we never submitted, we could not submit. . . . The legitimate powers of government extend only to such acts as are*

> Congress, and the Judiciary can make laws enjoining publication of current news and abridging freedom of the press in the name of "national security." . . . To find that the President has inherent "power" to halt the publication of news by resort to the courts would wipe out the First Amendment and destroy the fundamental liberty and security of the very people the Government hopes to make "secure." No one can read the history of the adoption of the First Amendment without being convinced beyond any doubt that it was injunctions like those sought here that Madison and his collaborators intended to outlaw in this Nation for all time.

injurious to others. But it does me no injury for my neighbour to say there are twenty gods, or no god. It neither picks my pocket nor breaks my leg.

The right to speak and to think as we wish is a "natural right"; it is neither given to us **by** law, nor derived **from** law, but antecedent to law—lower down in the protocol stack, if you will, than law. It derives not from the statute books but from what Jefferson called, in the Declaration of Independence, *the laws of Nature and of Nature's God*—it is just in the "nature" of things, the way the world is, that if you bring two human beings together, they will think, and they will attempt to communicate with one another about what they are thinking, even without any law to help them.

A *right of free correspondence between citizen and citizen on their joint interests . . . under whatever laws these interests arise (of the State, of Congress, of France, Spain, or Turkey), is a natural right. It is not the gift of law, either of England, or Virginia, or of Congress, but, in common with all our other natural rights, it is one of the objects for the protection of which society is formed and law established.*

Humans communicate with one another not because the law enables them to do so; they communicate with one another because—well, because that's the kind of beings we are, and that is what is in our nature. Law's job is not to enable that communication to occur but to protect it when it does occur—that is one of the *"objects for the protection of which"* we **make** law.

And finally, some powerful positive feedback: ONLY BY FORMING A GOVERNMENT THAT DOESN'T TRAMPLE UPON THESE RIGHTS CAN WE PRESERVE OUR ABILITY TO CREATE A GOVERNMENT THAT DOESN'T TRAMPLE UPON THESE RIGHTS. *Where the press is free, all is safe. Our liberty depends on the freedom of the press; it cannot be limited without being lost.* Limit our freedom to think and speak as we wish, and republican government can't work—that is, it can't produce a government that will protect and preserve our right to think and speak as we wish.

No other sure foundation can be devised for the preservation of freedom and happiness [than to] *enable every man to judge for himself what will secure, or endanger, his freedom. Without this no republic can maintain itself in strength.*

[The United States] *will demonstrate the falsehood of the pretext that freedom of the press is incompatible with orderly government. To open the doors of truth, and to fortify the habit of testing everything by reason, are **the most effectual manacles we can rivet on the hands of our successors** to prevent their manacling the people with their own consent. Where the press is free, and every man able to read, all is safe.*

"Where the press is free and every man able to read." Jefferson's lifelong devotion to what he called the *holy cause* of public education is also part of this interlocking system of republican government and free communication. *What government a nation can bear depends on the condition of the general mind; if a nation expects to be igno-rant and free, it expects what never was and never will be.* Jefferson practically invented public education.[4] He was, I believe, the first person to propose a comprehensive system of free public schooling, in his "Bill for the General Diffusion of Knowledge" that he introduced into the Virginia Assembly in 1778—*by far the most important bill in our whole code,* he called it. And his most enduring monument—after a lifetime filled with enduring monuments—may well be the magnificent public university, the University of Virginia, that he single-handedly created during the last twenty or so years of his life, securing its funding, devising its curriculum, designing its buildings, and hiring its faculty.

> *No one more sincerely wishes the spread of information among mankind than I do, and none has greater confidence in its effect towards supporting free and good govern-ment... The most effectual means of preventing the perversion of power into tyranny is to illuminate as far as possible the minds of the people. Enlighten the people generally, and tyranny and oppressions of body and mind will vanish like evil spirits at the dawn of day. Although I do not believe that the human condition will ever advance to such a state of perfection as that there shall no longer be pain or vice in the world, I believe it is susceptible of much improvement, most of all in matters of government and religion; the diffusion of knowledge among the people is to be the instrument by which it is to be effected.*

To a remarkable extent, Jefferson's vision has prevailed—certainly in the United States, and to some extent elsewhere around the globe—and we are considerably better off for it. The United States did, in fact, create, over the ensuing two centuries, a system of public education remarkably close to Jefferson's ideal, one so extraordinary that only a madman like Jefferson could possibly have imagined it in 1800: free, compulsory education for all, and a comprehensive postsecondary network of thousands upon thousands of state universities, colleges, junior colleges,

---

4   "The fact is, that Thomas Jefferson was the first conspicuous advocate in this country of free public education in common schools supported by local taxation as well as of state aid to higher institutions of learning...that it was the duty of the state to educate its citizens, both for their own and the republic's well-being...that the system should be unified from the grammar school at the bottom to the university at the top, with as much care given to the selection and encouragement up the ladder of the best talent as to the general diffusion of rudimentary knowledge among the mass of citizens on the lower rungs.... [and] that education should be secular and practical, a matter of local initiative and responsibility, and as free as possible of any coercive discipline. To him the schoolhouse was the fountainhead of happiness, prosperity and good government, and education was the "holy cause" to which he devoted the best thought and efforts of his life." (Merrill Peterson, *The Jefferson Image in the American Mind* [1998], 238–44)

community colleges,...a system that was and to a considerable extent remains the envy of the world (and which many have copied and, perhaps, even improved upon—and more power to them).

And while Jefferson's uncompromising and absolutist vision of free speech and the First Amendment has never quite taken hold as the governing legal standard—you cannot yell "Fire!" in a crowded theater, or conspire with your friends to commit murder, or display pornographic images of children, and the government can punish you if you do—when viewed in context, against the background of the competing Federalist vision in the late 1790s, there can be no doubt which was the victor. The Federalists, you may recall from high school history class, during John Adams's first (and, mercifully, only) term as president, enacted the most extraordinary restriction on the freedom of speech the United States had ever seen or ever was to see, the now-infamous Sedition Act of 1798. The Sedition Act, simply stated, made it a federal crime to criticize the government—to "write, print, utter, or publish," any "malicious writings against the government of the United States, or either House of Congress, or the President," or **anything** that would "bring them into disrepute"—punishable by up to two years in prison. Look out, Jon Stewart! Dozens of U.S. newspaper editors and pamphleteers had been rounded up and tossed in jail under its terms.[5]

The Sedition Act would have destroyed the United States before the United States had even had the chance to become the United States. It is impossible to imagine republican government, or meaningful elections, where people are thrown in jail for criticizing the government, and it is therefore impossible to imagine the United

---

5   Here's the full text of the Sedition Act:

Be it enacted, That if any person shall write, print, utter, or publish, or shall cause or procure to be written, printed, uttered or published, or shall knowingly and willingly assist or aid in writing, printing, uttering or publishing any false, scandalous and malicious writing or writings against the government of the United States, or either house of the Congress of the United States, or the President of the United States, with intent to defame the said government, or either house of the said Congress, or the said President, or to bring them, or either of them, into contempt or disrepute; or to excite against them, or either or any of them, the hatred of the good people of the United States, or to excite any unlawful combinations therein, for opposing or resisting any law of the United States, or any act of the President of the United States, done in pursuance of any such law, or of the powers in him vested by the constitution of the United States, or to resist, oppose, or defeat any such law or act, or to aid, encourage or abet any hostile designs of any foreign nation against the United States, their people or government, then such person, being thereof convicted before any court of the United States having jurisdiction thereof, shall be punished by a fine not exceeding two thousand dollars, and by imprisonment not exceeding two years.

States of the nineteenth and twentieth centuries had the Sedition Act remained in place—which, thanks to Jefferson's election in 1800, it did not.[6]

To a Jeffersonian, then, free speech questions are always simultaneously (a) of supreme importance and (b) pretty easy. The answer to free speech questions is always (or almost always) simple: The more protection for, and the fewer the restrictions on, speech, the better. *Lay down true principles, and adhere to them inflexibly.*

Not so for intellectual property. That's a different matter entirely.

Jefferson's interest and involvement in intellectual property law—the law of patents and copyrights—derived, at least in part, from his passion for invention and inventions. He played a prominent role in the development of patent law in the United States—he was, for example, the author of the Patent Act of 1793 and served for three years as America's first Commissioner of Patents[7]—and he was never more animated in his correspondence than when he was discussing some new method or machine for breaking hemp, or measuring wind velocity, or milling grain, or pumping water, or any of the thousands of other practical things with which he was fascinated. *I am not afraid of new inventions or improvements nor* [wedded] *to the practices of our forefathers; where a new invention is supported by well-known principles, it ought to be tried.*

He was himself an inventor of considerable skill, and occasional genius. Jefferson-the-Gadgeteer is, I think, the Jefferson that most visitors to Monticello find most

---

6 It is comforting to think that the Judiciary would have stepped in; to our twenty-first-century eyes, the Sedition Act looks like a blatant, and quite obviously unconstitutional, abridgement of "the freedom of speech" protected by the First Amendment. But it looks like that to us because we've been living for 200+ years **without** the Sedition Act, or anything like it, to warp our institutions of governance. In 1798 it wasn't yet clear exactly **what** the First Amendment meant, and in fact **all** of the judges who had occasion to pass on the constitutionality of the Sedition Act—Federalist appointees, every one, and including several sitting Supreme Court Justices who heard Sedition Act cases while "riding circuit" in the countryside—upheld it against all challenges.

It wasn't the Judiciary that consigned the Sedition Act to the proverbial dustbin of history but the Adams-Jefferson election of 1800, which was widely seen at the time, and is still viewed by many historians today, as a national referendum on the Sedition Act. The Federalists, fortunately for us, got their asses kicked. Jefferson's first act as new president was to pardon everyone who had been convicted of violating the statute.

7 The first U.S. Patent Act, enacted during the first Congress's first session in 1790, set up a committee, consisting of the secretary of state, the secretary of war, and the attorney general, to review all patent applications. Virtually all of the committee's work fell to Jefferson, then serving as secretary of state, inasmuch as he was the only one of the three remotely interested in the mechanical arts; it was enough of a drain on his time during his years in office that he did away with the committee entirely in his draft of a revised patent statute (enacted into law as the 1793 Patent Act).

engaging and the one they remember most vividly: the revolving bookstand (so he could keep five books open at once and keep them all at hand), the swivel-chair ("Mr. Jefferson's whirligig," his Federalist opponents called it, invented "so he could look all ways at once"), the weather vane (which allowed you to read wind direction while **inside** the house), the folding chair (that could be used as a walking-stick when in the closed position), the giant automated day-calendar hanging in the front hall and indicating the day of the week (which was driven by a gearing mechanism so complicated Jefferson had to build a special room for it in the basement)—all built to Jefferson's own original designs and specifications. In the final analysis, probably only three of Jefferson's inventions had truly long-lasting significance—though that is, I suppose, three more than most of us will ever come up with: A map-holder that could store several maps in horizontal tubes and that allowed the user to pull down one map at a time for examination (a design still in use in my elementary school in New York City in the late 1950s and, for all I know, still in use today), a plow whose "mould-board" was designed in accordance with the then-newfangled mathematical principles set forth in Isaac Newton's *Principia Mathematica*,[8] and a method for

---

8   *Ploughing deep is the recipe for almost every good thing in farming. The plow is to the farmer what the wand is to the sorcerer. It's effect is really like sorcery.*

The story of Jefferson's Plow is another too-good-to-omit bit of Jeffersoniana. Having carefully observed the various deficiencies in the designs of plows used on the farms of France during his stay there, he wrote a memorandum (1788) with his ideas for an improved "mould-board" (the portion of the plow that lifts up and turns over the soil). He realized that the most efficient mould-board, one that could accomplish that lifting and turning action with least effort, needed to have a curved shape: a *mould-board of least resistance*, he called it, in which *the fore end should be horizontal to enter under the sod, and the hind end perpendicular to throw it over, with the intermediate surface changing gradually from the horizontal to the perpendicular.*

Corresponding on the subject several years later with William Patterson, professor of mathematics at the University of Pennsylvania, Patterson reminded him that the problem of finding the shape of least resistance was a standard problem in Newton's calculus; Newton himself had devoted considerable space in the *Principia Mathematica* to the closely related problem of finding the fastest route down an inclined plane from point A to point B (not, as it turns out, a straight line, but rather a kind of cycloid known as a "'brachicostone"), and Newton had even pointed out (unusually, in a primarily theoretical work like the *Principia*) that this curve might have practical application in the design of ship hulls. Jefferson grasped the analogy right away, and, after spending some time with both Newton's treatise and an influential mathematics textbook (Emerson's *Doctrine of Fluxions*) that he borrowed from Patterson (having mislaid the copy that he had read years before while in college), he was able to re-create Newton's calculations as applied to the mould-board design. *It answers in practice to what it promises in theory*, he wrote; *it is so light that the two small horses or mules draw it with less labor than I have ever before seen necessary. It*

encoding and encrypting private conversations so sophisticated that it was used by U.S. Navy cryptographers almost up until the start of World War II.

Notwithstanding (or perhaps because of?) his deep and abiding interest and involvement in intellectual property matters, Jefferson was no intellectual property hard-liner or absolutist—quite the opposite, actually.[9] He summarized his views on the subject in a remarkable 1813 letter to Isaac McPherson—the only writing from any of the U.S. Founders dealing with the question of intellectual property, and a document that has become, as one scholar put it, "**the** historical policy foundation for American intellectual property law" (emphasis in original).[10]

In Jefferson's view, intellectual property rights—the rights to exclude others from using or selling or copying the products of the human imagination, whether

---

does beautiful work and is approved by everyone. His design was featured in James Mease's *Domestic Encyclopedia* (Philadelphia, 1803), and was awarded the gold medal by the French Society of Agriculture.

9 Regarding his own inventions, he was always rather proud that he had *never thought of monopolizing by patent any useful idea which happened to offer itself to me,* preferring instead to allow all who wished to use them *to do so without restriction or royalty* (even though, in one historian's words, "had [his plow design] been patented and exploited, it would probably have brought him wealth beyond the dreams of eighteenth century avarice").

> *You will be at perfect liberty to use the form of the mould board plow, as all the world is, having never thought of monopolizing by patent any useful idea which happens to offer itself to me; and the permission to do this is doing a great deal more harm than good.*

10 McPherson had written Jefferson seeking assistance in fending off the patent claims lodged against him by one Oliver Evans. Evans's patent—the third issued by Jefferson's Committee, in 1790—had a strange and tangled history. The patent was for a series of improvements in the use of "elevators, conveyors, and 'hopper-boys' for use in milling flour." After the patent expired in 1804, Evans had managed to convince Congress to give him **another** patent for the same invention in 1808 (on the grounds that his original patent had been deemed null and void by the courts because of certain procedural irregularities)—in effect, taking the invention out of the public domain into which it had fallen after expiration of the original patent and putting it back into Evans's private hands.

McPherson asked for Jefferson's opinion on whether or not he needed to respond to Evans's insistent demands for royalty payments. Jefferson expressed considerable sympathy for McPherson's position. For one thing, it was not clear that Evans's contraption was an "invention" deserving of the name (and of the patent rights granted to him):

> *Your letter points to the much broader question: whether what have received from Mr. Evans the new and proper name of Elevators, are of his **invention**, for if they are not, his patent can give him no right to obstruct others in the use of what they possessed before.*

that's the chemical formula for a new drug to treat Alzheimer's disease, the design of a new mousetrap, or the lyrics to "Like a Rolling Stone"—**are** the "gift of social law." Unlike free speech rights, they **don't** derive from the "nature of things," because it is in the nature of things that ideas move freely from one person to another: *That ideas should freely spread from one to another over the globe seems to have been peculiarly and benevolently designed by nature when she made them, like the air we breathe, incapable of confinement or exclusive appropriation, and, like fire, expansible over all space without lessening their density in any point.*

It appeared, rather, that Evans had merely brought together a number of previously known implements that *had been in use from time immemorial—the Persian wheel, the water-elevator, Archimedes' screw,* and others—for a new purpose (milling flour), and that this alone could not justify his exclusive rights:

> *If one person invents a knife convenient for pointing our pens, another cannot have a patent right for the same knife to point our pencils. A compass was invented for navigating the sea; another could not have a patent right for using it to survey land. A machine for threshing wheat has been invented in Scotland; a second person cannot get a patent right for the same machine to thresh oats, a third rye, a fourth peas, a fifth clover, etc. A string of buckets is invented and used for raising water, ore, &c., can a second have a patent right to the same machine for raising wheat, a third oats, a fourth rye, a fifth peas, &c? A man has a right to use a saw, an axe, a plane, separately; may he not combine their uses on the same piece of wood? He has a right to use his knife to cut his meat, a fork to hold it; may a patentee take from him the right to combine their use on the same subject?*

> *Such a law,* he went on, *instead of enlarging our conveniences, as was intended, would most fearfully abridge them, and crowd us by monopolies out of the use of the things we have.*

He was sympathetic, too, because he had lately seen the effects of *harrassment by lawsuits,* [and] *the abuse of frivolous patents that is likely to cause more inconvenience than is countervailed by those really useful.*

> *There is a late instance in this State of a rascal going through every part of it and swindling the mill-owners, under a patent of two years old only, out of 20,000 dollars for the use of winged-gudgeons* **which they have had in their mills for twenty years**, *every one preferring to pay ten dollars unjustly rather than be dragged into a Federal court, one, two, or three hundred miles distant. . . . We use a machine for crushing corncobs, and for which Oliver Evans has obtained a patent, although to my knowledge the same machine has been made by a smith in Georgetown these sixteen years for crushing plaster, and he made one for me twelve years ago, long before Evans's patent. The only difference is that he fixes his horizontally, and Evans vertically. Yet I chose to pay Evans's patent price for one rather than be involved in a lawsuit of two or three hundred dollars' cost. We are now afraid to use our ploughs, every part of which has been patented, although used ever since the fabulous days of Ceres.*

Ideas are "incapable of confinement" and "expansible without lessening their density"—what modern-day economists would call "nonappropriable" and "nonrivalrous." The only way to keep an idea to yourself is—well, to keep it to yourself:

> If nature has made any one thing **less** susceptible than all others of exclusive property, it is the action of the thinking power called "an idea"—the fugitive fermentation of an individual brain. An individual may exclusively possess an idea, but only as long as he keeps it to himself. The moment it is divulged, it forces itself into the possession of every one, and the receiver cannot dispossess himself of it.

Nor do ideas get "used up" as more people use them:

> Their peculiar character is that no one possesses them the less because others possess the whole; he who receives an idea from me receives instruction himself without lessening mine, [just] as he who lights his [candle] at mine receives light without darkening me.

Unlike free speech rights, intellectual property thus *cannot, in nature*, be a subject of property; they **do** derive from the "social law," from the laws of England, or Virginia, or wherever; they're not antecedent to the law, but entirely dependent on it.

That doesn't mean we shouldn't have intellectual property rights. It only means that we get to decide (and we have to decide) whether to have them or not, and how much of them to have. *Society may give an exclusive right to the profits arising from them, as an encouragement to men to pursue ideas which may produce utility*. Or it may not. *This may or may not be done, according to the will and convenience of the society, without claim or complaint from anybody*.

These are different sorts of questions than free speech questions. The answer to free speech questions is (almost) always "More." How long should free speech protection last? Forever. How broad should protection for speech be? Broader than it is. What kinds of speech should be protected? All of it.

But intellectual property questions—how long should copyrights and patents last? how broad should protection be? what kinds of inventions and creations should get protection and which shouldn't?—are harder, because More/Broader/Longer is not always the right answer. Intellectual property protection involves trade-offs—benefits and costs—that need to be balanced against one another in order to come up with the right answer.

The benefit side is easy to see and to appreciate. We give creators and inventors of new things—new farm implements, new poems, new kinds of cement, new songs—property rights (patents or copyrights) in their creations because that will stimulate the creation of still **more** new things. Absent that protection—*in nature*, as it were—should you come up with a new and better plow design there would be no way for you to stop others from copying and manufacturing and selling it; you're therefore unlikely to invest the time and effort and resources necessary to create the new design in the first place. The same goes for the poet, the cement developer, the songwriter. Giving creators and inventors the right to exclude others from making or using or selling or copying their creations or inventions gives them an incentive they would otherwise not have to create and invent; knowing in advance that the law will provide them with the exclusive right to exploit whatever they come up with—to make a buck from their creations—they're more likely to undertake the effort required to bring those creations and inventions into being.[11] We get more new things—more new plow designs, more new poems, more new kinds of cement, more new songs—than we would get if we didn't provide legal protection for creations and inventions, and we are all decidedly better off as a result.

The cost side is a little harder to see. At some point, as intellectual property rights get stronger, covering more kinds of things, or covering them for longer periods of time, they can become **too** strong, and they can choke off creativity rather than stimulate it. **Today's** inventors and creators—plow designers and songwriters alike—are always building upon and borrowing from **yesterday's** creations and inventions. The stronger the property rights given to yesterday's creations and inventions, the more difficult and costly that building-upon and borrowing process becomes for today's creators and inventors, who have to obtain permission, or pay a licensing fee, in order to use patented or copyrighted creations and inventions (or risk a lawsuit if they do not).[12] And similarly, just as stronger property rights for

---

BOX 12.1

The fact is, that one new idea leads to another, that to a third, and so on through a course of time until some one, with whom no one of these ideas was original, combines all together, and produces what is justly called a new invention. [Who was] the first inventor of a thousand good things? For example, who first discovered the principle of gravity? Not Newton, for Galileo, who died the year that Newton was born, had measured its force in the descent of gravid bodies. Who invented the Lavoiserian chemistry? The English say Dr. Black, by the preparatory discovery of latent heat. Who invented the steamboat? Was it Gerbert, the Marquis of Worcester, Newcomen, Savary, Papin, Fitch, Fulton?

TJ TO BENJAMIN WATERHOUSE, MARCH 3, 1818

---

11 *The just rewards of genius,* Jefferson called it:

> *Certainly an inventor ought to be allowed a right to the benefit of his invention for some certain time. Nobody wishes more than I do that ingenuity, which is spurred on by the hope of a monopoly for a limited time, should receive a liberal encouragement: nobody estimates higher the utility which society has derived from that.*

12 If this point is obscure, consider the following thought experiment: Suppose we could retroactively change patent or copyright law, declaring, say, that all patents previously granted

yesterday's creations makes it more difficult for today's creators, stronger property rights for **today's** creators makes it more difficult for **tomorrow's**.

That's the trade-off, the price we pay (tomorrow) for the intellectual property protection we bestow (today): We restrict—purposefully and intentionally—the freedom of future creators and inventors to borrow from and build upon what they find around them, in the hopes of increasing creative and inventive activity in the present.

It's a price worth paying—at least, it's worth paying if the legal protection does what it is supposed to do, i.e., if the additional incentive provided by the property right brings new creations and inventions into existence that would not otherwise exist. Tomorrow's creators and inventors are still better off—or at least they are no **worse** off—having to obtain permission, or pay a fee, to use/copy/borrow **those** creations and inventions, because those creations and inventions wouldn't even exist without the promise of property protection in the first place.

But what about the creations and inventions we would have gotten anyway, even **without** any promise of property protection? People create new things for many reasons, the prospect of being able to assert exclusive rights over their creations being only one of them. Even without a promise of exclusive property rights, creative and inventive activity will not cease entirely; farmers will still tinker with the design of their plows, musicians will still try out new versions of old songs, and cement manufacturers will continue to play around with the proper formulas for making cement. Bestowing property rights on **these** creations and inventions—the ones we'd get anyway, even without property protection—makes tomorrow's inventors **worse** off than they otherwise would have been, without providing society with any corresponding benefit; these creations would have appeared anyway and, without any property protection at all, they would have been free for tomorrow's creators to use and to make and to copy and to build upon. Giving property protection to **those** inventions is a net loss; it does nothing more than burden tomorrow's inventors to no purpose.

Intellectual property law in a Jeffersonian world, then, is always a matter of degree, of finding that balance, of *drawing the line*, as he put it, *between the things which **are** worth to the public the embarrassment of an exclusive patent and those which are not*. Because we pay a price, down the road, in the future, for the intellectual property protection we grant in the present, we have to always ask ourselves whether that price is worth paying. If it is, then intellectual property rights are a

for medical devices will last for thirty years instead of twenty, or that some forms of intellectual property that had previously **not** been protected by copyright (dress designs, or recipes) were in fact protected. One effect of that change, obviously, would be to make it more difficult or costly for today's creators to use those previously created inventions and designs.

good thing; if it's not, they're not. If they stimulate the creation of new things—as, surely, they sometimes do; nobody can read the history of the United States without acknowledging that the hunt for profit made possible by the patent law can help stimulate the creation new inventions—we should have them. But as to the things that aren't "worth...the embarrassment of an exclusive patent"—the things we'd get anyway—property protection is unnecessary and counterproductive.

I know well, Jefferson continued, *the difficulty of drawing that line.* If not forever, how long should copyrights last? If not all inventions are worth protecting with a patent, how do we distinguish the ones that are from the ones that aren't? It's inherently a messy and imprecise business, measuring and balancing speculative and uncertain estimates of present benefits and future costs. The Goldilocks Principle applies: Protection for intellectual property shouldn't be too weak (or it won't give creators enough of an incentive to create) or too strong (or it will choke off future creativity), but just right. We'll never get it exactly right, but it is what we are always aiming for—in a Jeffersonian world, at least.[13]

---

13 For instance, we need to draw the line circumscribing the duration of intellectual property rights. Intellectual property rights shouldn't last forever (although their close cousins, rights in "real property," generally do) because they don't need to last forever; it is hard to argue that today's creators need a promise of perpetual exclusivity, passing to their heirs and their heirs' heirs and on and on forever, to give them an incentive to create, that they somehow get any additional incentive whatsoever from knowing that their heirs five, or ten, or fifteen generations hence will still be able to cash in on whatever it is they are creating today.

> *Certainly an inventor ought to be allowed a right to the benefit of his invention for some time. It is equally certain it ought* **not** *be perpetual;* **for to embarrass society with monopolies for every utensil existing, and in all the details of life, would be more injurious to them than had the supposed inventors never existed,** *because the natural understanding of its members would have suggested the same things or others as good.*
>
> *[Precisely] how long the term should be is a difficult question.*

And we will need to draw the line separating inventions that are somehow trivial or obvious—of the kind we're likely to get anyway, in the ordinary course of tinkering and experimentation—from those which are not.

> *If a new application of our old machines be a ground of monopoly, the patent law will take from us much more good than it will give. If the bringing together under the same roof various useful things before known... entitles one to an exclusive use of all these, either separately or combined, every utensil of life might be taken from us by a patent. I might build a stable, bring into it a cutting-knife to chop straw, a hand-mill to grind the grain, a curry comb and brush to clean the horses, and by a patent exclude every one from ever more using these things without paying me.*

Cutting through the acronyms and argot . . . the Internet may fairly be regarded as a never-ending worldwide conversation. The Government may not . . . interrupt that conversation. As the most participatory form of mass speech yet developed, the Internet deserves the highest protection from governmental intrusion. . . . True it is that many find some of the speech on the Internet to be offensive, and amid the din of cyberspace many hear discordant voices that they regard as indecent. The absence of governmental regulation of Internet content has unquestionably produced a kind of chaos, but . . . the strength of the Internet is chaos, [and] the strength of our liberty depends upon the chaos and cacophony of the unfettered speech the First Amendment protects. (Judge Stephen Dalzell, ACLU v. Reno)

The perfect Jeffersonian world, then, is one that has as much protection for speech as it can have, but only as much protection for intellectual property as it needs.

Sounds like cyberspace! At least, it's not hard to see why Jeffersonians find cyberspace so congenial a place. There's certainly been a hell of a lot of "free speech"; if you truly believe in the power of human communication, and believe that it should be as unconstrained as possible—that *freedom of discussion is sufficient for the propagation and protection of truth*, and that *liberty depends on the freedom of the press, which* **cannot** be limited without being lost—cyberspace is surely your kind of place. As an engine for the propagation of human communications on a global scale, there's never been anything remotely like it, at least not since Gutenberg invented movable type. And it seems sometimes almost to have been *peculiarly and benevolently designed* to resist efforts to rein it in and get it under control.

As for intellectual property . . . has the Internet had (and does it now have) as much, but only as much, intellectual property protection as it needs?

That's a harder question, of course—unanswerable, really.

It's a useful question to ask, though. Even without knowing how much intellectual property protection it "needs," it's surely hard to argue that it has had "too much." The loudest complaint about the inter-network has, if anything, been that there has been so **little** protection for intellectual property. Copyright "piracy" has been, in the eyes of many people, the Big Story, the **absence** of effective protection for intellectual property, the remarkable facility with which Internet users have been able to reproduce and redistribute information of all kinds—music, text, video, etc.—whether ostensibly protected by some nation's copyright law or not, in quantities that truly stagger the mind. Sean Fanning comes up with a little string of program code—Napster—throws it onto the network, and a year later 70 million people are trading billions of songs every day. Shut down Napster, along comes Grokster, and BitTorrent, and file-sharing continues apace. And just when you thought it was safe, here comes YouTube.

But I don't think that really was the Big Story. Smuggling preexisting copyright-protected works across the border into new places where they are freely reproduced and redistributed and resold is a very old game—we did it ourselves, back in the day.[14] Many people, as the Internet was picking up steam back in the early '90s, saw that coming.

No, the Big Story—the Big Jeffersonian Story, at least—is that a place with so **little** intellectual property protection spawned such an extraordinary explosion of creative activity. **Nobody** saw Wikipedia coming. Or Seti@Home, or open source software, or Project Gutenberg, or Slashdot, or the NASA Clickworkers project, or Amazon's user-generated recommendations, or the Public Library of Science, or the Drudge Report and the rise of the blogosphere, or the possibility that one could lose oneself for days on end pursuing megabytes upon megabytes of freely accessible information on everything from the archeology of ancient Rome to the history of zoological nomenclature, from the best ways to fix 1950s Fiat carburetors to the poems of Walt Whitman, from the configuration of the night sky to the complete, annotated human genome...

Without the incentive to create, why would anyone create?

It turns out we didn't know nearly as much about creativity, or incentives, or the power of networks, as we thought we did. Yochai Benkler, in his marvelous book about the new forms of intellectual creativity that the Internet has helped spawn, describes a little thought experiment that illustrates the point well:

> Imagine that you are performing a web search with me. Imagine...that we wanted to answer the questions of an imaginative six-year-old about Viking ships. What would we get, sitting in front of our computers and plugging in a search request for "Viking Ships"? The first site is Canadian, and includes a collection of resources, essays, and work-sheets. An enterprising elementary school teacher at the Gander Academy in Newfoundland seems to have put these together. She has essays on different questions, and links to sites hosted by a wide range of individuals and organizations, such as a Swedish museum, individual sites hosted on geocities.com, and even to a specific picture of a replica Viking ship, hosted on a commercial site devoted to selling nautical replicas.... The second link is to a Norwegian site called "the Viking Network," a Web ring dedicated to preparing and hosting short essays on Vikings.... The third site is hosted by a Danish commercial photographer, dedicated to photographs of archeological finds and replicas of Danish Viking ships. A retired professor from the University of Pittsburgh runs the fourth. The fifth is somewhere between a hobby

---

14 The history of U.S. copyright law, in two sentences, goes something like this: Up until 1891, it was entirely lawful to bring books, paintings, maps, etc., in from over the border—from England, say—and then to copy, reprint, and resell them to your heart's content; U.S. copyright law did not protect works produced in other countries, so it was not infringement to reproduce and distribute them in the United States. Much of the U.S. book publishing industry was built, in part, on the ability of U.S. publishers to reprint English works—Dickens, Eliot, Scott, Thackeray, Austen, Carlisle, Gibbon, and the other great (and hugely popular) English authors of the eighteenth and nineteenth centuries—without paying any royalties.

and a showcase for the services of an individual independent Web publisher...The sixth and seventh are museums, in Norway and Virginia, respectively...[etc.]

Multiply that, Benkler suggests, by a billion—the billion or so people who live in societies sufficiently wealthy to allow cheap and ubiquitous Internet access, each of whom has a few minutes a day to spend on—well, on whatever he or she wants to spend it on. Small pieces, as David Weinberger put it, loosely joined.[15] It's not just an incomprehensibly vast compendium of information, though of course it is an incomprehensibly vast compendium of information—some of it reliable, some of it not, some of it hateful, much of it not, some of it useful, lots of it not—but a new mode of **creating** information. Benkler calls it "peer production"

> Why can fifty thousand volunteers successfully coauthor Wikipedia...and then turn around and give it away for free? Why do 4.5 million volunteers contribute their left-over computer cycles to create the most powerful supercomputer on earth, SETI@ Home? Without a broadly accepted analytic model to explain these phenomena, we tend to treat them as curiosities, perhaps transient fads,...We should try instead to see them for what they are: a new mode of production emerging in the middle of the most advanced economies in the world.

That we didn't see coming. The Internet should be a barren wasteland, if we truly needed copyright incentives to stimulate our collective creative juices. But it isn't. If the goal is to have only as much intellectual property protection as we need, it's hard to make the case that we needed any more than the little we had.

There's a great deal more to this story, of course; free speech and intellectual property questions, on the Internet as elsewhere, are vastly more complicated than this. They're more complicated because it turns out that not everyone is a Jeffersonian—who knew?! The perfect Jeffersonian world may have as much protection for speech as it can get and only as much protection for intellectual property as it needs, but there are lots and lots of Hamiltonians out there, and they don't buy it. They

---

15 Eben Moglen puts the point this way:

> "Incentives" is merely a metaphor, and as a metaphor to describe human creative activity it's pretty crummy. [A] better metaphor arose on the day Michael Faraday first noticed what happened when he wrapped a coil of wire around a magnet and spun the magnet. Current flows in such a wire, but we don't ask what the incentive is for the electrons to leave home. We say that the current results from an emergent property of the system, which we call induction....So Moglen's Metaphorical Corollary to Faraday's Law says that if you wrap the Internet around every person on the planet and spin the planet, software flows in the network. It's an emergent property of connected human minds that they create things for one another's pleasure and to conquer their uneasy sense of being too alone. (Eben Moglen, "Anarchism Triumphant: Free Software and the Death of Copyright.")

have a very different vision, a world governed by different principles, principles that are, rather remarkably, almost the perfect mirror image of Jefferson's. In that mirror-world, it is free speech that gets the cost-benefit balancing, while the inventors and creators hold "natural rights" to legal protection.

That mirror-world looks a good deal like France, actually—ironically enough, given Jefferson's own deep and abiding affection for all things French.[16] French law, as we saw earlier in the Yahoo! Problem, tolerates speech regulation of a kind entirely unacceptable in a more Jeffersonian place (like the United States). Contrast the absolute Jeffersonian negative of the U.S. Bill of Rights—"Congress shall **make no law** . . . abridging the freedom of speech"—with the corresponding provisions in the French Declaration of the Rights of Man: "Tout citoyen peut donc parler, écrire, imprimer librement, sauf à répondre de l'abus de cette liberté dans les cas déterminés par la Loi" ("Any Citizen can speak, write, and print freely, **except** to answer for the abuse of this freedom in cases determined by the Law"). In the U.S., Law with a capital "L"—the law of the statute books and court decisions—is subordinate to the freedom of speech, which "no law" may limit; in France, Law defines the limits of the right: "La Loi n'a le droit de défendre que les actions nuisibles à la Société" ("The Law has a right to forbid . . . those actions that are injurious to society"). Not surprisingly, the French statute books contain any number of restrictions—prohibitions on the use of hate speech, the use of racist epithets, the use of languages other than French in certain circumstances, and even the expression of opinions that "cast discredit on judicial opinions"—that make a Jeffersonian cringe.

And in that mirror-world, creators and inventors have the rights that are superior to Law—the "droit moral," the French call it, the **moral** right to protection for their intellectual property. In France, intellectual creations are treated as aspects of the creators' personality, part of the private space into which the Law may not intrude, and authors have perpetual and **inalienable** rights—rights that can never be waived, or transferred to others, or limited by contract—to publish (or to withhold publication of) their works, to be credited as the work's creator, to prevent others from claiming authorship, and to prevent others from making "deforming changes" in the

---

16 *I cannot leave this great and good country* [France] *without expressing my sense of its pre-eminence of character among the nations of the Earth. A more benevolent people I have never known, nor greater warmth and devotedness. Their kindness and accommodation to strangers is unparalleled, and the hospitality of Paris is beyond anything I had conceived to be practicable . . . Their eminence, too, in science, the communicative dispositions of their scientific men, the politeness of general manners, the ease and vivacity of their conversation, give a charm to their society to be found nowhere else. . . . Ask the travelled inhabitant of any nation: "In what country on earth would you rather live?" "Certainly in my own, where are all my friends, my relations, and the earliest and sweetest affections of my life." "Which would be your second choice?" "France."* (Thomas Jefferson, *Autobiography.*)

work that would be damaging to the author's reputation. The Jeffersonian cost-benefit intellectual property calculus doesn't apply to these "moral rights," because they reflect something more fundamental that society's particular utilitarian needs.

It's a perfectly coherent vision, and perfectly reasonable people hold it strongly and sincerely. Not just in France, of course—this isn't some part of "national character," it's an idea that, like all ideas, flows easily and naturally across national borders. Even in Jeffersonian places like the United States, there are plenty of reasonable people who find the mirror-world vision an attractive one (just as there are, I would imagine, plenty of disgruntled Jeffersonians in France). Self-government is a conversation, and there's a wide range of views in the United States about what the First Amendment means, a vigorous debate about whether (or to what extent) we should have similar restrictions on "hate speech," or pornography, and the like, and about whether creators and inventors have some "moral" right to control the use and distribution of their creations and inventions.

I'm on Jefferson's side, of course (could you tell?). But that's really neither here nor there. I wish everyone were, but, alas, that's not the case. And being on Jefferson's side means recognizing that everyone gets to decide these questions for him/herself.

> *Everyone takes his side, according to his constitution and the circumstances in which he is placed. Opinions, which are equally honest on both sides, should not affect personal esteem or social intercourse.*

"Chacun à son goût," as the French would say—to each his/her own, each to his/her taste.[17]

So that's the challenge, for "Internet law." We have created, all of a sudden, in the space of a couple of decades—"in einen Augenblick," as the Germans would say, in the twinkling of an eye—a global place, where the people of the world have gotten all mixed up together, interacting with one another in ways unimaginable a mere two decades ago. We often disagree—quite fundamentally—about the kind of law we want to have, about what Law is, and where it comes from. Nobody has the right answer, because these are not the sorts of questions that have right and wrong answers. And nobody has the right to impose his or her vision on others who do not share it, because all are created equal.

So who decides?

We are, I'm afraid, back where we were a couple of chapters ago. What else can we do but let people decide for themselves which vision they prefer? Jeffersonians want what Jeffersonians always want—the freedom to build their communities in the manner they find most congenial, and the freedom for the Hamiltonians to build theirs.

Isn't that, after all, what frontiers are for?

---

17 Or even better, perhaps, from the German: "Jedem Narren gefällt seine Kappe" (Each fool prefers his own hat).

EPILOGUE
JEFFERSON'S NATURE, AND THE NATURE OF CYBERSPACE

We shall not cease from exploration
And the end of all our exploring
Will be to arrive where we started
And know the place for the first time.

T. S. ELIOT, "LITTLE GIDDING"

Though my editor pressed me mercilessly to do so, I never could quite figure out whether this was a book about Jefferson or a book about cyberspace. Now that you've finished—and you're not one of those people who jumps ahead to the end, are you?—you can decide for yourself.

I suspect that I didn't answer any of the questions you might have had, at the start, about Internet law and regulation: about whether we should impose a rule of "Net Neutrality" on Internet Service Providers, or adopt more stringent privacy protections for data in electronic form, or require ISPs to keep track of user identities and to turn the information over to the authorities upon demand, or any of the other controversial current issues now under debate. That was intentional—not because they're unimportant questions, and not because I don't have opinions about most of them, but because that wasn't the point of this book. There will be time for them later. We are at the very beginning of what will become a centuries-long conversation about these questions, and my goal here was not to put anything to rest but to put everything in play, not to conclude any part of that conversation but to help it get started. We need, more than answers to today's questions about law and policy on the network, new ways of thinking about the questions themselves, new vocabularies, new visions of the possible, new ways of identifying and organizing what we know and what we don't know about the new place. Jefferson's ways of thinking, and his vocabulary, and his vision, are not the only ones suitable for the task, to be sure— they are not even necessarily the best ones for the task. But they have an integrity and a coherence that are difficult to match, and they can serve (again!) as the focus for discussion and debate, now on a global scale.

And what about that moose? We last saw it standing there in Jefferson's entry hall, on display for M. Buffon and all who cared to come see it. *An acquisition more precious than you can imagine.* What **was** he up to? Why did he care so much about stuff like that? And, more importantly, why should we care why he cared?

He wanted, as we saw earlier, simply to show Buffon how big animals were in the New World. But numbers in a table could do **that**. He needed the moose itself, I think, for the "Wow" factor, the "Aha!" moment: "Whoa—we've never seen anything like **that** before!" He wanted to dazzle—and a moose is, let's be honest, a pretty dazzling creature. He wanted to dazzle because he wanted people to believe that there really was a "new world" over there, and he wanted people to believe that because if they did, it was more likely to become true.

Wikipedia would serve, I think, as a pretty good moose, something we could bring with us (if we could only bring one thing) to show to people of the Old World. In this case, of course, the Old World is actually the **old** world—not the world on the other side of an ocean, but the world of 1985 or 1990, the world consisting of people who have no idea what a "Wikipedia" looks like, the world separated from us not in space but in time. "Come take a look," we would say to them: here's the world's single most widely consulted source of information, available in forty-odd languages, accessible (virtually instantaneously) to over a billion people, compiled by thousands of people working anonymously and for no pay. "Whoa—we've never seen anything like **that** before!"

But it wasn't just the dazzle. Jefferson found something in all that poking around in *the laws of Nature and Nature's God*, something that proved valuable for his thinking about the world. There were connections between the moose and the structure of the Northwest Ordinance, between the seashells in the mountains and the Bill for the General Diffusion of Knowledge, between the exponential growth of animal populations and the Problem of the Extended Republic, and there are connections between end-to-end design, distributed routing, the growth of the Internet, the decision-making structure of ICANN, the resolution of the Yahoo! Problem, and the scope of intellectual property protection in Second Life. I can't articulate, in a well-crafted sentence or two (or perhaps even in a whole book!) exactly what they are or how they manifest themselves; Jefferson couldn't, either (at least, he never did), which is some consolation, Jefferson being a much smarter guy, and a much better writer, than I am.

Many people then, and many people now, deny the existence of those connections, and would discourage us from looking for them. In a wonderful (though ultimately wrongheaded) essay titled "Jefferson's Nature," my friend and colleague Lawrence Lessig called the Jeffersonians to task for all their talk about the "nature" of cyberspace. "The strange thing about cyberspace," Lessig wrote, is that "it is said to **have** a nature."

> We are building the most important jurisdiction since the Louisiana Purchase, . . . and here's the central point: This space—this space that cyberspace is—this space is constituted by its code. Its nature, its values, the freedoms it protects, all these things are things only because of the architecture of the space. The architecture, the design, the constitution, the shape—these features that someone, some code writer, builds. This architecture makes cyberspace as it is, and this architecture can be different. . . . The nature of this space is not determined by god; **the nature of this space is ours to set.** Whether, in Jefferson's words, ideas will be free to flow is a decision we must make, not a decision that nature has made. Whether one may travel in this space with the right of anonymity is a choice that we must make, not a choice that the nature of the space will assure. The space has the nature that its code writers give it; yet we are the code writers, and we can do things differently.

"Vis-à-vis the laws of nature in this new space," Lessig went on, "we are gods; and the problem with being gods is that we must choose."

> We stand on the edge of an era when fundamental choices about what life in cyberspace, and therefore, life in real space, will be like. These choices will be **made**; there is no nature here to discover.

He railed against what he called the "is-ism" of the "modern Jeffersons," the idea

> that says that the way the Net is is the way the Net has to be...that makes it seem
> as if the values of that space are values we will simply find, given to us by the laws of
> quantum physics,

an "is-ism" that would have us

> watching as important aspects of privacy and free speech are erased by the emerging
> architecture of the panopticon, and [speaking], like modern Jeffersons, about nature
> making it so—forgetting that here, we are nature.

Well, yes and no. He's right about the choices we have to make. We do indeed, collectively, **make** cyberspace. That is surely one of the strangest things about it (and one of the things that makes it so different from Virginia): the Net is just the "space the code-writers give us," nothing more, nothing less. No gods give us that code; we are the code-writers, the architects and builders of the place.

But I'm not so sure that "the nature of this space is ours to set." There **are** laws of Nature—some that we understand, some that we don't (yet). Jefferson was surely right about **that**; he (along with his many, many collaborators in the global scientific enterprise) was getting closer all the time—closer than any of them could possibly have known—to one of the biggest of them all, one of the truly fundamental ones. There **are** laws of growth, and scale, and organization, reasons why website visits, Internet connectivity, the population of cities, and the frequency of words all follow the same pattern, reasons why the one global network is the one with end-to-end design and distributed routing, though we probably understand those laws about as well as Jefferson and Buffon understood why moose are the way they are—i.e., not very well.

And they matter—not just for the mouse and the moose, but for the design of human institutions; we can shake our fists at the law of gravity all we like, but if we don't pay close attention to it when building our bridges, they will all fall down. Those laws constrain the "should be" because they define the "could be," and it is not, as Lessig would have it, "is-ism" to keep looking for them and trying to understand how they work. Jefferson, surely, is proof of that; he can be charged with many failings, but "is-ism" is not among them, for few people in history were as successful at taking the "is" and turning it into the "should be" as he. He found a way, somehow, to get his ideas in line with those laws of Nature, to harness them, and to find in them something that helped enlarge and enrich the scope of human life.

Why should we care about that? How could we **not** care about that?

APPENDIX

FIGURE 5.3 The Internet as a Three-Layer System

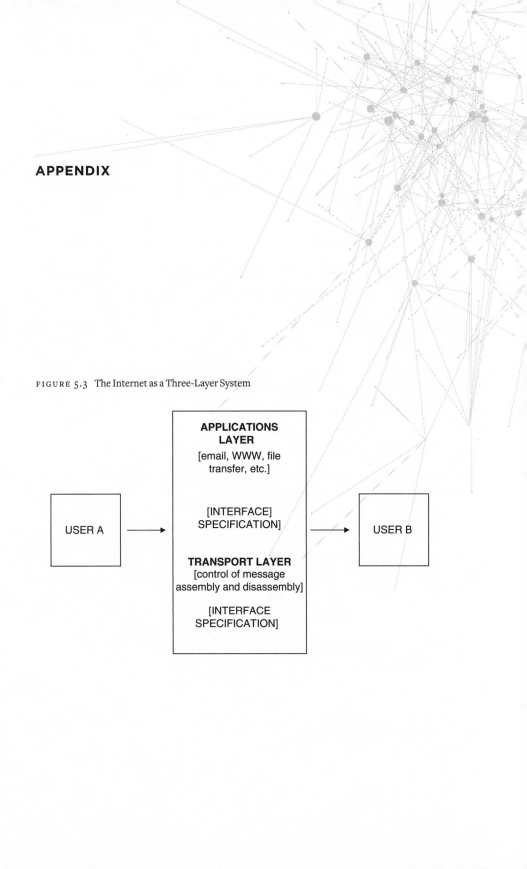

FIGURE 5.5   User A Using the Telephone Network to Communicate over the Internet with User B

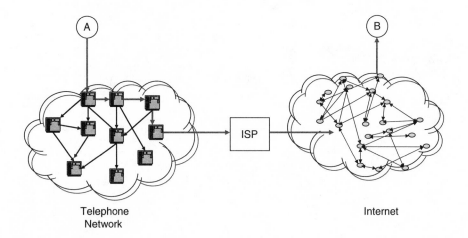

Telephone
Network

Internet

FIGURE 6.5

If we take our Normal Distribution:

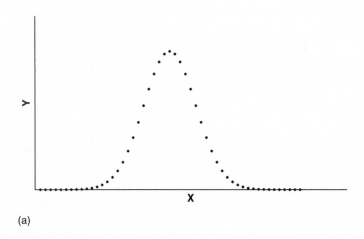

(a)

and change the scale by "zooming" in on some portion:

Hypothetical Normal Distribution

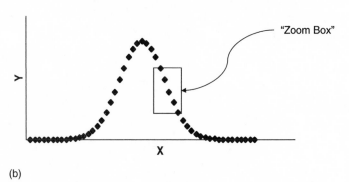

(b)

the distribution no longer has the same shape or symmetrical properties:

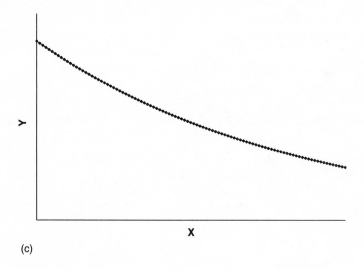

(c)

FIGURE 6.6

So if, for example, you were to count and weigh every living thing in a patch of forest, the distribution of weights across the whole population of organisms, from the smallest bacterium to the largest oak tree, you'd get a power law curve that would look something like this:

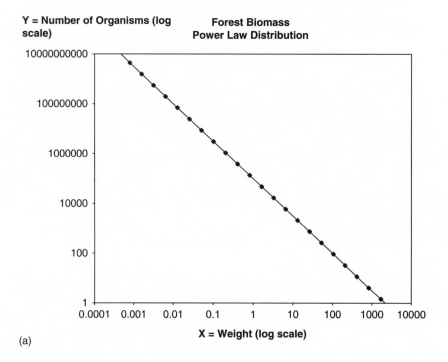

(a)

It will look the same even if you magnify the scale so that you're only looking at organisms weighing between 1,000 and 2,000 grams, or between 50,000 and 55,000 grams, or between 1 and 2 grams:

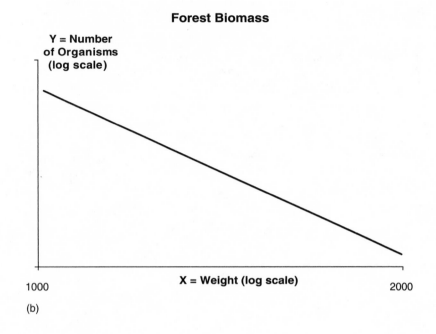

(b)

FIGURE 9.1 IETF Structure

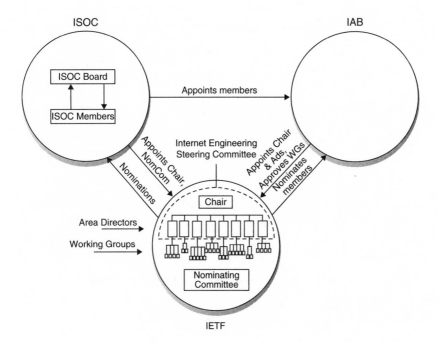

FIGURE 10.3   ICANN Board of Directors Selection Process

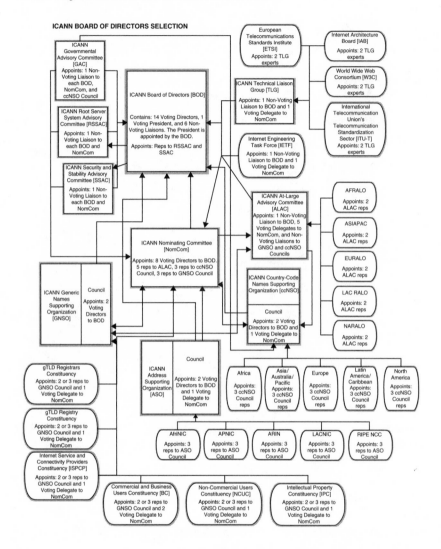

REFERENCES AND SUGGESTED READINGS

PROLOGUE

GENERAL BACKGROUND

On cyberspace: Excellent general treatments of the legal and social landscape in cyberspace include the books of Lawrence Lessig (*Code and Other Laws of Cyberspace* [1999], *Free Culture* [2004], and *Code v.2.0* [2006]); David Weinberger, *Small Pieces Loosely Joined: A Unified Theory of the Web* (2002); Adam Thierer and Wayne Crews, Jr., eds., *Who Rules the Net: Internet Governance and Jurisdiction* (2003); Jack Goldsmith and Tim Wu, *Who Controls the Internet?: Illusions of a Borderless World* (2006); Jonathan Zittrain, *The Future of the Internet (And How to Stop It)* (2008); Andrew Shapiro, *The Control Revolution* (2000); David Brin, *The Transparent Society* (1998); Daniel Solove, *The Digital Person: Technology and Privacy in the Information Age*, 2d ed. (2006); and Jessica Litman, *Digital Copyright* (2006).

On "cyberspace as 'place,'" the leading text is Dan Hunter, "Cyberspace as Place and the Tragedy of the Digital Anticommons," 91 *Calif. L. Rev.* 439 (2003); other useful treatments are in Julie Cohen, "Cyberspace As/And Space," 107 *Colum. L. Rev.* 210 (2007); Michael J. Madison, "The Narratives of Cyberspace Law (or, Learning from Casablanca)," 27 *Colum. J. L. & Arts* 249 (2004).

The technical side of the design of cyberspace networks is described (in a form accessible to the nonspecialist) at the Internet Society website (see esp. "What is the Internet" at www.isoc.org/internet/); E. Krol and E. Hoffman, "RFC 1462: What is the Internet?," available at www.ietf.org/rfc/rfc1462.txt?number=1462; Rus Shuler, "How Does the Internet Work," available at www.theshulers.com/whitepapers/internet_whitepaper.html; National Research Council, "*The Internet's Coming of Age* (2001); B. Carpenter, ed., "RFC 1958: Architectural Principles of the Internet," available at www.faqs.org/rfcs/rfc1958.html.

On Jefferson: Few people in history left a more complete written record of their ideas than Jefferson did—some twenty thousand letters, thousands of pages of journal entries, hundreds of speeches and official memoranda of one kind or another, his *Autobiography*, a "Memorandum of Service to My Country," several lengthy articles for Diderot's *Encyclopédie Methodique*, among other writings. The Library of America's one-volume selection from this material (*Thomas Jefferson: Writings* [1984]), edited by the great Jefferson scholar Merrill D. Peterson, collects a wonderful sample of the best of them, and is probably the single resource I would recommend first to anyone interested in a deeper understanding of those ideas than anything I can provide below. Other sources for the primary material on which I have relied:

The Adams-Jefferson Letters (Lester Cappon, ed., 1959) is another wonderful resource, the complete record of a remarkable fifty-plus-year relationship carried out mostly in writing and marked by just about every human emotion one can think of—love, hate, anger, despair, hope, envy, you-name-it. (The collection includes all of the Abigail Adams–Jefferson correspondence, as well.) Lester Cappon's notes are prodigiously helpful in setting out the background and context of the correspondence.

Princeton University Press's project on *The Papers of Thomas Jefferson*—now in its fifty-eighth year—is one of the great works of scholarship ever undertaken and should be declared a National Historical Monument or some-such. Everything Jefferson wrote, and everything he received, in chronological order, thoroughly annotated and cross-referenced. The first thirty-four volumes (of a projected sixty) have been released—and they haven't even reached the years of his presidency. A treasure trove of Jeffersoniana.

Other compilations of Jefferson's letters include *The Writings of Thomas Jefferson* (Paul L. Ford, ed., 1892–99) (10 vols.); *The Writings of Thomas Jefferson* (A. A. Lipscomb and A. E. Bergh, eds., 1903) (20 vols., available in electronic form); *The Commonplace Book of Thomas Jefferson* (G. Chinard, ed., 1926); *The Literary Bible of Thomas Jefferson* (G. Chinard, ed., 1928); *The Life and Selected Writings of Thomas Jefferson* (A. Koch and W. Peden, eds., 1944); *Jefferson: Political Writings* (J. Appleby and T. Ball, eds., 1999); *Thomas Jefferson: The Garden and Farm Books* (R. Baron, ed., 1987); *Jefferson Himself* (B. Mayo, ed., 1942); and *The Complete Jefferson* (S. Padover, ed., 1943).

There are also a number of outstanding online collections of Jefferson's writings in searchable, electronic form, most notably those at the University of Virginia (etext.virginia.edu/jefferson/) and at the Library of Congress (memory.loc.gov/ammem/collections/jefferson_papers/)—not coincidentally, two institutions Jefferson helped found.

Jefferson biographies number, by now, in the hundreds if not the thousands, with more seeming to appear every week. I found the following to be the most useful and have relied most heavily on them: Merrill D. Peterson, *Thomas Jefferson and the New Nation: A Biography* (1970) and *The Jefferson Image in the American Mind* (1998); Peter S. Onuf, ed., *Jeffersonian Legacies* (1993); Claude G. Bowers, *The Young Jefferson* (1969); Richard B. Bernstein, *Thomas Jefferson* (2003); Dumas Malone, *Jefferson and His Time* (6 vols., 1948–81); Willard Sterne Randall,

Thomas Jefferson (1993); W. H. Adams, *The Paris Years of Thomas Jefferson* (1997); Joseph J. Ellis, *American Sphinx: The Character of Thomas Jefferson* (1996).

Among the more off-beat writings about Jefferson (and there are many of those), I found two—John Dos Passos's *The Head and Heart of Thomas Jefferson* (1954) and Albert J. Nock, *Jefferson* (1926)—to be the most useful and interesting. And for the more poetically inclined, I recommend Ezra Pound's *Cantos XXXI–XXXIV* (one of which, titled "Nuovo Mondo," consists almost entirely of excerpts from Jefferson's own writings); Phillip Levine's *A Walk with Tom Jefferson* (1988); Mary Jo Salter's *A Phone Call to the Future* (2008) (especially the poem titled "The Hand of Thomas Jefferson"); and Amy Clampitt's *Westward* (1990).

CHAPTER REFERENCES

The opening quotations are from Lytton Strachey, *"Eminent Victorians* (1918); Søren Kierkegaard, *The Concluding Unscientific Postscript to the Philosophical Fragments* (1846); and Bob Dylan, "Lily, Rosemary, and the Jack of Hearts" (from the album *Blood on the Tracks*).

Berlin's discussion of foxes and hedgehogs comes from his essay "The Hedgehog and the Fox: An Essay on Tolstoy's View of History" (1953).

The reader interested in more information on Jefferson-the-Fox would do well to consult, in addition to the general Jefferson biographies listed above, any one or more of the following: Silvio Bedini, *Thomas Jefferson and His Copying Machines* (1984) and *Thomas Jefferson: Statesman of Science* (1990); Daniel J. Boorstin, *The Lost World of Thomas Jefferson* (1948); I. Bernard Cohen, *Science and the Founding Fathers: Science in the Political Thought of Thomas Jefferson, Benjamin Franklin, John Adams, and James Madison* (1995); Edward T. Martin, *Thomas Jefferson: Scientist* (1952); Brooke Hindle, ed., *Early American Science* (1976).

On *Notes on the State of Virginia*: the best currently available edition of *Notes on the State of Virginia* is the one edited by William Peden (1954). I drew much of the general background on the book, and on the circumstances surrounding its publication, from the following: Henry Steel Commager, "Thomas Jefferson and the Character of America," in *Thomas Jefferson: The Garden and Farm Books* (Robert C. Baron, ed.); Peter S. Onuf, *Jefferson's Empire: The Language of American Nationhood* (2000); John Dos Passos, *The Head and Heart of Thomas Jefferson* (1954); Donald Jackson, *Thomas Jefferson and the Stony Mountains* (1981); Harvey Mansfield, "Thomas Jefferson," in *"American Political Thought"* (Morton Frisch and Richard Stevens, eds., 1983).

On Jefferson's moose, see Anna Clark Jones, "Antlers for Jefferson," *New Eng. Quart.* 21: 333–48 (1939); Ruth Henline, "A Study of *Notes on the State of Virginia* as Evidence of Jefferson's Reaction Against the Theories of the French Naturalists," *Virg. Mag. of Hist. and Biog.* 55: 233–46 (1946); Paul Semonin, *American Monster: How the Nation's First Prehistoric Creature Became a Symbol of National Identity* (2000); Gilbert Chinard, "Eighteenth Century Theories of America as a Human Habitat," *Proc Am Phil. Soc.* 91: 27–57 (1947); Henry Steel Commager, "Thomas Jefferson and the Character of America," in *Thomas Jefferson: The Garden and Farm Books* (Robert C. Baron, ed.); and Donald Jackson, *Thomas Jefferson and the Stony Mountains* (1981).

JEFFERSON QUOTATIONS

There is not a sprig of grass . . . TJ to Martha Jefferson Randolph, Dec. 23, 1790

I think public service . . . TJ to James Madison, May 20, 1782

Nature intended me for the tranquil pursuits of science . . . TJ to P. S. Dupont de Nemours, March 2, 1809

I had always made it a practice . . . TJ, *Autobiography*

Is not the Caribou and Black Moose . . . *tamed to any purpose?* TJ to Governor John Sullivan of New Hampshire (1783)

CHAPTER 1

On Jefferson's map, and his mapmaking exploits in general, see: A. W. Greely, "Jefferson as a Geographer," in Lipscomb and Bergh, *The Writings of Thomas Jefferson*; Walter W. Ristow, "Maps," *Library of Congress Quarterly Journal,* vol. 23: 231–42 (July 1966); Donald Jackson, *Thomas Jefferson and the Stony Mountains* (1981), 86–163; John Logan Allen, "Imagining the West: The View from Monticello," in *Thomas Jefferson and the Changing West* (James P. Ronda, ed., 1997); Silvio Bedini, *Thomas Jefferson: Statesman of Science* (1990), 11–15, 131–33, 447–48. Also The University of Virginia online exhibit at www.lib.virginia.edu/small/exhibits/lewis_clark/albemarle2.html.

On mapping cyberspace: The preeminent resource is Martin Dodge's wonderful collection of maps and information and discussion at www.cybergeography.org, along with his books *Atlas of Cyberspace* (with R. Kitchin, 2001) and *Mapping Cyberspace* (with R. Kitchin, 2000).

The Peacock Map is available at www.peacockmaps.com/ and at www.lumeta.com/research/. Used by kind permission of Lumeta Corporation. Information on methodologies can be found at research.lumeta.com/ches/map.

On the history of TCP/IP: The two indispensable (and hugely entertaining) resources are Janet Abbate, *Inventing the Internet* (2000), and Katie Hafner and Matthew Lyon, *Where Wizards Stay Up Late* (1996). For other useful compendia of information on the development of the inter-network, see Leinert et al., "A Brief History of the Internet," available at www.isoc .org/internet/history/brief.shtml (along with the other outstanding material collected at the Internet Society website at www.isoc.org); National Research Council, *Internet's Coming of Age*; Peter Salus, *Casting the Net: From ARPANET to INTERNET and Beyond* (1995); Richard Griffiths, "The History of the Internet/The Internet for Historians (and just about everyone else)," available at www.let.leidenuniv.nl/history/ivh/frame_theorie.html.

Figure 1.4 is from www.directionsmag.com/images/articles/125_figure_1.gif.

JEFFERSON QUOTATIONS

I consider . . . *the idea of preparing a new copy* . . . TJ to John Melish, Dec. 10, 1814

My father's education . . . TJ, *Autobiography*

Everything I can lay my hands on ... TJ to William Dunbar, March 13, 1804

... *based on an accurate chart of each county* ... TJ to Gov. Wilson Nicholas, April 19, 1816

CHAPTER 2

Data in table 2.1 on Internet host counts are from the Internet Systems Consortium (www.isc.org/index.pl).

On the eighteenth-century debates over population size in the New World, see Antonello Gerbi, *The Dispute of the New World: The History of a Polemic 1750–1900* (trans. J. Moyle, 1973); Henry Steele Commager and Elmo Giordanetti, *Was America a Mistake: An Eighteenth-Century Controversy* (1967); G. Chinard, "Eighteenth Century Theories on America as a Human Habitat," *Proc Am Phil. Soc.* 91: 27–57 (1947); I. Bernard Cohen, *Science and the Founding Father* (1995); Daniel J. Boorstin, *The Lost World of Thomas Jefferson* (1948); Henry Steel Commager, "Thomas Jefferson and the Character of America," in *Thomas Jefferson: The Garden and Farm Books* (Robert C. Baron, ed., 1987); Peter Gay, *The Enlightenment: An Interpretation* (1968).

On Malthus, and the connections between Malthus's Essay and the theory of natural selection, see David Quammen, *The Song of the Dodo: Island Biogeography in an Age of Extinctions* (1996); Philip G. Fothergill, *Historical Aspects of Organic Evolution* (1952); Michael T. Ghiselin, *The Triumph of the Darwinian Method* (1969); and the generally excellent Wikipedia entries on each of Malthus, Darwin, and Wallace.

On Franklin's demographic work, see Conway Zirkle, "Benjamin Franklin, Thomas Malthus, and the United States Census," in *Early American Science* (Brooke Hindle, ed., 1976); Alfred Aldridge, "Franklin as Demographer," *J. Econ. Hist* 9: 25–44 (1949–50); Brooke Hindle, *The Pursuit of Science in Revolutionary America* (1956); I. Bernard Cohen, *Science and the Founding Fathers* (1995); Bernard Jaffe, *Men of Science in America* (1944); Gordon S. Wood, *The Americanization of Benjamin Franklin* (2004).

On Jefferson and Adams's negotiations with the Amsterdam bankers, see George Green Shackelford, *Thomas Jefferson's Travels in Europe 1784–1789* (1995).

On Virginia's cession of territory to the United States, see Claude Bowers, *The Young Jefferson* (1969).

On the many different networking and inter-networking protocols developed during the 1970s and 1980s, see Janet Abbate, *Inventing the Internet* (2000); Gregory White, *Understanding Networks and TCP/IP*, available at 216.239.53.100/isapi/authorid%7E%7B2EE28A7C-1138–435C-A3AD-F648BB1A6707%7D/authors/author.asp; National Research Council, *Global Networks and Local Values: A Comparative Look at Germany and the United States* (2001); Jeannette A. Hoffmann, *Governing Technologies and Techniques of Government: Politics on the Net* (available at duplox.wz-berlin.de/final/jeanette.htm#toc3); Paul A. David and Mark Shurmer, "Formal Standards-setting for Global Telecommunications and Information Services: Towards an Institutional Regime Transformation?" *Telecommunications Policy* 20 (10): 789–815 (1996); Shirley M. Radack, "The Federal Government and Information Technology Standards: Building the National Information Infrastructure," *Government Information Quarterly* 11 (4): 373–85 (1994);

Marshall T. Rose, *The Open Book—A Practical Perspective on OSI*" (1996); Todd Shaiman, "The Political Economy of Anticipatory Standards: The Case of the Open Systems Interconnection Reference Model (Master's thesis, University of Oxford, M.Sc. in Economic and Social History); Paul A. David, "The Internet and the Economics of Network Technology Evolution," in *Understanding the Impact of Global Networks on Local Social, Political and Cultural Values* (Christoph Engel and Kenneth H. Keller, eds., 1999); A. Michael Froomkin, "Habermas@Discourse. Net: Toward a Critical Theory of Cyberspace," 116 *Harv. L. Rev.* 749 (2003).

JEFFERSON QUOTATIONS

Among the debilities of the government ... TJ, *Autobiography*

... daily dunned by a company ... TJ, *Autobiography*

... the money negotiations in Holland, ... TJ to James Madison, Aug. 2, 1787

Your knowledge of the subject enables you to give the best opinion, ... TJ to John Adams, Feb. 6, 1788

The danger of our incurring something like a bankruptcy ... TJ to George Washington, May 2, 1788

The moment of paying a great sum ... Ibid.

... the most amiable and the greatest of men ... TJ to Samuel Smith, Aug. 22, 1798

On being present to anyone ... TJ to William Smith, Feb. 19, 1791

CHAPTER 3

On network scaling laws, see David P. Reed, "The Law of the Pack," *Harv. Bus. Rev.* (Feb. 2001); David Weinberger, *Small Pieces Loosely Joined*; David Reed and David Weinberger, "Reed's Law: An Interview," *J. of the Hyperlinked Organization* (2001), available at www.hyper-org.com/backissues/joho-jan19-01.html#reed; James Hendler and Jennifer Golbeck, "Metcalfe's Law, Web 2.0, and the Semantic Web," available at www.cs.umd.edu/~golbeck/downloads/Web20-SW-JWS-webVersion.pdf; Jim Robertson, "The Fundamentals of Information Science: Metcalfe's Law," available at www-ec.njit.edu/~robertso/infosci/index.html#metcalf.

On roads in eighteenth-century America, see Joel Achenbach, *The Grand Idea: George Washington's Potomac and the Race to the West* (2004).

On Jefferson's efforts to clear the Rivanna River, see Willard Sterne Randall, *Thomas Jefferson* (1993); Claude G. Bowers, *The Young Jefferson* (1969).

On Jefferson's canal-building and canal-designing efforts, see George Green Shackelford, *Thomas Jefferson's Travels in Europe 1784–1789* (1995); TJ, "Memoranda Taken on a Journey from Paris into the Southern Parts of France, and Northern Parts of Italy, in the Year 1787."

On Jefferson, New Orleans, and the Louisiana Purchase, see James E. Lewis, *The Louisiana Purchase: Jefferson's Noble Bargain?* (2003); Charles Emory Smith, "The Louisiana Purchase," in Lipscomb and Bergh, *The Writings of Thomas Jefferson*; Donald Jackson, *Thomas Jefferson and the Stony Mountains* (1981); John Logan Allen, "Imagining the West: The View from

Monticello," in *Thomas Jefferson and the Changing West* (Ronda, 1997); Bernard deVoto, *The Course of Empire* (1952); Stephen E. Ambrose, *Undaunted Courage: Meriwether Lewis, Thomas Jefferson, and the Opening of the American West* (1996).

JEFFERSON QUOTATIONS

I rejoice at your success in your steamboats ... TJ to Robert Fulton, April 16, 1810

The roads are under the government of the county courts ... TJ, *Notes on the State of Virginia*

The Rivanna had never been used for navigation ... TJ, "A Memorandum (Services to My Country)"

Our towns, but more properly our villages or hamlets, ... TJ, *Notes on the State of Virginia*

There are other places at which ... *and they remain unworthy of enumeration.* TJ, *Notes on the State of Virginia*

... a canal of no great expense ... TJ to George Washington, Aug. 15, 1787

Opening a canal between these two watercourses ... *established in another channel.* TJ to George Washington, May 2, 1788

A competition between the Hudson and Patowmac rivers ... *are yet to be cleared of their fixed obstructions.* TJ, *Notes on the State of Virginia*

40 miles of very mountainous road ... *as to be little used.* Ibid.

The country watered by the Misisipi ... *half of our inhabitants.* Ibid.

There is on the globe one single spot ... TJ to Robert Livingston, April 18, 1802

Spain might have retained it quietly ... *to make arrangements on that hypothesis.* Ibid.

Nothing since the revolutionary war has produced more uneasy sensations ... Ibid.

We must know at once ... TJ To Robert Livingston, Feb. 3, 1803

... to procure cession of New Orleans ... TJ to James Monroe, Jan. 13, 1803

... the object of your mission ... *for the purposes of commerce.* TJ, Instructions to Captain Lewis, June 20, 1803

CHAPTER 4

On scaling in nature, see James H. Brown and Geoffrey B. West, eds., *Scaling in Biology* (2000); J. T. Bonner, *Why Size Matters* (2006); J. B. S. Haldane, "On Being the Right Size," in *The World of Mathematics*, vol. 2 (J. Newman ed., 1952); J. T. Bonner, *The Evolution of Complexity by Means of Natural Selection* (1998); Geoffrey B. West, J. H. Brown, and B. Enquist, "A General Model for the Origin of Allometric Scaling Laws in Biology," *Science* 276: 122–26 (1998); P. D. Gingerich, "Rates of Evolution: Effects of Time and Temporal Scaling," *Science* 222: 159–61 (1983); J. E. Cohen et al., "Body Sizes of Animal Predators and Animal Prey in Food Webs," *J Animal Ecology* 62: 389–97 (1993); S. M. Stanley, "An Explanation of Cope's Rule," *Evolution* 27: 1–26 (1973).

On Jefferson's discovery (or nondiscovery) of the *Megalonyx*, see Julian P. Boyd, "The Megalonyx, the Megatherium, and Thomas Jefferson's Lapse of Memory," *Proceedings of the*

American Philosophical Society 102: 420–35 (1958); Paul Semonin, *American Monster* (2000); and TJ, "A Memoir on the discovery of certain Bones of a Quadruped of the Clawed Kind in the Western parts of Virginia," *Trans. Am Phil Soc* 4 (1799), reproduced in *Selected Works in Nineteenth-Century North American Paleontology* (Keir B. Sterling, ed., 1974).

On Buffon and his contributions to paleontology and natural history, see Semonin, *American Monster* (2000); Charles Singer, *A Short History of Scientific Ideas to 1900* (1959); Philip G. Fothergill, *Historical Aspects of Organic Evolution* (1952); William Peden, Introduction to *Notes of the State of Virginia* (1954).

On the controversy over the degenerate animals of the New World, see Gilbert Chinard, "Eighteenth Century Theories on America as a Human Habitat," *Proc Am Phil. Soc.* 91:27–57 (1947); Donald Jackson, *Thomas Jefferson and the Stony Mountains* (1981); Antonello Gerbi, *The Dispute of the New World: The History of a Polemic 1750–1900* (trans. J. Moyle, 1973); Daniel J. Boorstin, *The Lost World of Thomas Jefferson* (1948); I. Bernard Cohen, *Science and the Founding Fathers* (1995)

On the study of island ecosystems and their significance for the development of evolutionary theory, see David Quammen, *The Song of the Dodo: Island Biogeography in an Age of Extinctions* (1996).

On distributed routing, see Edward Felten, "The Nuts and Bolts of Net Neutrality," available at itpolicy.princeton.edu/pub/neutrality.pdf; Rus Shuler, "How does the Internet Work," available at www.theshulers.com/whitepapers/internet_whitepaper/index.html; Theodore John Socolofsky and Claudia Jeanne Kale, "Request for Comments (RFC) 1180, A TCP/IP Tutorial" (1991), available at www.rfc-editor.org/rfc/rfc1180.txt; Janet Abbate, *Inventing the Internet* (2000); E. Krol and E. Hoffman, "RFC 1462, What is the Internet?" (1993), available at www.ietf.org/rfc/rfc1462.txt?number=1462; Christian Huitema, *Routing in the Internet* (2000).

JEFFERSON QUOTATIONS

Of all the charges . . . the best qualification for their service. TJ to Charles F. Welles, Dec. 12, 1809

. . . the most flattering incident of my life. TJ to secretary of the American Philosophical Society, Jan. 28, 1797

an acquisition more precious than you can imagine . . . TJ to Governor John Sullivan, Jan. 7, 1786

a good deal of the hair has fallen off . . . TJ to Sullivan, Oct. 5, 1787

I had the honour of informing you . . . which it will always be pleasing to me to have procured . . . TJ to Buffon, Oct. 1, 1787

The most important consideration . . . general consent to receive another. TJ to John Manners, Feb. 22, 1814

CHAPTER 5

On the Internet's "layered architecture," see Tim Wu, "Application-centered Internet analysis," 85 *Va. L. Rev.* 1163 (1999); T. Socolofsky and C Kale, "RFC 1180: A TCP/IP Tutorial," available at www.rfc-editor.org/rfc/rfc1180.txt; Charles Hedrick, "Introduction to the Internet Protocols," available at www.linuxjunkies.org/network/tcpip/introo.html; Shvetima Gulati, "The Internet Protocol, Part One: Foundations," available at www.acm.org/crossroads/ columns/connector/july2000.html; Kevin Werbach, "A Layered Model for Internet Policy," *J. Telecom. & High Tech. L.* 37, 1 (2002); "The TCP/IP Guide," available at www.tcpipguide. com/index.htm; and the Cisco Guide to the Internet Protocols, available at www.cisco.com/ univercd/cc/td/doc/cisintwk/ito_doc/ip.htm. The Wikipedia entries (en.wikipedia.org/wiki) under the headings Internet_Protocol_Suite, Internet_Protocol, and Transmission_Control_Protocol are also extremely helpful.

On end-to-end design, the original article laying out the idea in J. H. Saltzer, D. P. Reed, and D. D. Clark, "End-to-end arguments in System Design" (1981), available at web.mit.edu/ Saltzer/www/publications/endtoend/endtoend.pdf, reprinted in *Innovation in Networking* (Craig Partridge, ed., 1988). Other good references include Mark A. Lemley and Lawrence Lessig, "The End of End-to-End: Preserving the Architecture of the Internet in the Broad-band Era," 48 *UCLA Law Review* 925 (2001); Edward Felten, "Nuts and Bolts of Net Neutral-ity," available at itpolicy.princeton.edu/pub/neutrality.pdf; Christian Huitema, *Routing in the Internet* (2000); David Clark and Marjory S. Blumenthal, "Rethinking the Design of the Inter-net: The End-to-End Arguments vs. the Brave New World," available at itc.mit.edu/itel/docs/ jun00/TPRC-Clark-Blumenthal.pdf; David P. Reed et al., Commentaries on "Active Network-ing and End-to-End Arguments," 12 IEEE Network 66(1998), available at ieeexplore.ieee. org/iel4/65/15117/ 00690972.pdf; Scott R. Bradner, "Where-to Where? [Was End-to-End?]," (2005), available at www.sobco.com/sob/.

On the contrasts between telephone network and TCP/IP network design, see Kevin Wer-bach, "Digital Tornado: The Internet and Telecommunications Policy" (FCC Office of Plans and Policy Working Paper No. 29, 1997); Susan Crawford, "The Ambulance, the Squad Car, and the Internet," 21 *Berkeley Tech. L. J.* 873 (2006); Jason Oxman, "The FCC and the Unregu-lation of the Internet," (FCC Office of Plans and Policy Working Paper No. 31, 1999), available at www.fcc.gov/Bureaus/OPP/working_papers/oppwp31.pdf.

CHAPTER 6

There is an immense and growing literature on the significance of power law distribu-tions generally; for good general introductions, see Mark Newman, Albert-Laszlo Barabási, and Duncan Watts, eds., *The Structure and Dynamics of Networks* (2006); Albert-Laszlo Barabási, *Linked: The New Science of Networks*(2002); Manfred Schroeder, *Fractals, Chaos, Power Laws* (1991); Guido Caldarelli, *Scale-Free Networks: Complex Webs in Nature and Tech-nology* (2007); and Mark Buchanan, *Ubiquity: The Science of History ... Or Why the World is Simpler Than We Think* (2000). A wealth of material on the subject can be found at the home pages of Albert-Lazslo Barabási (www.nd.edu/~networks/), Mark Newman (www-personal .umich.edu/~mejn/pubs.html), and Jon Kleinberg (www.cs.cornell.edu/home/kleinber/ kleinber.html).

On the power law character of Internet connectivity specifically, see G. Caldarelli, R. Marchetti, and L. Pietronero, "The Fractal Properties of the Internet," 52 *Europhys. Lett.* 386 (2000); R. Albert, H. Jeong, and A.-L. Barabási, "Diameter of the World Wide Web," 401 *Nature* 130 (1999); available at www.nd.edu/~networks/Publication%20Categories/ 03%20Journal%20Articles/Computer/Diameter_Nature%20401,%20130–131%20(1999).pdf; M. Faloutsos, P. Faloutsos, and C. Faloutsos, "On Power Law Relationships of the Internet Topology," 29 *Comp Comm. Rev* 251 (1999); Bernardo A. Huberman, *The Laws of the Web: Patterns in the Ecology of Information* (2001); L. Adamic, "The Small World Structure of the WWW," available at www.hpl.hp.com/research/idl/papers/smallworld/smallworldpaper.html; L. Adamic and B. Huberman, "The Nature of Markets on the World Wide Web," available at www.parc.xerox. com/istl/groups/iea/www/webmarkets.html; B. Huberman, P. Pirolli, J. Pitkow, and R. Lukose, "Strong Regularities in World Wide Web Surfing," 280 *Science* 95 (1998).

Figure 6.1 is from Lada Adamic and Bernardo Huberman, "Zipf's Law and the Internet," 3 *Glottometrics* 143 (2002).

On the divergent properties of power law and normal distributions, see T. B. Flowler, "Heavy Tails and the Central Limit Theorem," 27 *Telecomm. Review* 25 (2007).

On the structure and dynamics of "small world" networks, see Duncan Watts and Steven Strogatz, "Collective Dynamics of Small World Networks," 393 *Nature* 440 (1998), and Duncan J. Watts, *Small Worlds: The Dynamics of Networks between Order and Randomness* (2000).

JEFFERSON QUOTATIONS

Doubt is wisdom ... TJ to Marquis de Chastellux, June 7, 1785

Ignorance is preferable to error ... *what is wrong.* TJ, *Notes on the State of Virginia*, Query 7

The wise know too well ... *how little he knows.* TJ, "The Batture at New Orleans: The proceedings of the Government of the United States in maintaining the public right to the beach of the Mississippi, adjacent to New Orleans, against the intrusion of Edward Livingston" (1809)

All quotations in footnote 1 are from *Notes on the State of Virginia.*

The general spread of the light of science ... TJ to Roger Weightman, June 24, 1826

When I contemplate ... *burners of witches.* TJ to Dr. Benjamin Waterhouse, March 3, 1818

I brand as cowardly ... *will proceed in improvement.* TJ to William Mumford, June 18, 1799

What a field we have ... *proportion as it is free.* TJ to Josiah Willard, March 24, 1789

CHAPTER 7

On the origins and growth of the World Wide Web, see "The website of the world's first-ever web server" available at info.cern.ch/; Tim Berners-Lee, "The World Wide Web: Past, Present, and Future" (1996), available at www.w3.org/People/Berners-Lee/1996/ ppf.html; "Tim Berners-Lee and Robert Cailliau Develop the World Wide Web," available at www.livinginternet.com/w/wi_lee.htm; Robert Cailliau, "A Short History of the Web" (1995) available at www.netvalley.com/archives/mirrors/robert_cailliau_speech.htm.

JEFFERSON QUOTATIONS

A language cannot be too rich ... TJ To J. Evelyn Denison, Nov. 9, 1825

The variety of dialects ... TJ to John Waldo, Aug. 16, 1813

INTERLUDE

There is a vast literature on the contrasts between Hamilton and Jefferson and their long-standing relationship. I found the following particularly helpful: Gordon Wood's magisterial *The Creation of the American Republic, 1776–1787* (1969); Joseph Ellis, *Founding Brothers* (2000); Richard Brookhiser, *Alexander Hamilton: American* (1999); Robert A. Hendrickson, *The Rise and Fall of Alexander Hamilton* (1981); Stanley Elkins and Eric McKitrick, *The Age of Federalism* (1993); Peter S. Onuf, *Jefferson's Empire: The Language of American Nationhood* (2000); Merrill Peterson, *The Election of 1800: Context and Implications for 'A Rising Nation...'* (1998); Gerald Stourzh, *Alexander Hamilton and the Idea of Representative Government* (1970).

Jonathan Spence's marvelous aphorism ("one of history's uses is to remind us how unlikely things can be") is from *Treason of the Book* (2003), ix.

The Merrill Peterson quote ("One despised, the other idolized, rulership") is from Peterson, *Election of 1800: Context and Implications* (1998).

On the definition of "republic," see Akhil R. Amar, *America's Constitution: A Biography* (2005) at 276–81; Gary Hart, *Restoration of the Republic: The Jeffersonian Ideal in 21st-Century America* (2004).

On the Problem of the Extended Republic and Montesquieu's Law, see Gary Hart, *Restoration of the Republic* (2004); Peter S. Onuf, "Thomas Jefferson, Missouri, and the 'Empire for Liberty,'" in *Thomas Jefferson and the Changing West* (Ronda, 1997); Jack Rakove, *James Madison and the Creation of the American Republic* (2006); Bernard Bailyn, *The Ideological Origins of the American Revolution* (1967); Peter S. Onuf, *Jefferson's Empire: The Language of American Nationhood* (2000).

The Gordon Wood quote ("The best political science of the century") is from Wood, *The Creation of the American Republic, 1776–1787* (1969), 499.

The Peter Onuf quotation ("have to be jettisoned") is from Onuf, "Thomas Jefferson, Missouri, and the 'Empire for Liberty,'" in *Thomas Jefferson and the Changing West* (Ronda, 1997), 118.

On Hamilton and the Whiskey Rebellion, see Hendrickson, *The Rise and Fall of Alexander Hamilton* (1981); Stanley Elkins and Eric McKitrick, *The Age of Federalism* (1993); Ellis, *Founding Brothers* (2000).

On Hamilton and the Louisiana Purchase, see Brookhiser, *Alexander Hamilton: American* (1999) ; Peter S. Onuf, *Jefferson's Empire: The Language of American Nationhood* (2000); Peterson, *Election of 1800* (1998); Stourzh, *Alexander Hamilton*; Peter S. Onuf, *Statehood and Union: A History of the Northwest Ordinance* (1987); Douglass Adair, "Hamilton on the Louisiana Purchase," 12 *William and Mary Quarterly* 268 (1955); James E Lewis, *The Louisiana Purchase:*

Jefferson's Noble Bargain? (2003); James P. Ronda, *Jefferson's West: A Journey with Lewis and Clark* (2000).

JEFFERSON QUOTATIONS

Men by their constitution are naturally divided into two parties...TJ to Henry Lee, Aug. 10, 1824

The division is founded in the nature of man...future time. TJ to John Adams, June 27, 1813

In every country...pursue the same objects. TJ to Henry Lee, Aug. 10, 1824

Everyone takes his side...social intercourse. TJ to John Adams, June 27, 1813

Difference of opinion leads to inquiry, and inquiry to truth....rigorous examination. TJ to P. H. Wendover, March 15, 1815

The term 'republic'...TJ to John Taylor, May 28, 1816

The mother principle...TJ to Samuel Kercheval, July 7, 1816

Government by its own citizens...TJ to John Taylor, May 28, 1816

The excise tax...& determined in the mind of every man. TJ to James Madison, Dec. 28, 1794

Governments are republican only in proportion...TJ to Samuel Kercheval, July 12, 1786

I have much confidence...compact and equality. TJ to François Marbois, June 14, 1817

It would furnish proof of the falsehood of Montesquieu's doctrine...The reverse is the truth. TJ to Nathaniel Niles, March 22, 1801

Our Revolution presented us an album...engraved on our hearts. TJ To John Cartwright, June 5, 1824

[This] chapter of our history furnishes a lesson to man perfectly new. TJ to Nathaniel Niles, March 22, 1801

We can no longer say there is nothing new under the sun...the mighty wave of public opinion which has rolled over it is new. TJ to Dr. Joseph Priestly, March 21, 1801

Before the establishment of the American States...for the man of these States. TJ to John Adams, Oct. 28, 1813

My hope of its duration...the flatteries of hope are as cheap, and pleasanter, than the gloom of despair. TJ to François Marbois, June 14, 1817

CHAPTER 8

On linguistic evolution, see generally Stephen Pinker, *The Language Instinct* (1994), 332–69, and the outstanding entry at en.wikipedia.org/wiki/Comparative_linguistics#Language_evolution_and_the_comparative_method.

JEFFERSON QUOTATIONS

a pursuit to which I felt great attraction...TJ to Herbert Croft, Oct. 30, 1798

how many ages have elapsed...TJ, *Notes on the State of Virginia a hobby which too often runs away with me* ... TJ to J. Evelyn Denison, Nov. 9, 1825

Great question has arisen ... TJ, *Notes on the State of Virginia*

to arrest the progress ... TJ to John Waldo, Aug. 6, 1813

What a language has the French become ... TJ to John Adams, Aug. 15, 1820

I am no friend to what is called Purism ... *adds to its copiousness.* TJ to John Waldo, Aug. 6, 1813

If dictionaries are to be the arbiters ... TJ to John Adams, Aug. 15, 1820

Dictionaries are but the depositories of words already legitimated by usage ... Ibid.

The horrors of Neologism ... TJ to Joseph Milligan, April 6, 1816

Uncouth words will sometimes be offered ... *is it the worse for these?* Ibid.

A language cannot be too rich. TJ to J. Evelyn Denison, Nov. 9, 1825

The greater the degree of enlargement ... TJ to John Waldo, Aug. 6, 1813

Had the preposterous idea of fixing the language ... TJ to Joseph Milligan, April 6, 1816

Nothing is more evident than that as we advance in the knowledge ... Ibid.

Without neologism we should still be held ... TJ to John Adams, Aug. 15, 1820

*Necessity obliges **us** to neologize* ... *the transfer of old words to new objects.* TJ to John Waldo, Aug. 6, 1813

The institution of parliamentary assemblies ... Ibid.

CHAPTER 9

On the UN's "World Summits on the Information Society," see the main WSIS web page at www.itu.int/wsis/index.html. Internet Governance Project www.internetgovernance.org. The quotations in the text are from the "Tunis Agenda for the World Summit on the Information Society" (available at www.itu.int/wsis/docs2/tunis/off/6rev1.html) and the "Geneva Declaration of Principles" of (available at www.itu.int/wsis/docs/geneva/official/dop.html).

"If code is law, then, as William Mitchell writes ..." Lawrence Lessig, *Code v. 2.0* (2007), 79; the argument that "code is law" was first laid out in Lawrence Lessig, *Code and Other Laws of Cyberspace* (1999).

Thanks to Kevin Werbach, who provided the HTTP Referrer example used in the text.

On IPv6, see Christian Huitema, *Routing in the Internet* (2000); National Research Council, *Global Networks and Local Values: A Comparative Look at Germany and the United States* (2001); Jeannette A. Hoffmann, "Governing Technologies and Techniques of Government: Politics on the Net" (available at duplox.wz-berlin.de/final/jeanette.htm#toc3); National Technical Information Agency, "Technical and Economic Assessment of Internet Protocol, Version 6 (available at www.ntia.doc.gov/ntiahome/ntiageneral/ipv6/final/ipv6finalTOC.htm); William Stallings, "IPv6: The New Internet Protocol," available at www.csipv6.lancs.ac.uk/ipv6/documents/papers/stallings/; see generally the IPv6 forum at www.ipv6forum.org.

On the structure and organization of the IETF and related organizations, see "Overview of the IETF," available at www.ietf.org/overview.html; P. Hoffman, "The Tao of the IETF," available at www.ietf.org/tao.html; G. Simonellis, "A Concise Guide to the Major Internet

Bodies," available at www.acm.org/ubiquity/views/v6i5_simoneli.html; Scott Bradner, "The Internet Engineering Task Force," available at www.linuxjunkies.org/articles/bradner.pdf; H. Alvestrand, "RFC 3935: A Mission Statement for the IETF" (2004), available at www.ietf.org/rfc/rfc3935.txt; J. Galvin, "RFC 2727: IAB and IESG Selection, Confirmation, and Recall Process: Operation of the Nominating and Recall Committees," available at www.ietf.org/rfc/rfc2727.txt; R. Hovey and Scott Bradner, "RFC 2028: The Organizations Involved in the IETF Standards Process," available at www.ietf.org/rfc/rfc2028.txt?number=2028; Vinton Cerf, IETF and ISOC, available at www.isoc.org/isoc/related/ietf/.

On the RFC process, see B. Carpenter, ed., "The IETF Process: A Roadmap," available at tools.ietf.org/id/draft-carpenter-procdoc-roadmap-04.txt; Scott Bradner, "RFC 2026: The Internet Standards Process," available at www.ietf.org/rfc/rfc2026.txt. The entire RFC series is catalogued at the Internet Society website, ietfreport.isoc.org/index.html.

"the IETF has agreed that..." H. Alvestrand, "RFC 3935: A Mission Statement for the IETF" (2004), available at www.ietf.org/rfc/rfc3935.txt.

On the IETF processes and general models of democratic governance, see Pauline Borsook, "How Anarchy Works," *Wired* (Oct. 1995), available at www.wired.com/wired/archive/3.10/ietf.html; A. Michael Froomkin, "Habermas@Dicourse.net: Toward a Critical Theory of Cyberspace," 116 *Harv. L. Rev* 749 (2003); Philip J. Weiser, "Internet Governance, Standard Setting, and Self-Regulation," 28 *N. Kent. L. Rev* 822 (2001); Jeannette A. Hoffmann, "Governing Technologies and Techniques of Government: Politics on the Net" (available at duplox.wz-berlin.de/final/jeanette.htm#toc3); L. Jean Camp and Charles Vincent, "Setting Standards: Looking to the Internet for Models of Governance."

On OSI and other protocol-development projects in the mid to late 1980s, see Janet Abbate, *Inventing the Internet* (2000); National Research Council, *Global Networks and Local Values: A Comparative Look at Germany and the United States* (2001); Marshall T. Rose, *The Open Book—a Practical Perspective on OSI* (1999); Marvin A. Sirbu and Laurence E. Zwimpfer, "Standards Setting for Computer Communication: The Case of X.25," 23 *IEEE Communications* 35 (1985); Paul A. David and Mark Shurmer, "Formal Standards-setting for Global Telecommunications and Information Services," 20 *Telecommunications Policy* 789 (1996); Shirley M. Radack, "The Federal Government and Information Technology Standards," 11 *Government Information Quarterly* 373 (1994); Todd Shaiman, *The Political Economy of Anticipatory Standards*, (1995); Paul A. David, "The Internet and the Economics of Network Technology Evolution," in Christoph Engel and Kenneth H. Keller, *Understanding the Impact of Global Networks on Local Social, Political and Cultural Values* (2000).

Special thanks to Michelle Arnold for her assistance in putting together the diagrams in this chapter and the next.

CHAPTER 10

On the operation of the DNS, see the excellent ISOC briefing available at www.isoc.org/briefings/016/index.shtml; National Research Council, *Internet's Coming of*

Age,; P. Mockapetris, "RFC 1034, Domain Names—Concepts and Facilities," available at www.ietf.org/rfc/rfc1034.txt (Nov. 1987); Theodore Socolofsky and Claudia Jeanne Kale, "RFC 1180: A TCP/IP Tutorial" (1991), available at www.rfc-editor.org/rfc/rfc1180 .txt; A. Michael Froomkin, "Wrong Turn in Cyberspace: Using ICANN to Route around the APA," 50 *Duke L. J.* 17 (2000) and available at personal.law.miami.edu~froomkin/ articles/icann-main.pdf; Jeannette Hoffmann, "Topological Ordering in Cyberspace," available at www.wz-berlin.de/tau/ot/member/hoffmann.en.htm#vortrage.

On the events leading up to and culminating in the DNS crisis and the formation of ICANN, the works of Milton Mueller (especially his *Ruling the Root: Internet Governance and the Taming of Cyberspace* [2002]); Michael Froomkin (especially "Wrong Turn in Cyberspace: Using ICANN to Route around the APA," 50 *Duke L.J.* 17 [2000]) and "ICANN and Antitrust" (with Mark A. Lemley), available at papers.ssrn.com/paper.taf?abstract_id=291221); Jon Weinberg (especially "ICANN and the Problem of Legitimacy," 50 *Duke L.J.* 187, 2000); and Ellen Rony and Peter Rony, *The Domain Name Handbook: High Stakes and Strategies in Cyberspace* (1998) were indispensable.

"By virtue of the structure of the DNS..." Jonathan Weinberg, "ICANN and the Problem of Legitimacy," 50 *Duke L. J.* 187 (2000).

"Coordination of the root server network..." "Management of Internet Names and Addresses," 63 *Fed. Reg.* 31,741 (1998) [the "White Paper"], available at www.ntia.doc.gov/ ntiahome/domainname/6_5_98dns.htm.

"The U.S. Government should end its role..." Ibid.

The Joshua Quittner article referenced in the footnote is "Billions Registered: Right Now, there are no rules to keep you from owning a bitchin' corporate name as your own Internet address," *Wired* (Oct. 1994), available at www.hotwired.com/wired/2.10/departments/electrosphere/mcdonalds.html.

On the UDRP, see Uniform Dispute Resolution Policy, available at www.icann.org/dndr/ udrp/policy.htm; A. Michael Froomkin, "ICANN's UDRP: Its Causes and (Partial) Cures," 67 *Brook. L. Rev.* 605 (2002).

The *Livingston v. Jefferson* lawsuit, and its implications for the development of the notions of "in rem" and "in personam" legal jusrisdiction, is discussed at length in R. Kent Newmyer, *John Marshall and the Heroic Age of the Supreme Court* (2001); Jefferson's (lengthy) legal defense was published as "The Batture at New Orleans: The proceedings of the Government of the United States in maintaining the public right to the beach of the Mississippi, adjacent to New Orleans, against the intrusion of Edward Livingston" (1809).

CHAPTER 11

The opening hypothetical ("A, in Austria...") is adapted from Jonathan Zittrain, "Be Careful What You Ask For: Reconciling a Global Internet and Local Law," in *Who Rules the Net?* (Adam Thierer and Wayne Crews, 2003).

On the Yahoo! Problem, see Joel Reidenberg, "The Yahoo! Case and the International Democratization of the Internet," Fordham University School of Law Research Paper 11 (2001); and the Center for Democracy and Technology's "Jurisdiction" collection (at www .cdt.org/jurisdiction/), and its various Policy Posts on the Yahoo! dispute.

For general treatments of the Exceptionalist-Unexceptionalist debate, see the papers collected in *Who Rules the Net*; Brian Kahin and Charles Nesson, eds., *Borders in Cyberspace: Information Policy and the Global Information Infrastructure* (1997); Susan Crawford, David R. Johnson, and John G. Palfrey, "The Accountable Net: Peer Production of Internet governance," 9 *Va. J. Law & Tech.* 2 (2004); Susan Crawford, "Someone to Watch Over Me: Social Policies for the Internet," Cardozo Legal Studies Research Working Paper No. 129 (available at papers.ssrn.com/sol3/papers.cfm?abstract_id=796825); Viktor Mayer-Schönberger and David Lazer, eds., *Governance and Information Technology—From Electronic Government to Information Government* (2007). For a quick overview of this debate, see the "Brain Tennis" exchange between David Post and Jack Goldsmith, available at www.hotwired.com/synapse/braintennis/97/34/ncleft intro.html.

Major "Unexceptionalist" writings include Jack L. Goldsmith, "Against Cyberanarchy," 65 *U. Chi. L. Rev.* 1199 (1998); Jack L. Goldsmith, "The Internet and the Abiding Significance of Territorial Sovereignty," 5 *Ind. J. Global Legal Stud.* 475 (1998); Timothy S. Wu, Note, "Cyberspace Sovereignty?—The Internet and the International System," 10 *Harv. J.L. & Tech.* 647 (1997); Neil Weinstock Netanel, "Cyberspace Self-Governance: A Skeptical View from Liberal Democratic Theory," 88 *Calif. L. Rev.* 395 (2000); Allan R. Stein, "The Unexceptional Problem of Jurisdiction in Cyberspace," 32 *International Lawyer* 1167 (1998); Goldsmith and Wu, *Who Controls the Internet*. The "Exceptionalist" position is laid out in David R. Johnson and David Post, "Law and Borders— The Rise of Law in Cyberspace," 48 *Stan. L. Rev.* 1367 (1996); Lawrence Lessig, "The Zones of Cyberspace," 48 *Stan. L. Rev.* 1403 (1996); Henry H. Perritt Jr., "The Internet as a Threat to Sovereignty?: Thoughts on the Internet's Role in Strengthening National and Global Governance, 5 *Ind. J. Global Legal Stud.* 423 (1998); David G. Post, "Against 'Against Cyberanarchy," 17 *Berkeley Tech. L.J.* 1365, 1366 (2002); Viktor Mayer-Schönberger, "The Shape of Governance: Analyzing the World of Internet Regulation," 43 *Virginia Journal of International Law* 605 (2003); Robert Corn-Revere, "Caught in the Seamless Web: Does the Internet's Global Reach Justify Less Freedom of Speech?" in *Who Rules the Net?* (Thierer and Crews, 2003); Daniel Benoliel, "Law Geography and Cyberspace: The Case of Online Territorial Privacy," 23 *Cardozo Art. & Ent. L.J.* 125 (2005).

Other useful reference to the jurisdictional and governance debates in cyberspace include Viktor Mayer-Schönberger and John Crowley, "Napster's Second Life? The Regulatory Challenges of Virtual Worlds," 100 *Northwestern Law Review* 1775 (2006); Susan Crawford, "The Ambulance, the Squad Car, and the Internet," 21 *Berkeley J. Law & Tech.* 873 (2006); Jonathan Zittrain, "The Generative Internet," 119 *Harv. L. Rev.* 1974 (2006); Peter Swire, "Of Elephants, Mice, and Privacy: International Choice of Law and the Internet" 32 *Int. Law.* 991 (1998); Patricia Bellia, "Chasing Bits Across Borders," 2001 *U. Chi. Legal Forum* 35 (2001).

I have also benefited particularly from the work of Paul Schiff Berman on these questions; see Berman, "From International Law to Law and Globalization," 43 *Colum. J. Transnat'l L.* 485

(2005); Berman, "Towards a Cosmopolitan Vision of Conflict of Laws: Redefining Governmental Interests in a Global Era," 153 *U. Pa. L. Rev.* 1819 (2005).

"Transactions in cyberspace involve..." from Jack Goldsmith, "Against Cyberanarchy," 65 *U. Chi. Law Rev.* 1199, 1239–40 (1998).

"A government's responsibility for redressing..." Goldsmith and Wu, *Who Controls the Internet?*, 156.

"It is settled, with respect to realspace activity, . . " Goldsmith, "Against Cyberanarchy," 1239.

"When French citizens..." Goldsmith, "Yahoo! Brought to Earth," *Financial Times* (Nov. 26, 2000), available at news.ft.com/ft/tfc?Article&cid=FT3W85A41GC.

"A nation can purport..." Goldsmith, "Against Cyberanarchy," 1216–17.

"The practical answer is that C can sue A..." Jonathan Zittrain, "Be Careful What You Ask For: Reconciling a Global Internet and Local Law," in *Who Rules the Net?* (Thierer and Crews, 2003), 15.

"What we once called a global network..." Goldsmith and Wu, 149.

"To suffer a wide extended Country..." George Washington to James Duane, Sept. 7, 1783.

"the settling—or rather overspreading..." Ibid.

"The United States would be something new under the sun..." Peter S. Onuf, *Jefferson's Empire* (2000), 75.

On the Ordinance of 1784, see Editorial Note, "Plan for the Government of the Western Territory," 7 Papers of Thomas Jefferson, 581 ff. (J. Boyd, ed.); Peter S. Onuf, *Jefferson's Empire* (2000); Merrill D. Peterson, *The Jefferson Image in the American Mind*, (1998); Editorial Note, "Report of a Committee to Establish a Land Office," 7 Papers of Thomas Jefferson, 140 ff. (J. Boyd, ed.); Claude G. Bowers, *The Young Jefferson* (1969); Peter S. Onuf, "Thomas Jefferson, Missouri, and the 'Empire for Liberty,'" in *Thomas Jefferson and the Changing West* (Ronda, 1997); Peter S. Onuf, *Statehood and Union: A History of the Northwest Ordinance* (1987); Merrill Peterson, *Jefferson and the New Nation* (1970); Gordon S. Wood, *The Creation of the American Republic 1776–1789* (1969).

On Jefferson's plans for his "ward republics," see the excellent treatment in Gary Hart, *Restoration of the Republic* (2004).

On virtual worlds, generally, see the work of Edward Castronova, notably *Synthetic Worlds: The Business and Culture of Virtual Worlds* (2006) and *Exodus to the Virtual World: How Online Fun Is Changing Reality* (2007). On law in virtual worlds, see Dan Hunter and Greg Lastowka, "The Laws of Virtual Worlds," 92 *Cal. L. Rev.* 1 (2004); Beth Simone Noveck and Jack Balkin, *State of Play: Law, Games, and Virtual Worlds* (2006); Joshua Fairchild, "Virtual Property," 85 *B.U. L. Rev.* 1047 (2005); James Grimmelmann, "Virtual Worlds as Comparative Law," 49 *NYLS L. Rev* 147 (2004); David Post and David R. Johnson, "The Great Debate: Law in Virtual Worlds," available at firstmonday.org/Issues/issue11_2/post/index.html; and the excellent blogs at terranova.blogs.com/ and virtuallyblind.com/.

The material on virtual world economies in note 9 comes from Edward Castronova, "Virtual Worlds: A First Hand Account of Market and Society on the Cyberian Frontier"

(Center for Economic Studies & Institute for Economic Research, Working Paper No. 618, 2001), available at papers.ssrn.com/sol3/papers.cfm?abstract_id=294828.

JEFFERSON QUOTATIONS

...free and independent of all the world... TJ, draft of Virginia Constitution, quoted in Editorial Note, "Plan for the Government of the Western Territory," 7 Papers of Thomas Jefferson, 582 (J. Boyd, ed.)

The question 'How may the western territory be disposed of...? TJ to James Monroe, July 9, 1786

The moment we sacrifice the settlers' interests to our own... TJ to James Madison, Dec. 16, 1786

Conquest is not in our principles... TJ, Travelling Notes for Mr. Rutledge and Mr. Shippen, June 3, 1788

...a gradation of authorities... TJ to John Cabell, Feb. 2, 1816

The secret is in making... Ibid.

What has destroyed liberty... Ibid.

These wards, called townships in New England... TJ to Samuel Kercheval, July 12, 1816

...an empire built not on conquest... TJ to Marbois, June 14, 1817

Upon my plan we treat them as fellow citizens... TJ to James Monroe, July 9, 1786

CHAPTER 12

On the early battles over "cyberporn" and the Communications Decency Act, see Michael Godwin, *Cyber Rights* (1998), and Nadine Strossen, "Childrens' Rights vs. Adult Free Speech: Can They Be Reconciled?" 29 *Conn. L. Rev.* 873 (1997).

On the relationship between Hugo Black and Jefferson, see Daniel J. Meador, "Hugo Black and Thomas Jefferson: A Memoir," 79 *Virg. Quart. Rev.* 459 (2003); Akhil Reed Amar, "Hugo Black and the Hall of Fame," 53 *Ala. L. Rev.* 1221 (2002).

On Jefferson's role in the development of public education in the United States, see James Gilreath, ed., *Thomas Jefferson and the Education of a Citizen* (1999); Merrill D. Peterson, *The Jefferson Image in the American Mind* (1998); Albert J. Nock, *Jefferson* (1926); Garry Wills, *Mr. Jefferson's University* (2002). Jefferson's role in the development of public education in Washington, D.C., is treated at length in Saul Padover, ed., *Thomas Jefferson and the Nation's Capital* (1946).

On Jefferson's role in the history of U.S. intellectual property law, see Adam Mossoff, "Who Cares What Thomas Jefferson Thought About Patents?" 92 *Cornell. L. Rev* 953 (2007); Levi N. Fouts, "Jefferson the Inventor," 4 *J. Patent Off. Soc.* 316 (1922); E. C. Walterscheid, "Thomas Jefferson and the Patent Act of 1793," available at etext.lib.virginia.edu/journals/EH/EH40/walter40.html; Kenneth W. Dobyns, *The Patent Office Pony: A History of the Early Patent Office* (1994).

On Jefferson's inventions generally, see Silvio Bedini, *Thomas Jefferson and His Copying Machines* (1984); Bedini, *Thomas Jefferson: Statesman of Science* (1990); Daniel J. Boorstin, *The*

Lost World of Thomas Jefferson (1948); I. Bernard Cohen, *Science and the Founding Fathers* (1995); Edward T. Martin, *Thomas Jefferson: Scientist* (1952); Brooke Hindle, ed., *Early American Science* (1976). On the "mould-board plow" design, see Russell Martin and Lucia Stanton, "Jefferson's Plow of Least Resistance," available at monticello.org/reports/interests/moldboard.html; I. Bernard Cohen, *Science and the Founding Fathers*; Edwin M. Betts, ed., *Thomas Jefferson's Farm Book*, 47–64, and Betts, ed., *Thomas Jefferson's Garden Book,* 649–54. On Jefferson's accomplishments as a cryptographer, see David Kahn, *The Codebreakers: The Story of Secret Writing* (1967); "Thomas Jefferson's Wheel Cipher," available at monticello.org/reports/interests/wheel_cipher.html and "Jefferson's Cipher for Meriwether Lewis," available at monticello .org/jefferson/lewisandclark/cipher.html.

"Had [his mouldboard] been patented and exploited, it would probably have brought him wealth beyond the dreams of eighteenth century avarice," from Levi N. Fouts, "Jefferson the Inventor," 4 *J. Patent Off. Soc.* 316, 317 (1922).

"...**the** historical policy foundation for American intellectual property law..." from Adam Mossoff, "Who Cares What Thomas Jefferson Thought About Patents?" 92 *Cornell L. Rev* 953, 962 (2007).

On the history of U.S. copyright law, the essential reference is Paul Goldstein, *Copyright's Highway* (1994); see also Henry G. Henn, "The Quest for International Copyright Protection," 39 *Cornell L. Quart.* 43 (1954); Max Kampelman, "The United States and International Copyright," 41 *Am. J. Intl Law* 406 (1947); Lyman Ray Patterson, *Copyright in Historical Perspective* (1968); Jessica Litman, "Copyright Legislation and Technological Change," 68 *Or. L Rev* 275 (1989); David Post, "His Napster's Voice," 20 *Temple Env. & Tech. L.J.* 35 (2002) (reprinted in W. Crews and A. Thierer, eds., *Copy Fights: The Future of Intellectual Property in an Information Age* [2002]).

"Imagine that you are performing a web search with me..." from Yochai Benkler, *The Wealth of Networks: How Social Production Transforms Markets and Freedom* (2006), 53–54. "Why can fifty thousand volunteers successfully coauthor Wikipedia..." Ibid., 4.

JEFFERSON QUOTATIONS

Were it left to me to decide whether we should have a government without newspapers or newspapers without government... TJ to Edward Carrington, Jan. 16, 1787

To preserve the freedom of the human mind... TJ to William Mumford, June 18, 1799

The true foundation of republican government... they embody the will of their people and execute it. TJ to Samuel Kercheval, July 12, 1816

No other sure foundation can be devised... TJ to George Wythe, Aug. 13, 1786

It is honorable for us to have produced... TJ to James Madison, Dec. 16, 1786

Reason and free enquiry are the only effectual agents against error. TJ, *Notes on the State of Virginia*

Difference of opinion leads to inquiry, and inquiry to truth... TJ to P. H. Wendover, March 15, 1815

Subject opinion to coercion... TJ, *Notes on the State of Virginia*

Freedom of discussion, unaided by power... TJ, Second Inaugural Address

It is error alone which needs the support of government. TJ, *Notes on the State of Virginia*

The error seems not sufficiently eradicated that the operations of the mind . . . Ibid.

A right of free correspondence between citizen and citizen on their joint interests . . . TJ to James Monroe, Sept. 7, 1797

Where the press is free, all is safe . . . TJ to Charles Yancey, Jan. 6, 1816

[The United States] will demonstrate the falsehood of the pretext . . . TJ to Thomas Seymour, Feb. 11, 1807

To open the doors of truth, and to fortify the habit of testing everything by reason . . . TJ to John Tyler, June 28, 1804

by far the most important bill . . . TJ to George Wythe, Aug. 13, 1786

No one more sincerely wishes the spread of information among mankind . . . *minds of the people.* TJ to Hugh White, May 6, 1810

Enlighten the people generally . . . TJ to Pierre DuPont de Nemours, April 24, 1816

Lay down true principles, and adhere to them inflexibly. TJ to Samuel Kercheval, July 12, 1816

I am not afraid of new inventions . . . TJ to Robert Fulton, March 17, 1810

. . . never thought of monopolizing by patent . . . TJ to Charles Willson Peale, June 13, 1815

Ploughing deep . . . TJ to Charles Willson Peale, April 17, 1813

You will be at perfect liberty . . . TJ to Charles Willson Peale, June 13, 1815

Your letter points to the much broader question . . . TJ to Isaac McPherson, Aug. 13, 1813

There is a late instance in this State . . . TJ to Charles Willson Peale, June 13, 1815

That ideas should freely spread . . . TJ to Isaac McPherson, Aug. 13, 1813

If nature has made any one thing . . . Ibid..

Their peculiar character . . . Ibid.

Society may give an exclusive right . . . Ibid..

The just rewards of genius . . . TJ to Oliver Evans, Jan. 16, 1814

The fact is, that one new idea leads to another . . . TJ to Benjamin Waterhouse, March 3, 1818

. . . drawing the line between the things which are worth to the public . . . TJ to Isaac McPherson, Aug. 13, 1813

I know well the difficulty . . . Ibid.

Certainly an inventor ought to be allowed . . . TJ to Oliver Evans, May 2, 1807

If a new application of our old machines . . . TJ to Oliver Evan, Jan. 16, 1814

freedom of discussion is sufficient . . . TJ, Second Inaugural Address

liberty depends on the freedom of the press . . . TJ to Dr. James Currie, Jan. 28, 1786

Everyone takes his side, according to his constitution . . . TJ to John Adams, June 27, 1813

EPILOGUE

For general reference on the moose episode, see references for the Prologue.

On Jefferson's activities while in Paris, see generally William Howard Adams, *The Paris Years of Thomas Jefferson* (1997); George Green Schackleford, *Thomas Jefferson's Travels in Europe, 1784–1789* (1995).

"The strange thing about cyberspace...do things differently," from Lawrence Lessig, "Jefferson's Nature," available at www.lessig.org/content/articles/works/NatureD3.pdf.

"Vis-a-vis the laws of nature..." from Lessig, "Reading the Constitution in Cyberspace," 45 *Emory L. J.* 869 (1996).

"We stand on the edge of an era..." Lessig, "Jefferson's Nature."

"...the is-ism that says..." Ibid.

"...watching as important aspects of privacy..." Lessig, *Code and Other Laws of Cyberspace* (1999), 233.

JEFFERSON QUOTATIONS

...the experiment was expensive to me... TJ to John Rutledge, Sept. 9, 1788

An acquisition more precious than you can imagine... TJ to Governor John Sullivan, Jan. 7, 1786

The readiness with which you undertook... Ibid.

...all in good enough condition...and me little expense. TJ to Governor John Sullivan, Oct. 5, 1787

INDEX